IMAGES
of America

BENSENVILLE

On the Cover: Taking the name Peace Church, this place of worship was constructed on Center Street just north of Wood Street in 1903. (Courtesy of the Bensenville Community Public Library.)

IMAGES
of America

BENSENVILLE

Jonathan W. Sebastian

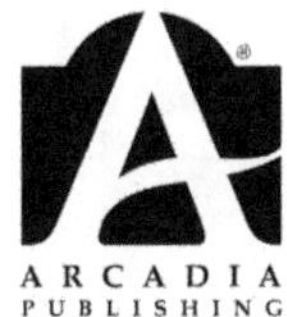

ARCADIA
PUBLISHING

ISBN 9781540235510

Published by Arcadia Publishing
Charleston, South Carolina

Library of Congress Control Number: 2018930082

For all general information, please contact Arcadia Publishing:
Telephone 843-853-2070
Fax 843-853-0044
E-mail sales@arcadiapublishing.com
For customer service and orders:
Toll-Free 1-888-313-2665

Visit us on the Internet at www.arcadiapublishing.com

Contents

ACKNOWLEDGMENTS

The author would like to express his thanks to Chris Sloan, the adult services coordinator at the Bensenville Community Public Library. Chris, thank you for all your help in the preparation of this book and for answering all my technology-related questions. Additionally, Janis Arquette was a tremendous resource and help. Janis, thank you for all the time you put in to help locate images and information for this book. You provided me the foundation in the history of Bensenville that I have needed in this project and the work at Fischer Farm. Thank you for all you do. Samantha Parkison, thank you for taking pictures to be used in this book. David Sieffert, thank you for your support and assistance. Finally, thank you to the Fischer Farm volunteers for all you do to preserve and share the history of this great community.

Unless otherwise noted, the pictures used in this book were obtained from the archives of the Bensenville Community Public Library.

INTRODUCTION

It has been called the fastest-dying town in the United States. The village of Bensenville, with its slogan, "Gateway to Opportunity," is known—if indeed, known at all—as the home of light industry, manufacturing, and warehouses. It is the immediate neighbor of O'Hare International Airport, which, to some degree, is actually on land that used to be a part of the village of Bensenville.

The village, however, is not dying. On the contrary, it has shown modest growth since the expansion of O'Hare Airport between 2010 and 2013. New businesses and new residents have arrived. In fact, 2,424 businesses now call the village home, as does a diverse population including Euro-American, Latino, African American, Asian, Pacific Islander, and Native American residents.

Crowds gather for Music in the Park on Wednesday evenings all summer long. Athletic leagues through the recreation department of the village continue to grow. The opportunities at the Bensenville Park District are expanded every year at the Deer Grove Leisure Center, the Water Park and Splash Pad, and White Pines Golf Club and Banquets. A preschool, a school of dance and movement, art and music classes, water aerobics, and athletic programs all thrive—and this is just some of what is offered. The same can be said for the programs and services of the Bensenville Community Public Library. Fulfilling all the traditional roles of a library through its collections, it is also reaching into the community. From guest speakers on a variety of topics, to book clubs, to English/Spanish discussion groups, there is truly an array for all ages encouraging patrons to read, think, dream, and create. Running through the life of this vibrant community is a rich cord of history, which is preserved and celebrated.

The Bensenville Park District and the Bensenville Community Public Library have been at the forefront of this work in their efforts to enrich the lives of residents and visitors. The former has done so through its operation of Fischer Farm, one of the oldest homesteads in DuPage County, and its maintenance of a historical locomotive. The latter has contributed to this work through its extensive local history collection and its preservation of the Korthauer Log House, the oldest structure in the village proper.

It is in the work done at these sites and the collections held that a surprisingly clear picture of the history of this village can be seen. The "Gateway to Opportunity" was at one time known as Tioga, meaning "the gateway" in the languages of the Native Americans that originally called this land home. Several tribes of the Algonquian language group had lived in northeastern Illinois for hundreds of years prior to the arrival of European settlers. Having entered the region from the south or southeast, Sauk, Fox, Kickapoo, Winnebago, Miami, Ottawa, and Ojibwa ranged across much of what is now Illinois. These became the principal nations in the region after having defeated the Illinois Nation and causing it to virtually cease to exist after 1766. The last of the Native Americans to arrive, the Potawatomi entered the region from the east, moving around the northern and southern ends of Lake Michigan. They may have originally been driven westward by the tribes belonging to the Iroquois Confederacy. Siding with the British in the War of 1812, the Potawatomi hoped to resist American expansion into the land they had come to call home. With American victory in that conflict, a blow was struck to their remaining here. Many Native Americans had already moved westward beyond the Mississippi River following the end of the War of 1812, while some remained hoping to retain their land. Conflict was the result, though in Illinois, it was mostly one-sided.

The first European settlers began to arrive in the mid-1830s. These families were German and came from the Kingdoms of Hanover and Prussia. They staked out claims, cleared land, and built homes. These were not isolated islands of existence, but rather individual plots that formed a vibrant community. Their Christian faith led them to construct churches of both the Lutheran and Reformed denominations. Education was also a priority, with the first school built in 1851. This issue was also the impetus for a village government, which was created in 1884. Businesses were established including a flaxseed mill, two general stores, a hotel, a butcher shop, and a cheese factory. Connections were made into the city of Chicago. The tangible items of this connection centered on the dairy industry—eggs, milk, butter, and cheese, which were produced in abundance in and around the little village of Bensenville, as the German families referred to their community. The connection from the village to the city was first made on the roads, Grand Avenue and Irving Park Road. These were dirt and plank roadways. By the 1870s, the connection was made with iron and steel. The dairy products were loaded onto railroad cars and transported to market on the same line that exists today, taking commuter passengers to work and leisure in the city of Chicago.

The railroad also inaugurated the diversification of the population. Immigrants from Mexico and, later, from other Latin American countries arrived. Eastern Europeans, especially Polish, began to come to the village as well. Industry and manufacturing of other products began to take shape in Bensenville. Then, during the Great Depression, the village made the national news. Alvin Karpis, at one time in the employ of Al Capone, struck out on his own and pulled not one, but two kidnapping jobs. He brought his hostages to Bensenville. He was eventually arrested after the use of a new policing technique: dusting for fingerprints. But, the village was also known for more positive stories. With the creation of a women's baseball league during World War II, Audrey Wagner went to a tryout at Wrigley Field and was offered a contract. She ended up being recognized (along with the rest of the All-American Girls Professional Baseball League) in the National Baseball Hall of Fame after her career was over.

The nation would change after World War II. The railroad was soon to be eclipsed by air travel, and trains coexisted with airplanes in Bensenville with the establishment of Orchard Field. This airfield became O'Hare International Airport and, in more recent years, would consume part of the village.

Bensenville responded and reinvented itself. Today, metal finishing services, precision machining, industrial equipment manufacturing, and banner and sign production can all be found here. Ethnic businesses are also present with Mexican grocery stores, Mexican bakeries, and a Punjabi Indian banquet hall. Dental, medical, and chiropractic practices all call Bensenville home. The village itself provides many services beyond its municipal responsibilities, maintaining its own athletic department with three ice rinks, an indoor pool, baseball, softball, and soccer fields. The Bensenville Park District provides recreation and leisure experiences, and the Bensenville Community Public Library serves its patrons with a variety of programs and services.

One

Pioneer Village

The 1833 Treaty of Chicago only finalized what had begun with the Treaty of Prairie du Chien eight years earlier. The Native Americans residing in northern Illinois had to move west of the Mississippi River. Already, the first white settlers had ventured into this land. Christian Fischer made his way west out of Chicago on Grand Avenue and staked a claim of nearly one thousand acres immediately south of what was to become the village of Bensenville. In 1836, he was joined by his brother and sister-in-law Conrad and Louisa Fischer and five of their children (one was lost to drowning during their journey). The Franzen family arrived the following year. They staked a claim just north of the Fischers. The Korthauer family arrived in 1838 and claimed the land just east of the Franzens. After that, the Koehlers and Lessemans came. All of these immigrants had come from the Kingdom of Hanover, which roughly corresponds to the province of the same name in northwestern Germany today. While seeking to escape the crop failures and the resulting famines that plagued the Germanic states during the 1840s, they desired the opportunities to be had in the New World, not the least of which was the opportunity to own land.

These German pioneers cut down trees, plowed the soil, planted crops, and raised animals. But almost from the beginning, this was not an isolated existence. A community-oriented life began to take shape. It centered first around the church. Johann Schmidt had claimed a parcel of land immediately north of the Fischers. A site was selected near the southwest corner of his land as an ideal location for a church. Funds were raised, this portion of the property was purchased from Schmidt, and the families built their house of worship. August Fischer, youngest son of Conrad and Louisa, donated land for a schoolhouse, which he and his older brother Henry built in 1851.

Just over a mile to the north, the Franzens built a gristmill. Soon, a blacksmith shop was opened nearby, then a saloon, and two general stores. Here, in the extreme northeast corner of DuPage County, a town was beginning to take shape.

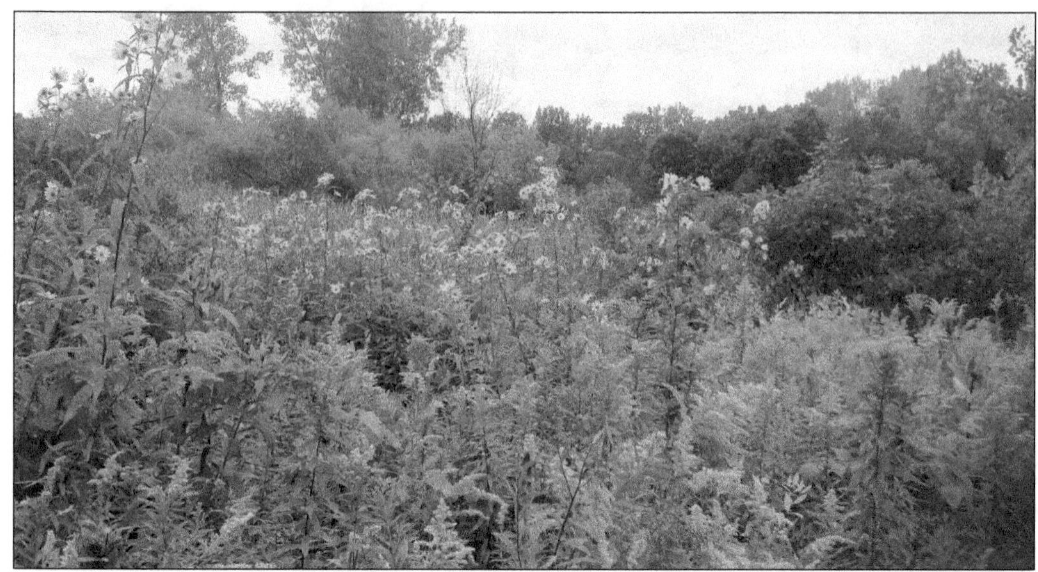

As late as the early 1830s, the northern tier of Illinois remained largely unsettled. The natural landscape was relatively unspoiled. Here, there were old-growth forests. White oak, red oak, bur oak, bitternut hickory, and American elm trees could be found across the region. These were trees that reached heights of 70 or 80 feet, sometimes more. The trunks of these trees could be as much as five feet thick. (Author's collection.)

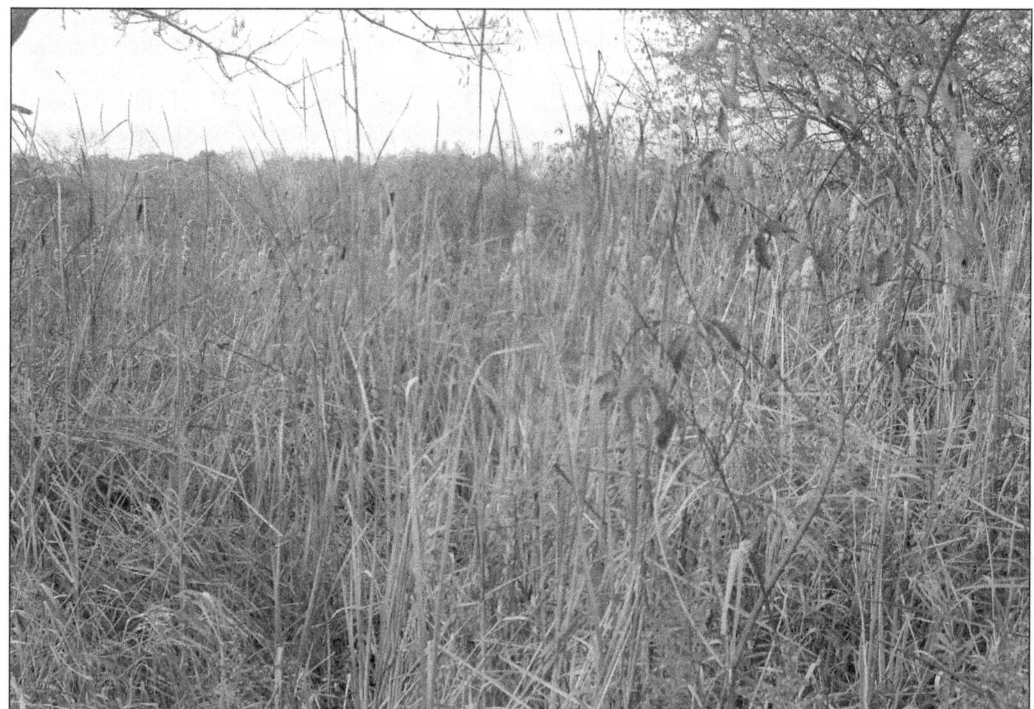

Large areas of northern Illinois were prairie. Big bluestem and prairie cordgrass grew to be eight feet tall. Purple coneflower, cardinal flower, and white indigo brought vibrant color to the landscape. Periodically catching on fire, this flora returned due to the plants' incredibly intricate root systems reaching far down into the rich soil. (Author's collection.)

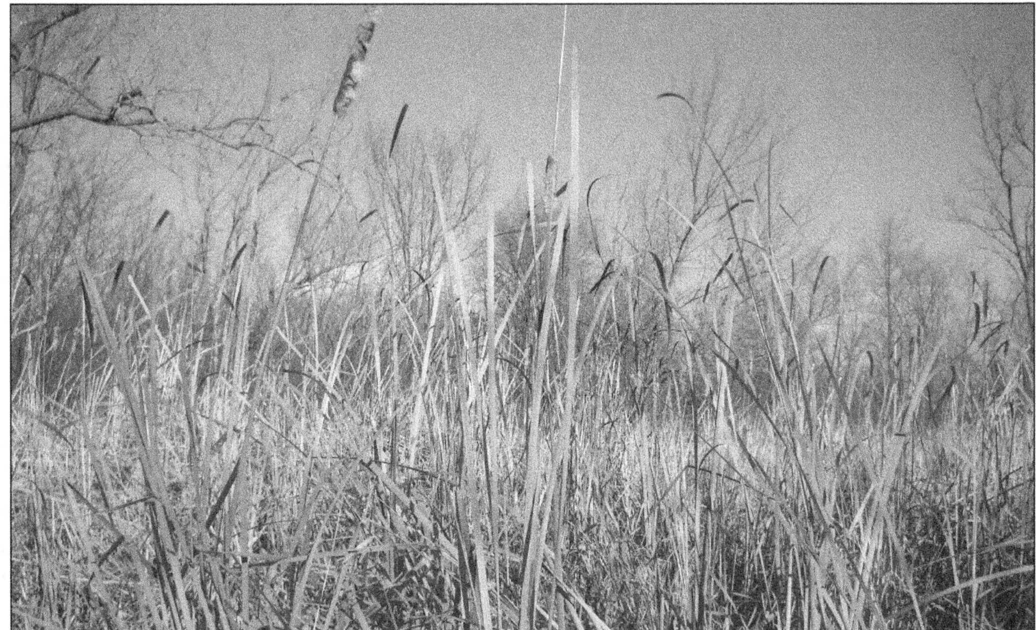

Wetlands were also present—that is, those areas where the soil was saturated for most, if not all, of the year. Water collected in these areas forming small streams or ponds. Common cattails, lily pads, and marsh violet predominated here, adding even more to the biodiversity originally present in northern Illinois. (Author's collection.)

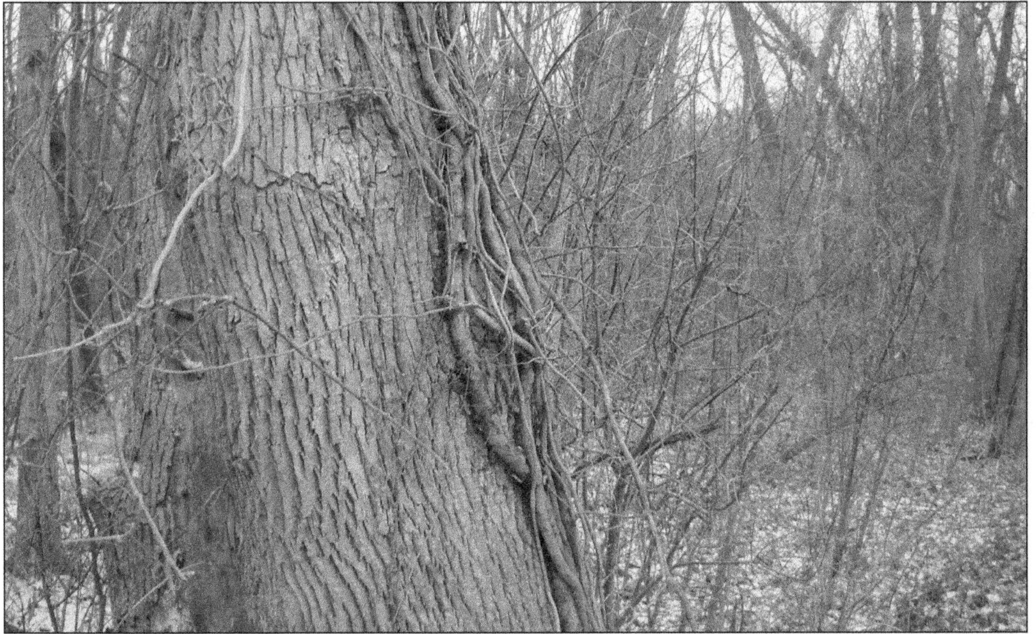

The land also teemed with a great variety of animals. Some of the species still call this region home, while others have vanished due to man-made pressures. Dragon- and damselflies, cardinals, robins, and hawks took to the air. On the ground, deer, coyotes, foxes, bobcats, rabbits, squirrels, chipmunks, skunks, beavers, and muskrats abounded. Bass, yellow perch, ducks, frogs, and toads were also prevalent. (Author's collection.)

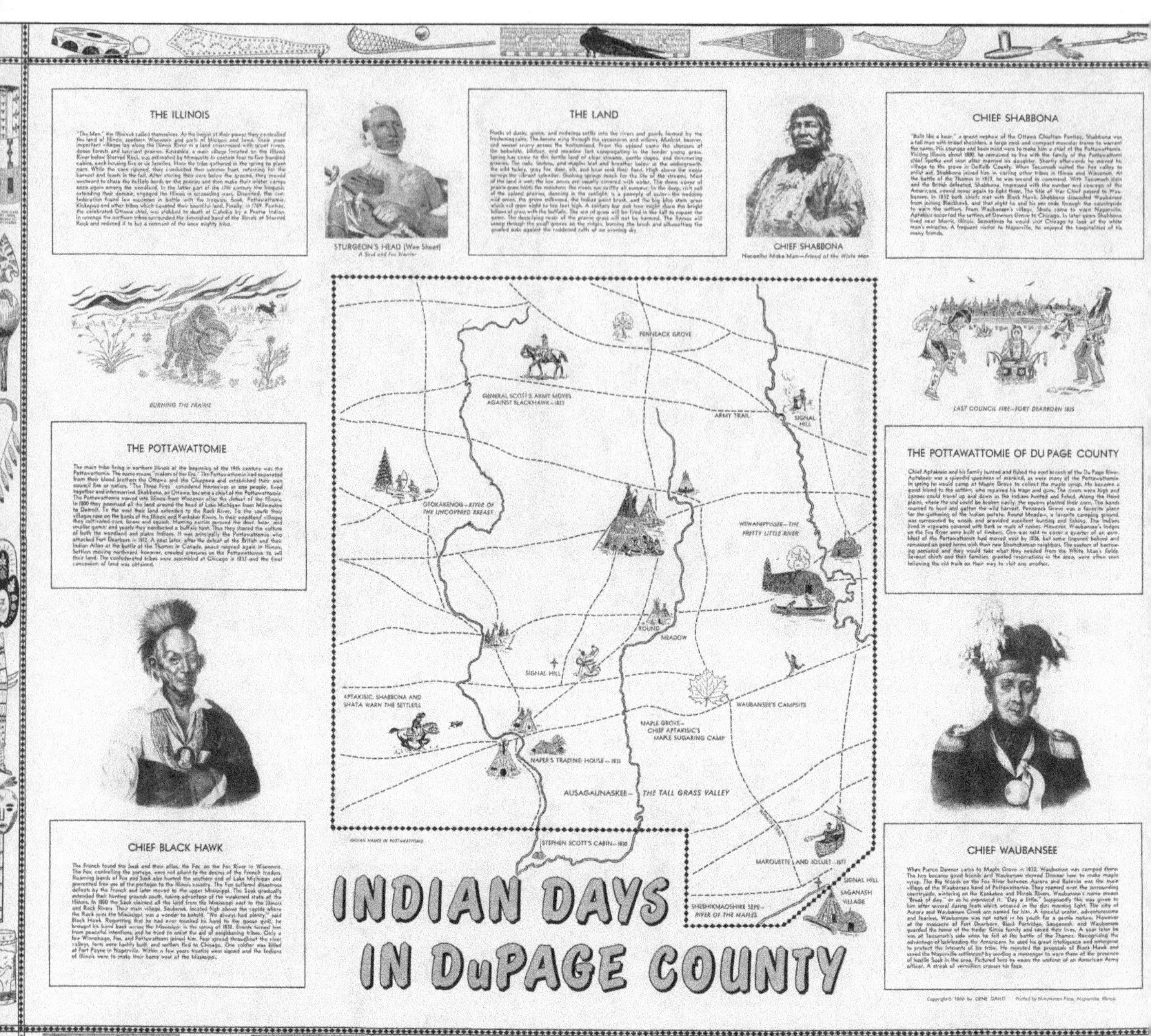

Native Americans lived here for centuries before the first white settler arrived. In northeastern Illinois, Sauk, Fox, Winnebago, and Potawatomi peoples hunted and fished, collected fruits and nuts, and cultivated corn, beans, and squash. They traded with the first Europeans to enter the region. Their autonomy on this land was forcibly ended with the signing of the Treaty of Chicago in 1833, compelling them to move west of the Mississippi River. They received their final payments at Fort Dearborn in August 1835 and then had to leave the land they called home. (Courtesy of the DuPage County Historical Museum.)

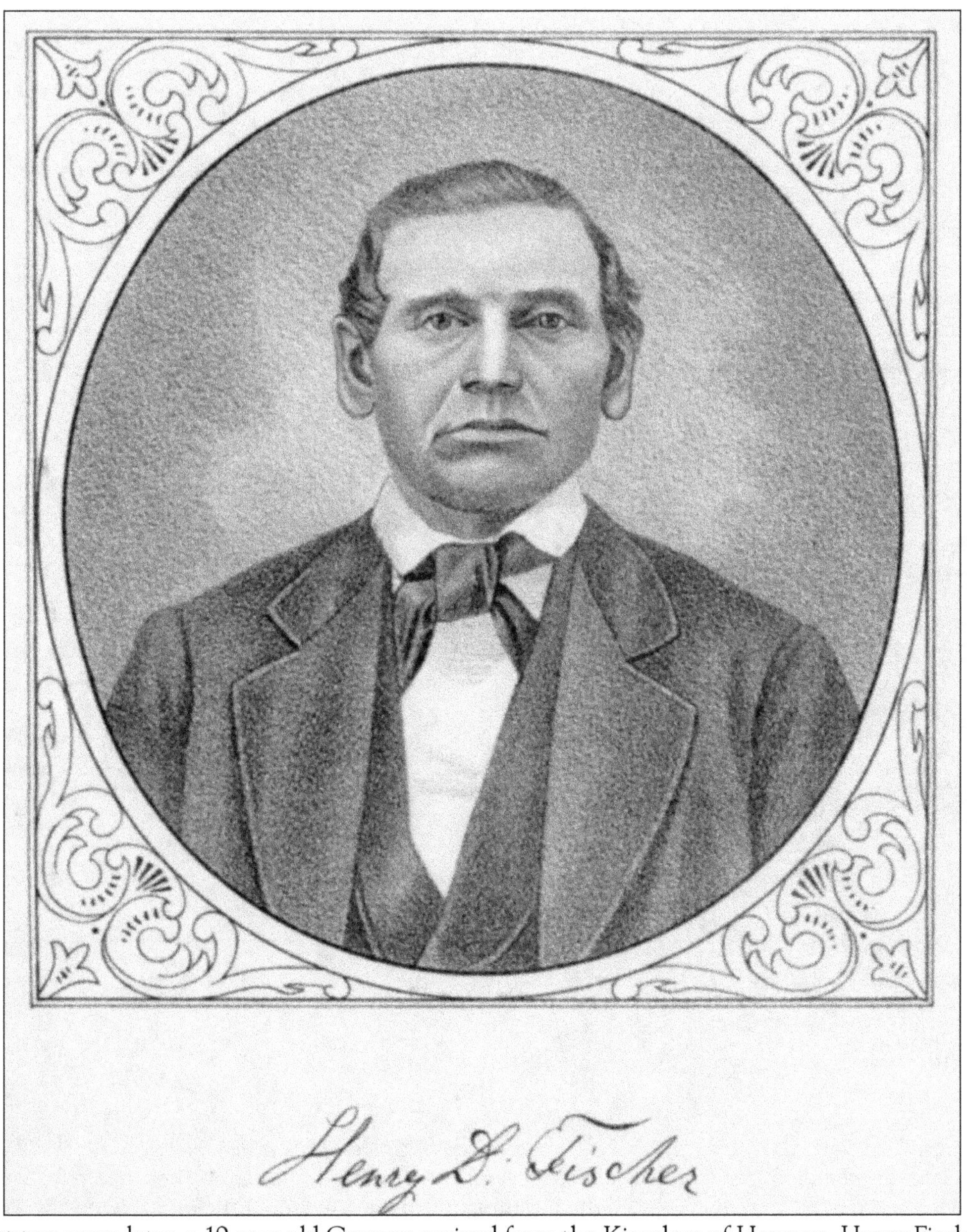

Just two years later, a 19-year-old German arrived from the Kingdom of Hanover. Henry Fischer had been preceded by his uncle, Christian, also from Hanover and two other settlers, Hezekiah Dunklee and Mason Smith, from New Hampshire. These were the first white men to settle in what would become the northeast corner of DuPage County. Dunklee and Smith chose a location just east of Salt Creek and north of what is now Irving Park Road. Extending south from that location was a large old-growth forest that came to be referred to as Dunklee's Grove. Christian Fischer staked out his claim, encompassing nearly 1,000 acres, immediately south of this grove near Grand Avenue and Church Road. Meanwhile, his nephew Henry worked to carry ashes for soapmaking in the frontier town of Chicago while he waited for the rest of his family to arrive. He decided, however, to make his way north, as far as Green Bay and found work in a lumber mill. (Courtesy of Fischer Farm.)

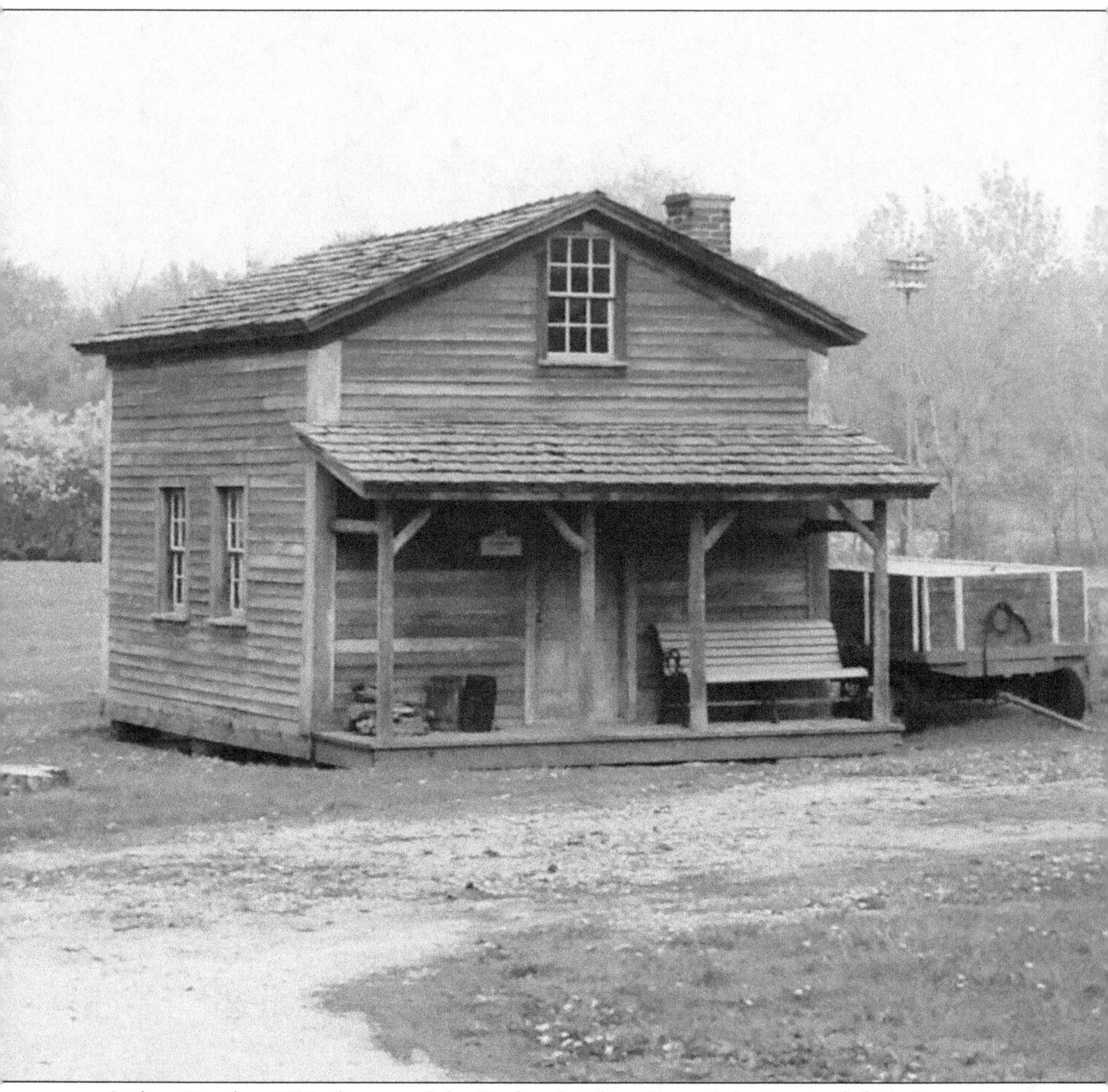

In late October 1836, the rest of the Fischer family—Conrad, Louisa, and their five remaining children—arrived. They had crossed the Atlantic and arrived in New York City. Then they went by boat up the Hudson River, unfortunately losing one young daughter to drowning on this leg of the journey. Reaching Albany, the family traveled westward on the Erie Canal and then by ship across the Great Lakes. Henry having learned of his family's arrival walked to Chicago from Green Bay. With the family assembled, Christian walked his brother's family from Lake Michigan to what was to become the northeast corner of DuPage County. They cut down trees from Dunklee's Grove and built their new home. The 14-by-16-foot log house was home to all eight members of the family. This remains the oldest extant structure in the county. (Author's collection.)

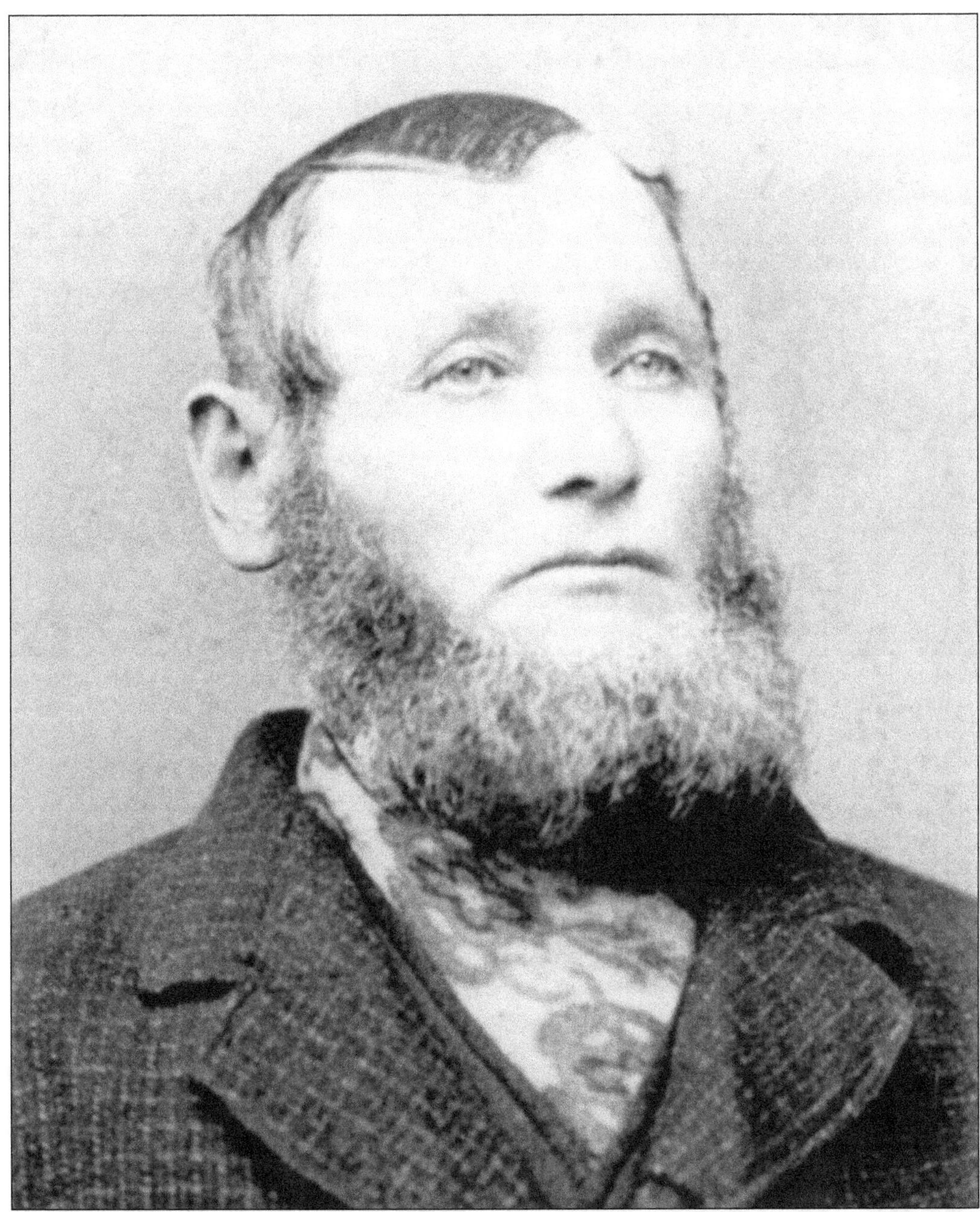

Henry's youngest brother, August, inherited the middle part of the family's original claim. Here, August would build a successful dairy farm. He grew the herd of cows and acquired horses, pigs, chickens, ducks, and geese. On the south side of Grand Avenue, he broke the prairie sod and planted feed corn, oats, and barley to feed his livestock. The eggs from the various birds along with the milk from the cows and butter that was churned was loaded on the wagon and transported to Chicago. There, it was sold to the rapidly growing population. (Courtesy of Fischer Farm.)

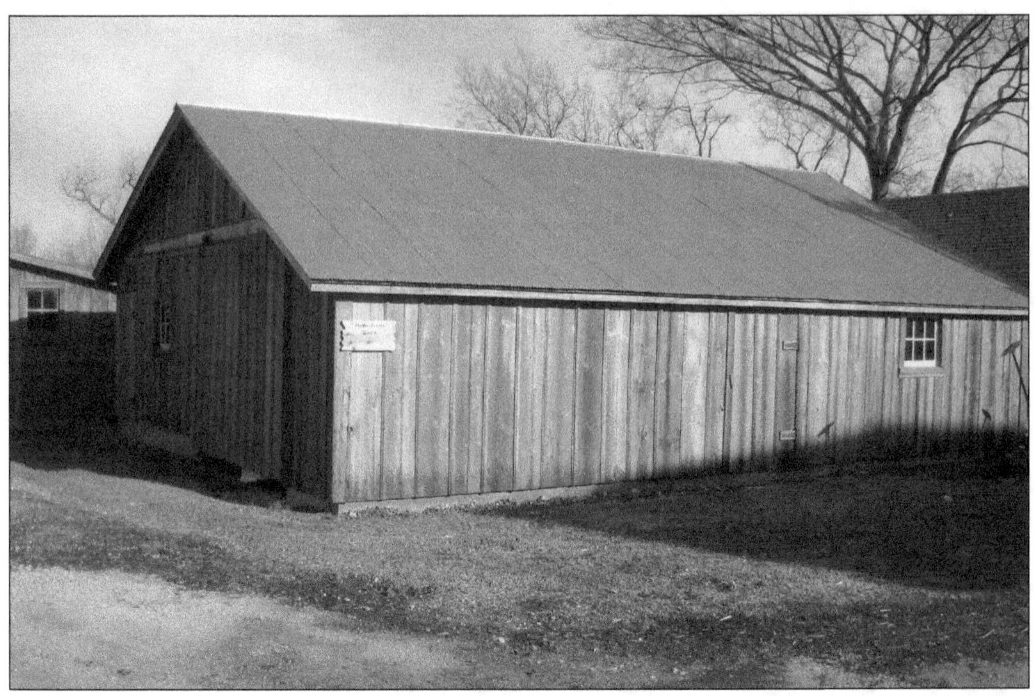

In order to operate this farm, the Fischers constructed their second building. This barn appears to have been patterned after a three-bay threshing barn. Likely, it was never used that way. The north bay was fitted with stanchions and served as the milking area. The other two bays served to house other farm implements and provided space to conduct the initial dairy work. (Author's collection.)

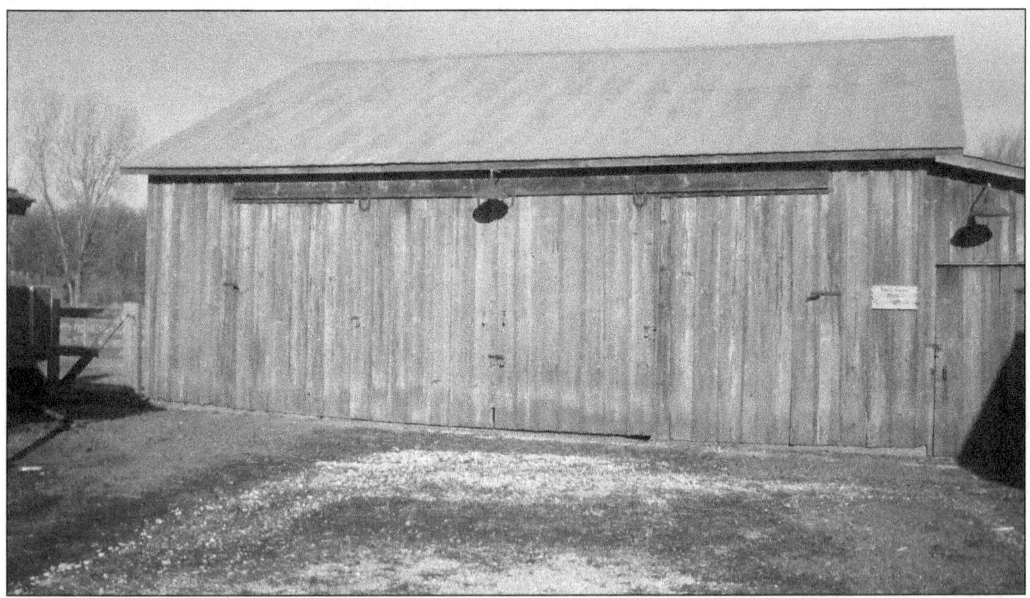

Horses were farmers' most valuable possessions. They provided the power necessary to plow the prairie into cultivated fields. They also provided the means of moving the wagons loaded with the dairy production into the city. This barn was constructed to shelter workhorses after a day of labor. It remained that way for years, until horses were replaced by tractors. (Author's collection.)

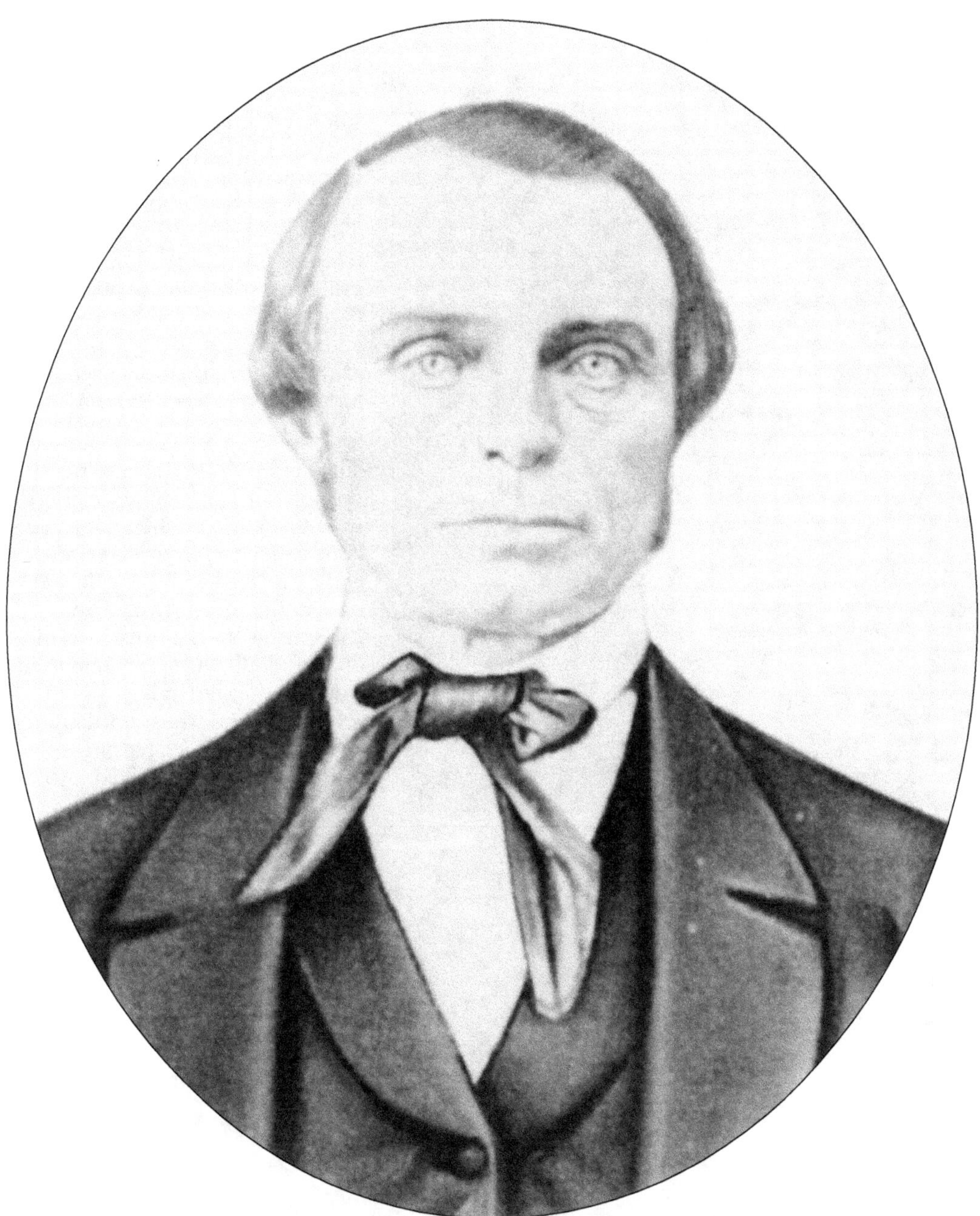

Departing their German home two years before the Fischers, the Franzen family had entered the United States through Baltimore in 1834. After brief stays in that city and then in Cincinnati, they arrived in Chicago in fall of 1835 and stayed for two years. In 1838, they established a farm just north of the Fischers and their youngest daughter, Maria, married Henry Fischer. (Courtesy of Rick Franzen.)

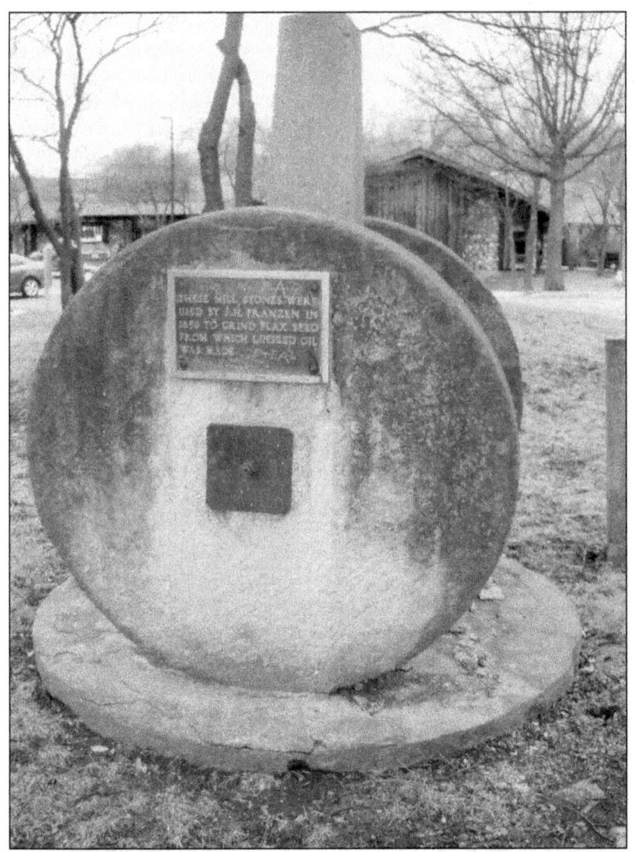

In 1847, Maria's elder brother, John Henry Franzen, built a mill and a brick factory. The stones pictured here were used to grind the flaxseed in order to extract linseed oil. This was used as sealant on bricks. The flax fibers were also used to make linen cloth. The mill originally stood between Memorial and Wood Streets and Mason and Barron Streets. Only the grinding stones remain today. (Author's collection.)

The Fischers sold the eastern portion of their claim to relatives in 1847. Henry Fischer, not to be confused with Henry described earlier, arrived with his wife and nine children. He farmed and then turned to the construction of a windmill with parts imported from the Netherlands. It would grind corn and wheat until 1916. Edward Ehlers operated the mill after the Fischers sold it to him and moved to Oregon.

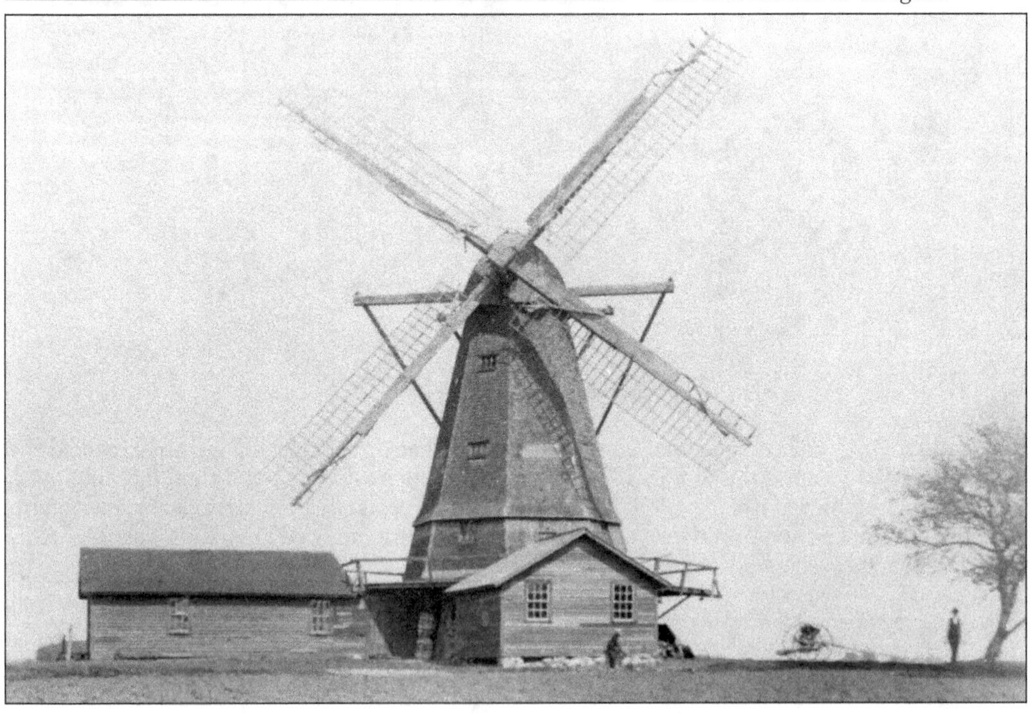

Just to the east of the Franzens, another claimed was made. This was the Korthauer family. Henry and Maria along with their three children—Caroline, William, and Herman—had also emigrated from the Kingdom of Hanover. They too constructed their new home. Henry would open a store and work as a cabinetmaker. Their first home survives, making it the oldest structure in the village of Bensenville proper.

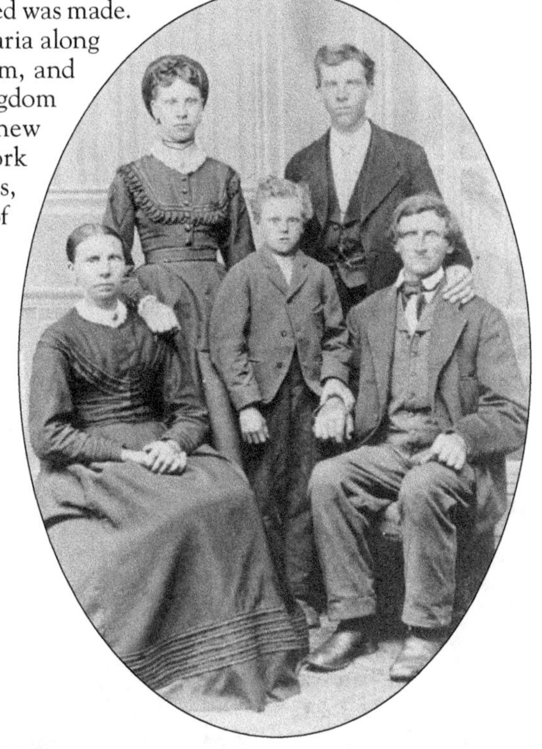

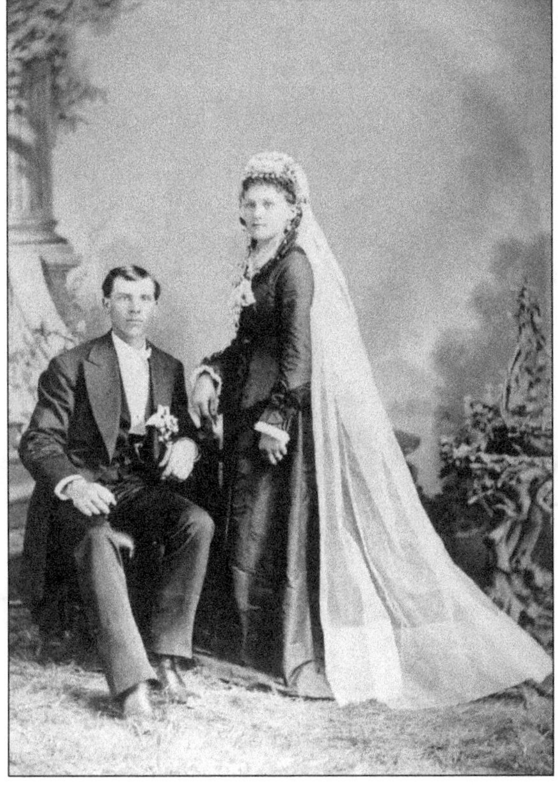

Herman Korthauer, the eldest son of Henry and Maria, would become a central figure in the early years of Bensenville. He would take over the family business running a hardware store. Herman would also help organize the village and the fire department.

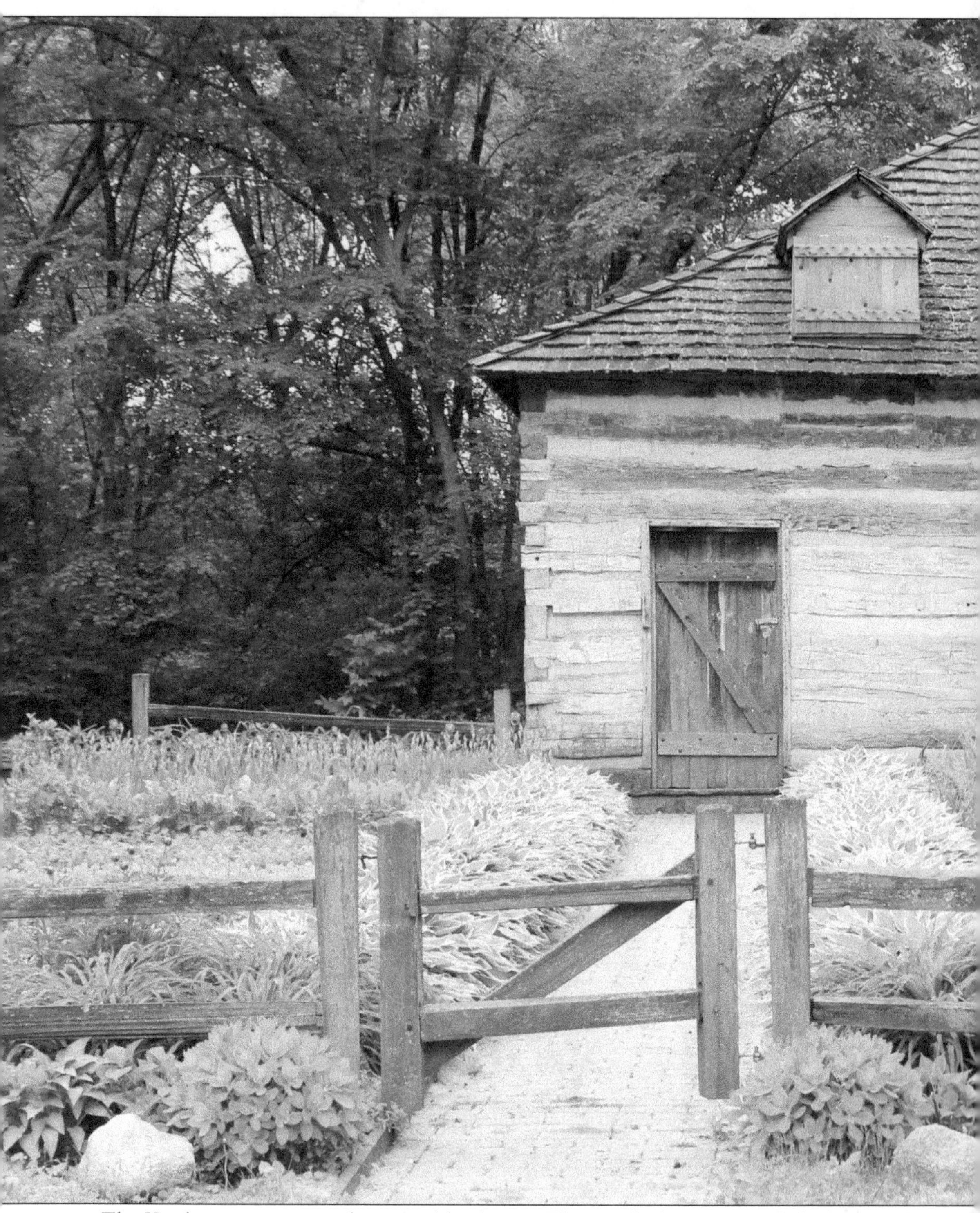

The Korthauers constructed a typical log house. They worked to square off the beams, thus differentiating the structure from a log cabin. The loft was accessed by a steep riser stairway. The back of the structure provided access to a root cellar, the primary way to store foodstuffs.

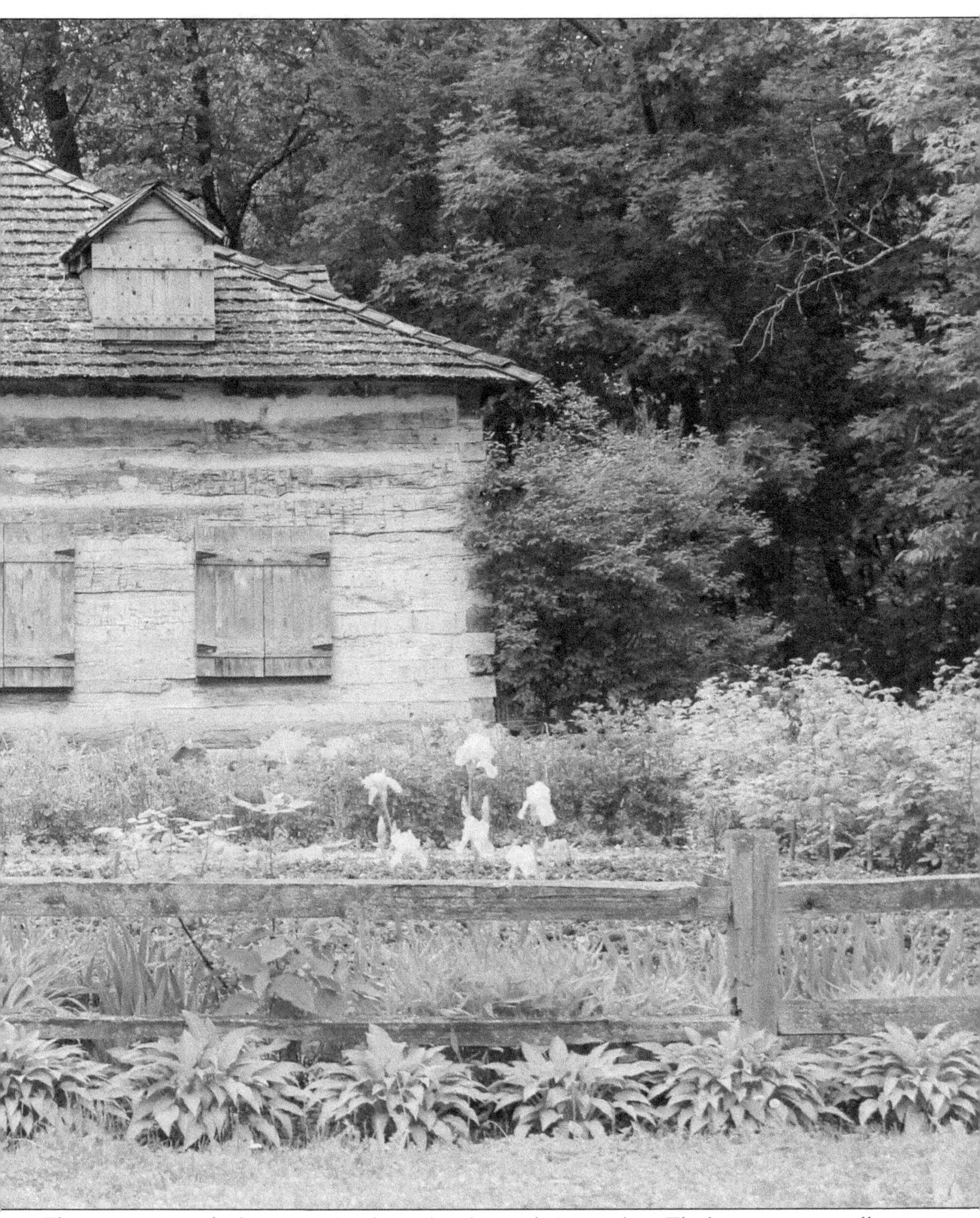

The property stretched out east of York Road to the Cook County line. The house was originally located on Green Street near Evergreen Street.

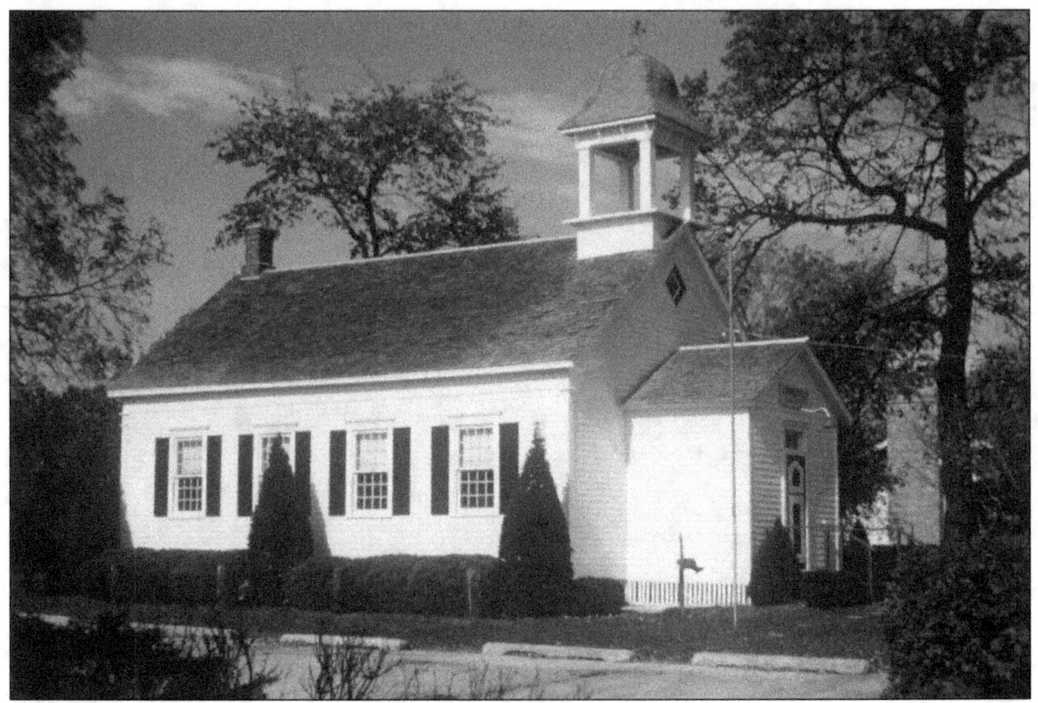

The families that settled in the northeast corner of DuPage County wanted to provide for their children in their new home. Education was a priority. Within 10 years, a school board was established. One of its members, August Fischer, donated a parcel of his property for the building of a school. August, his brother Henry, and several others worked together and the school, Fischer Schoolhouse, became a reality in 1851.

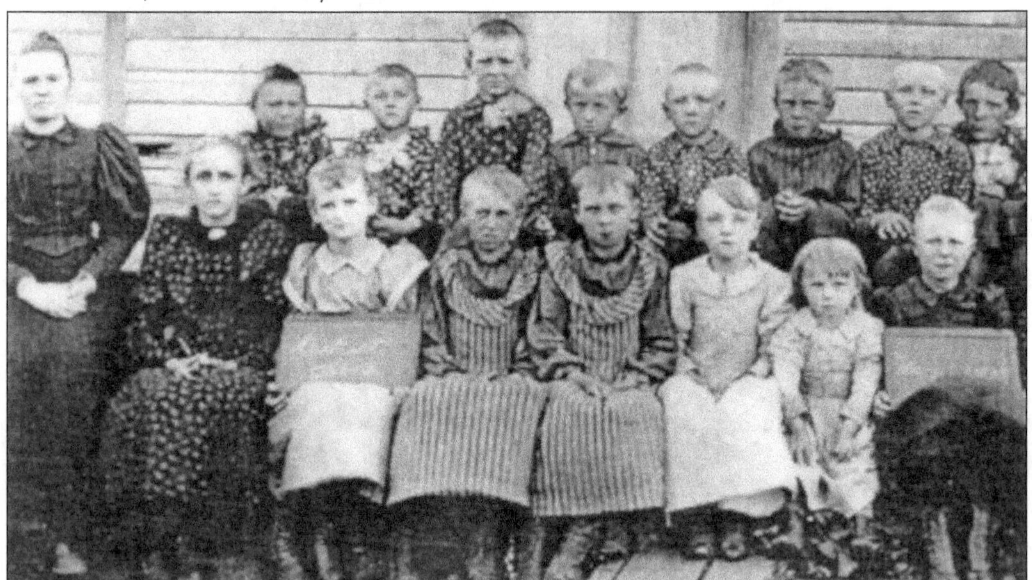

The children came when they could, and were frequently prevented by work on the farm. When they were able, they were often eager to learn all they could. There was one teacher, and the students ranged in age from five to fifteen. The teacher taught all subjects to all grades. Pay was low, and the teacher often had to stay with one of the student's families.

The only entity of greater importance than the school was the church. The families from the Kingdom of Hanover had been Lutheran. Their faith brought them together to meet in one another's homes until funds were raised for the purchase of property and the construction of a church building. Zion Lutheran Church was born.

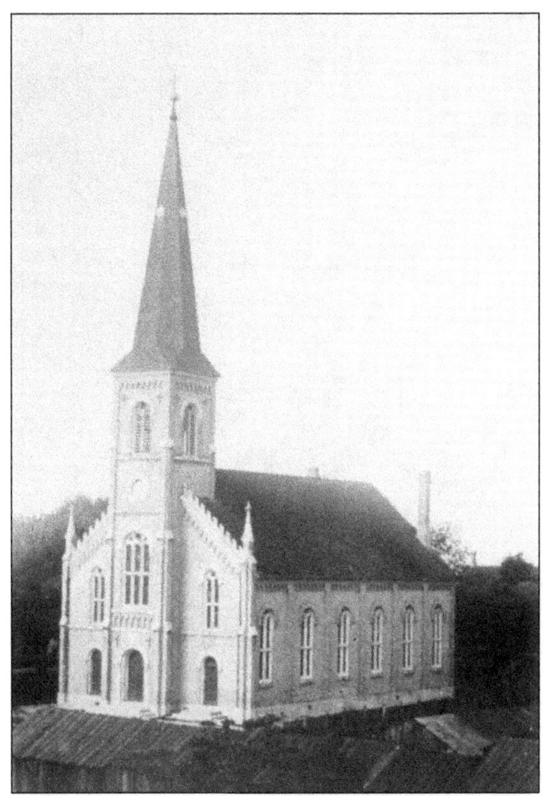

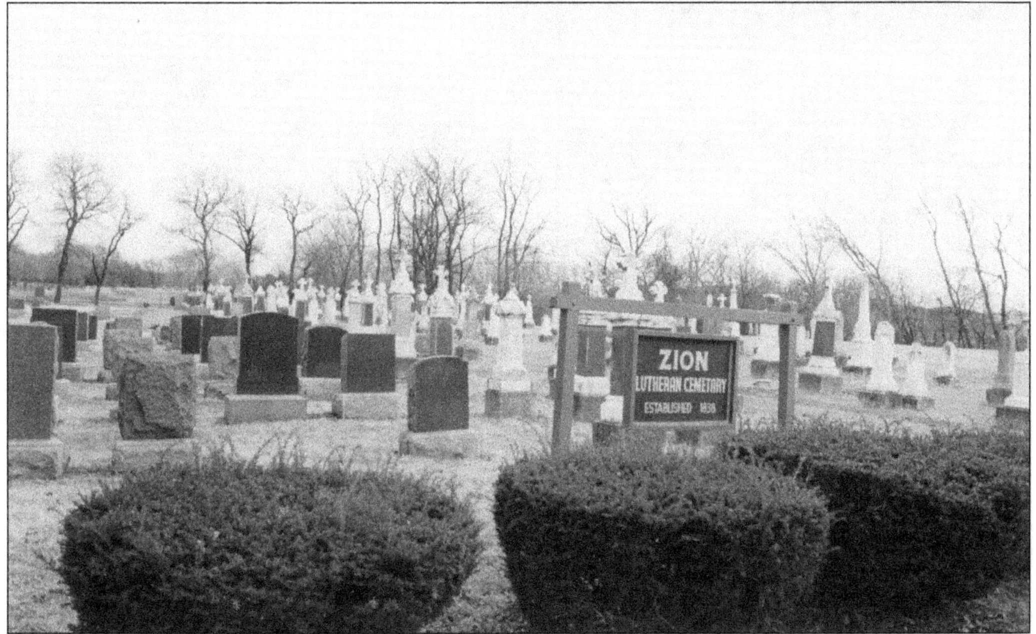

At the church, the ordinances of baptism and holy communion were observed, and weddings were celebrated. Here, also, funerals were observed. The faithful members of the congregation were laid to rest in the very shadow of the steeple. The records of birth, baptism, and death were carefully recorded. These practices kept the faith, traditions, and history preserved.

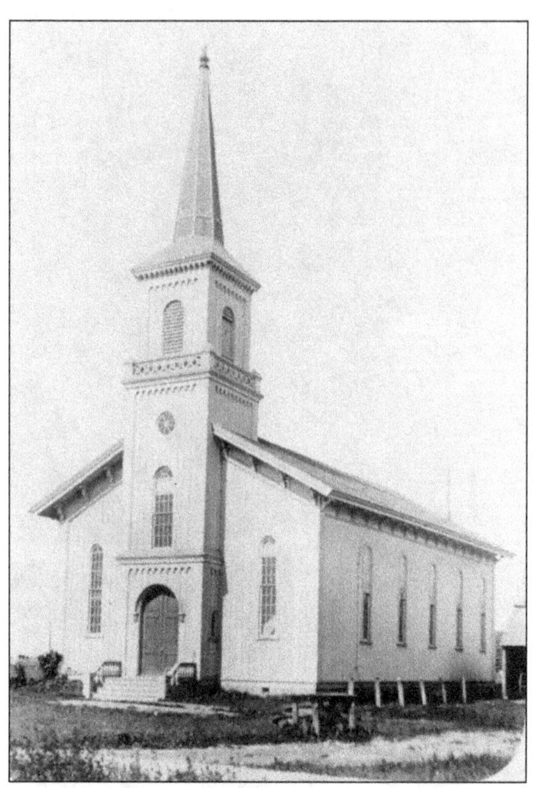

There was not always agreement within the church. After 10 years of meeting together, Rev. E.A. Brauer asked that one tradition of Lutheran practice be given priority. Evangelical and Reformed Lutherans parted company amicably. The Fischers, part of those withdrawing, again donated land and a new church was constructed. Immanuel Church grew into a vibrant congregation.

The parcel also included space for another cemetery, referred to as Churchville Cemetery. The first burial took place in 1859. Here are found the graves of the first to settle: Conrad and Louisa Fischer. Their grandson, killed in battle just outside of Atlanta in 1864, would be interred here as well. In 2000, a formal sign for the cemetery was finally placed. (Author's collection.)

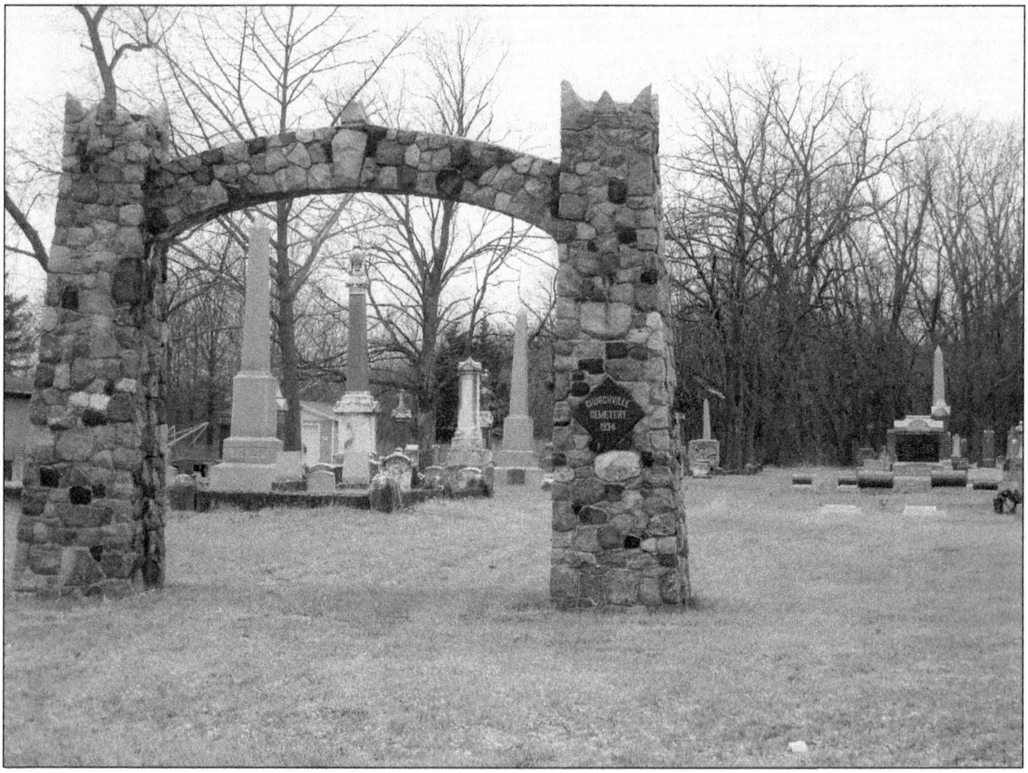

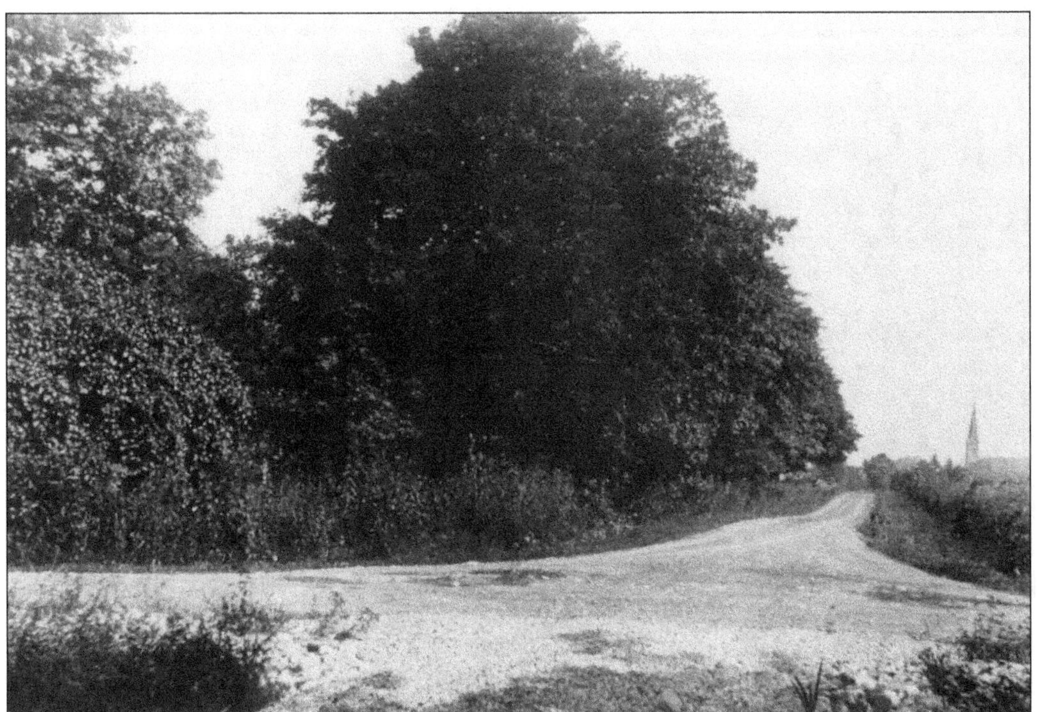

It had originally been the meeting point of all three ecosystems: the hardwood forest extending from the north met the wetland, which gave way to prairie stretching away for miles to the south. Now, that prairie was being plowed under. The Fischers put in rows of feed corn, oats, and barley on the south side of Grand Avenue. So did the Franzens, the Korthauers, and other families that arrived.

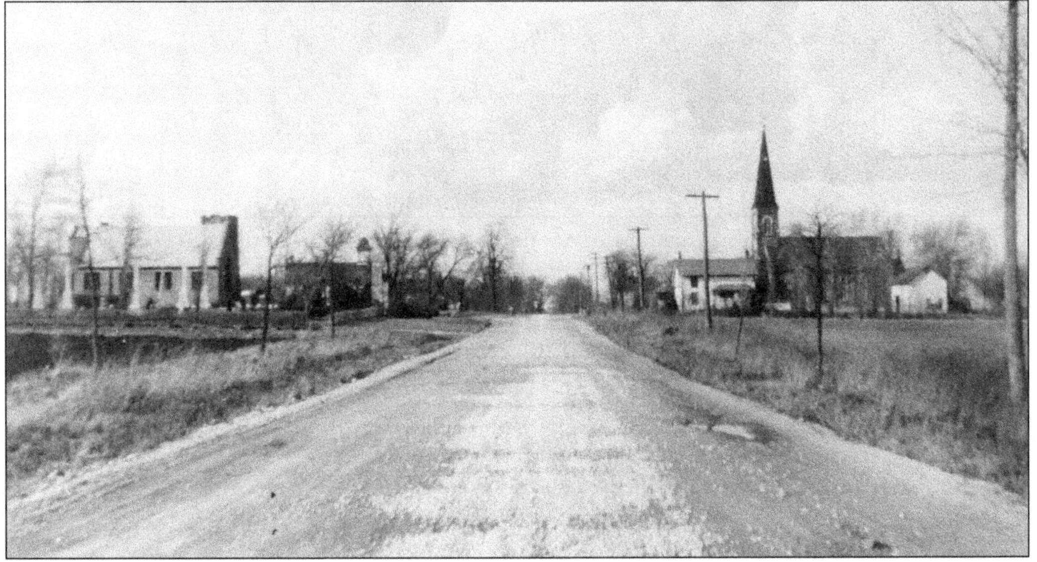

Between these first farms on a stretch of Church Road just north of Grand Avenue, a community was taking shape. Zion Lutheran Church stood on the east side of the road. Across the street stood Immanuel Church, the schoolhouse, and a store operated by the Fischers. People took to calling it Churchville.

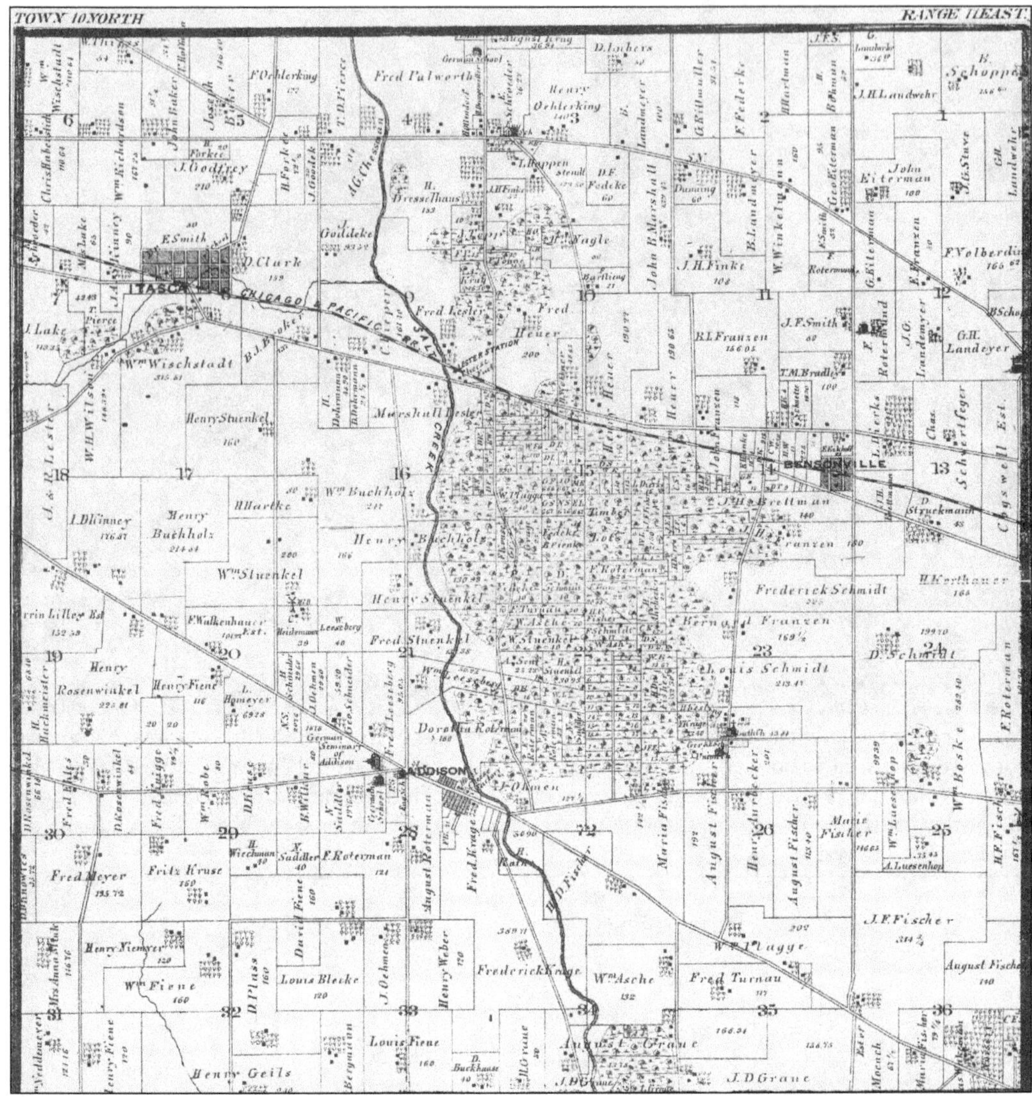

This plat of survey from 1874 includes many names of the original families to settle the area. Parcels owned by Fischers, Franzens, Korthauers, Koehlers, and Schmidts clearly reveal the German heritage of the area. They worshiped on Sunday and worked all week long. Dairy production and other related services were taking these hardworking settlers to Chicago and back again often. The connection was growing stronger. The community was going to change.

Two

Railroad

The Chicago & Pacific Railroad began laying tracks early in 1873. Before the first of March, the rails stretched out of Chicago on a northwesterly route that passed the green park at Humboldt, skirted the orchards in Dunning, passed through River Grove, crossed the Des Plaines River, and climbed the grade to Bensenville.

A village plat was drawn in the late summer of 1873 and officially recorded on October 10. That same year, the town received a post office, which was initially housed inside Heibenthal's Store on the north side of Main Street between Center and Addison Streets.

Bensenville, however, lacked a school. The Churchville Schoolhouse was nearly two miles to the southwest. On April 5, 1884, residents gathered in Herman Korthauer's hardware store to discuss the need for a school as well as the issue of incorporation. A six-member committee was created to poll residents on these issues and determine costs. One week later, residents gathered and, accepting the report, authorized the committee to file the petition for incorporation. The vote, held on May 10, passed 42 to 7.

The Chicago, Milwaukee, & St. Paul Railway bought out the Chicago & Pacific in 1898. The railroad was already transporting 300,000 gallons of milk in addition to large quantities of butter and cheese to Chicago. The Milwaukee Road (Chicago, Milwaukee, St. Paul & Pacific Railroad) operated Godfrey Yard immediately east of Bensenville, which had the potential to be enlarged and was near an artesian well. This well was immediately on the south side of the tracks in the center of the village. Artesian water was preferred for steam engines, as it did not result in any buildup inside the locomotives' flues and pipes. A roundhouse and turntable were built there in 1916. The entrance of the United States into World War I in April 1917 greatly spurred railroad traffic and launched the era of railroad dominance. The staff at the yard increased accordingly.

Some lived in Chicago, taking a company-provided train to and from the yard. Some, especially those who had families, moved to Bensenville. Others began to rent rooms in one of the few hotels in Bensenville. Railroads continued to grow throughout the 1920s, and an ever-increasing level of freight was moved through the yard, which soon stretched three miles in length and, by 1945, had a capacity of 8,323 cars. In 1953, the Milwaukee Road installed electronic controls.

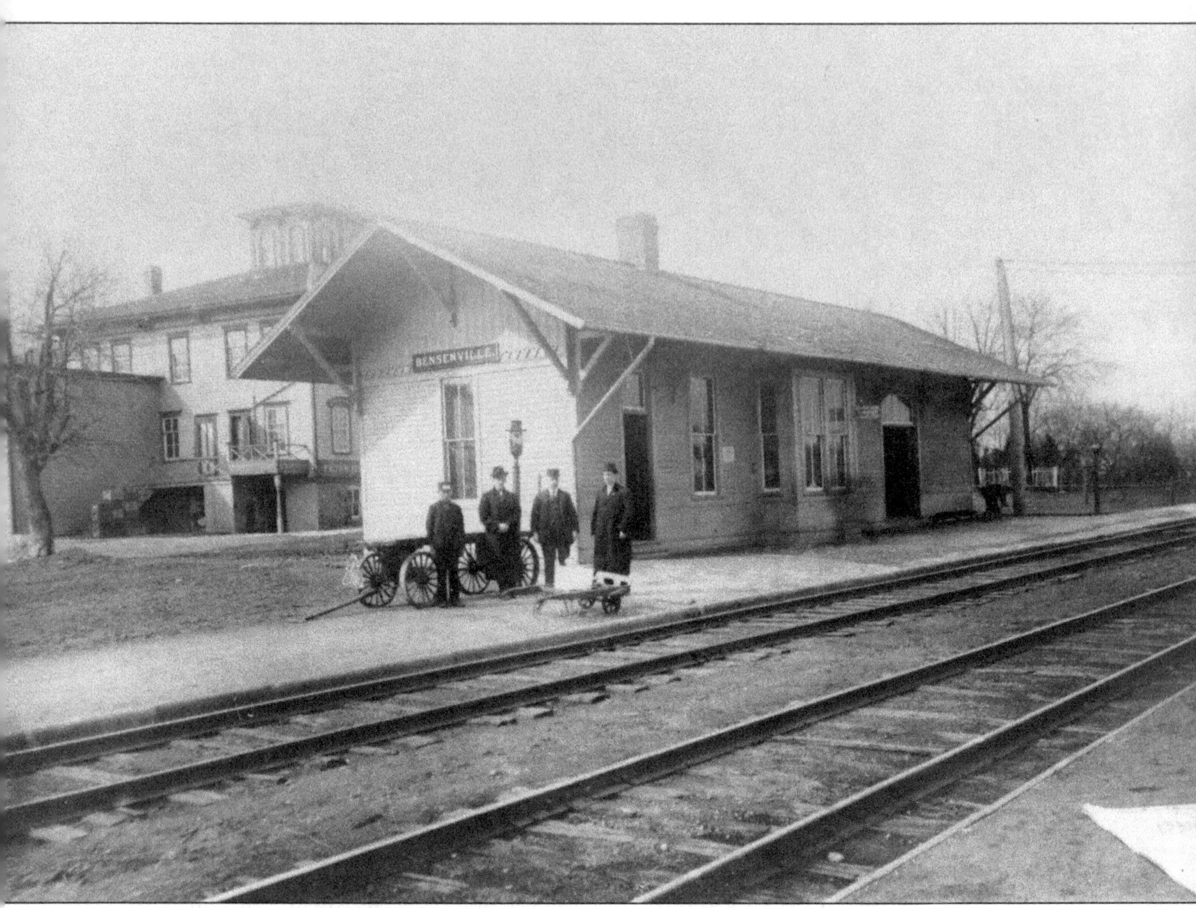

The laying of the railroad tracks only made final what had already been happening. The center of activity had shifted one and a half miles to the northeast. The blacksmith shop, saloon, and general stores were built just northeast of the Franzen mill. The railroad depot was built in 1873 on the south side of the tracks between what were being called Center and Addison Streets.

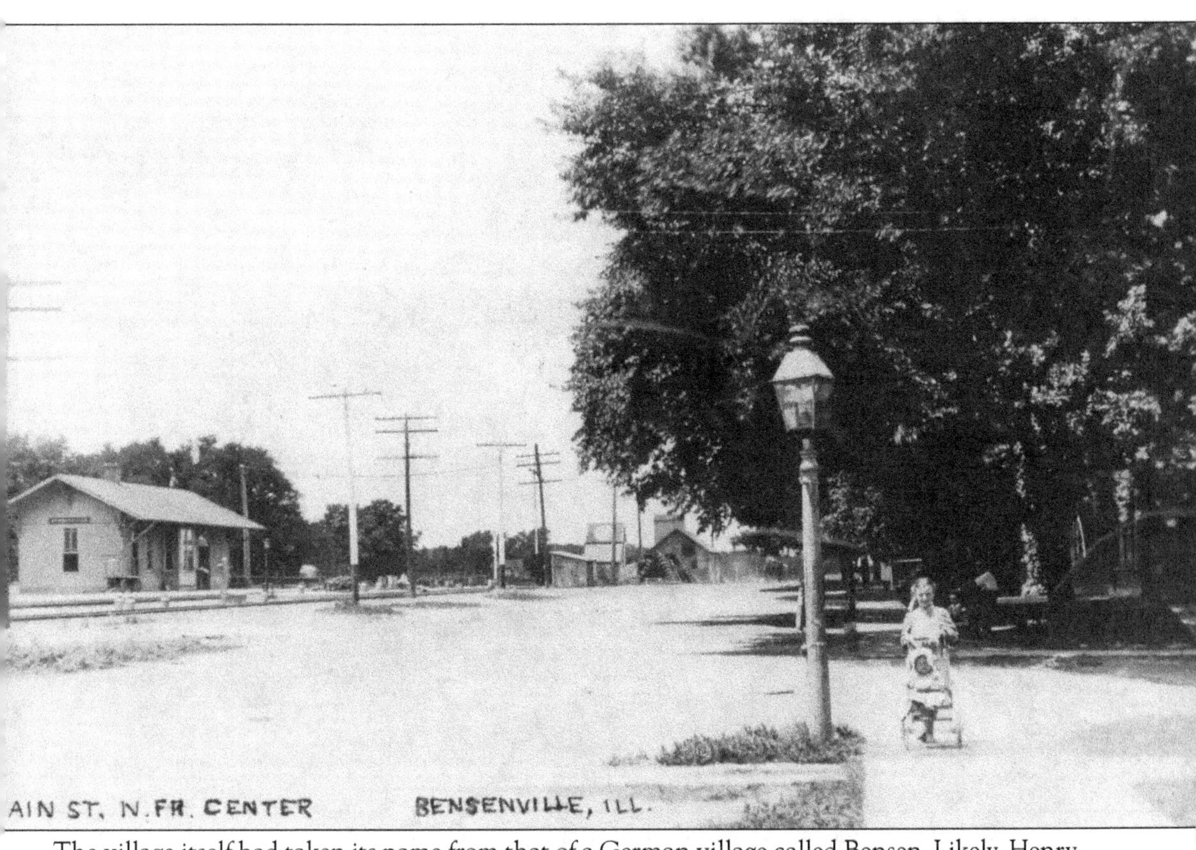

The village itself had taken its name from that of a German village called Bensen. Likely, Henry Schutte suggested the name as it had been his birthplace. The town was located in the Kingdom of Hanover, from which many of the other residents had emigrated as well. Agreement was found on the variation of the name as Bensenville.

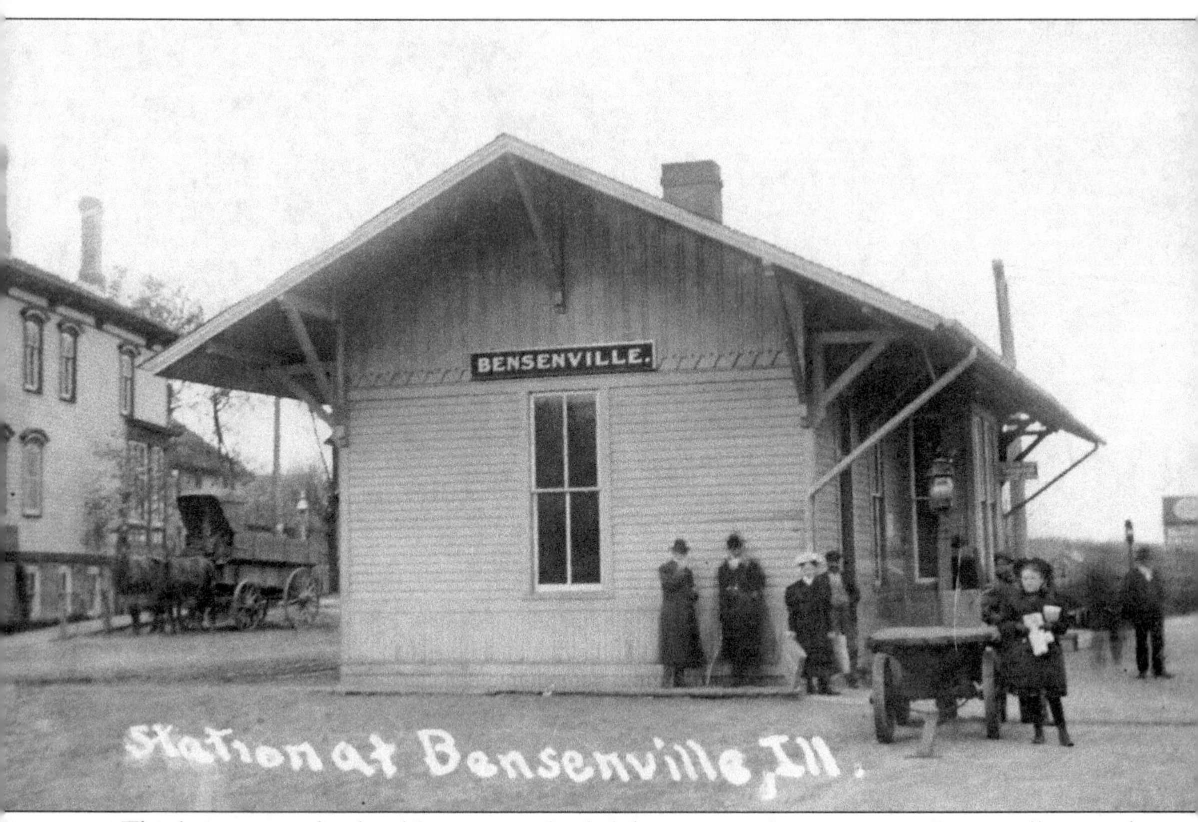

The depot meant that local farmers now loaded their wagons for transport to Bensenville, a much shorter trip. From there, it would go into Chicago by train. The milk cans, crates of eggs, and cheese piled up on the platform waiting for shipment. The depot is shown here in 1908.

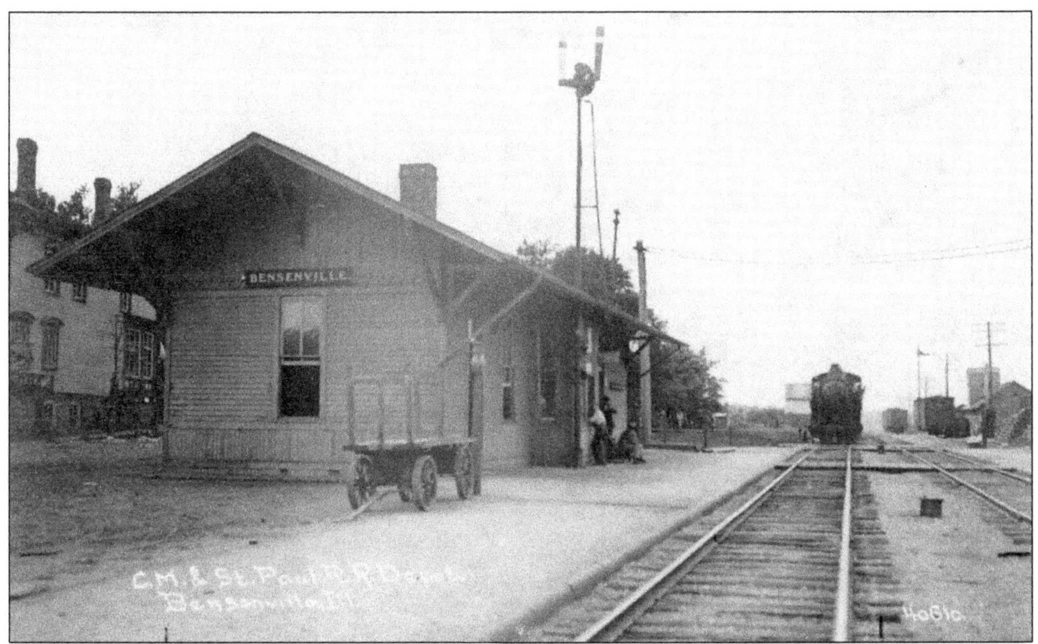

The Atlantic & Pacific Railroad had been chartered in 1865, but shortly, the stockholders changed the name to the Chicago & Pacific. It did not last long. Its lines and rolling stock were leased by the Chicago, Milwaukee, & St. Paul Railway, better known as the Milwaukee Road, beginning in 1880. Here, a train bound for Chicago pulls into Bensenville from the west. On the right-hand side, structures of the Franzen lumberyard can be seen.

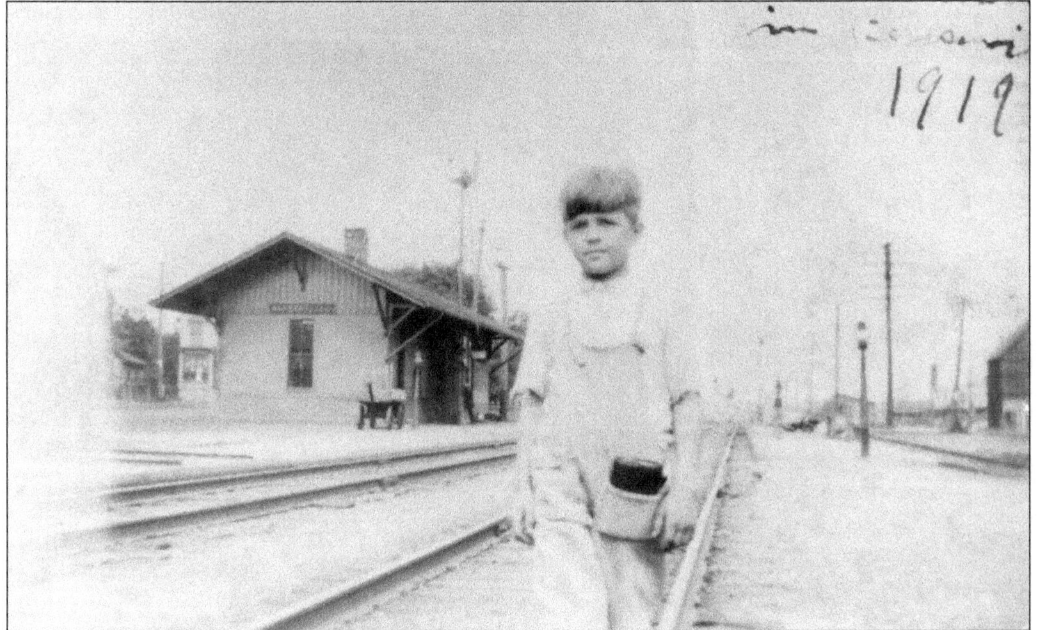

In 1898, the Milwaukee Road bought out the Chicago & Pacific, with the transfer completed in 1900. It placed this line in the Dubuque and Illinois Division and designated it as the West Line. The name lives on under Metra, which refers to this line as the Milwaukee District West Line. Here, Louis Cornille Jr. is walking on the railroad tracks in 1919.

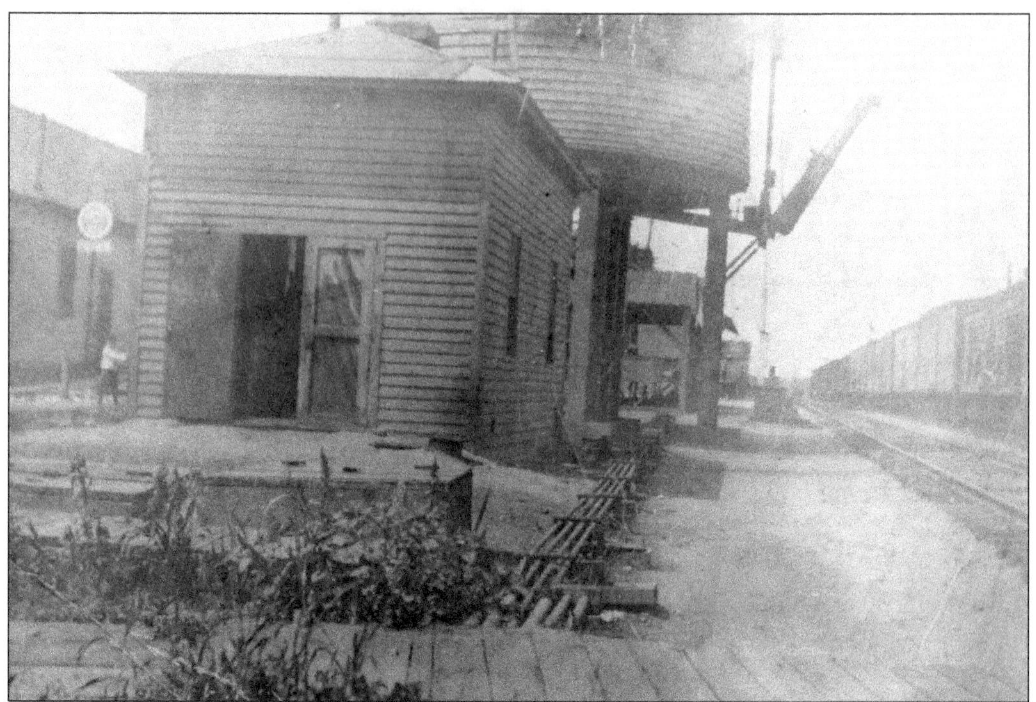

The Milwaukee Road was operating two yards in Chicago, one along Western Avenue and one in Galewood. The development of the city around these yards prevented their expansion. A third yard was located on the east side of Bensenville. Here was open land along with an artesian well. The railroad companies preferred using that water, as it did not cause any buildup in the flues and pipes of the steam locomotives.

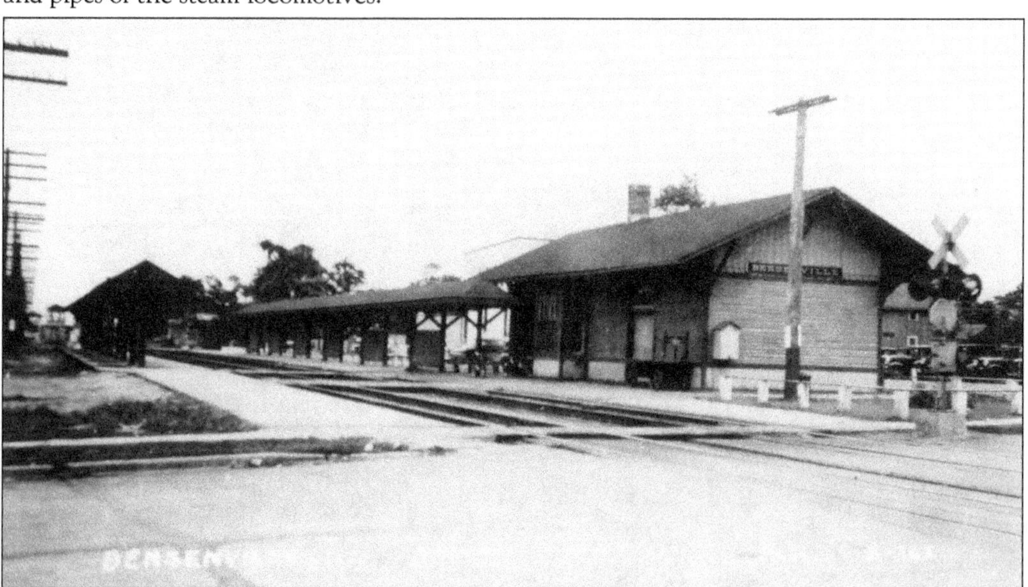

This view shows the Bensenville depot from the west in 1932. Accommodations for passenger service have been added. Note the covered portions of the platform on both north and south sides of the tracks. A parking lot now extends to the south as well. Lights have also been added to the crossing at Addison Street at the right of the picture.

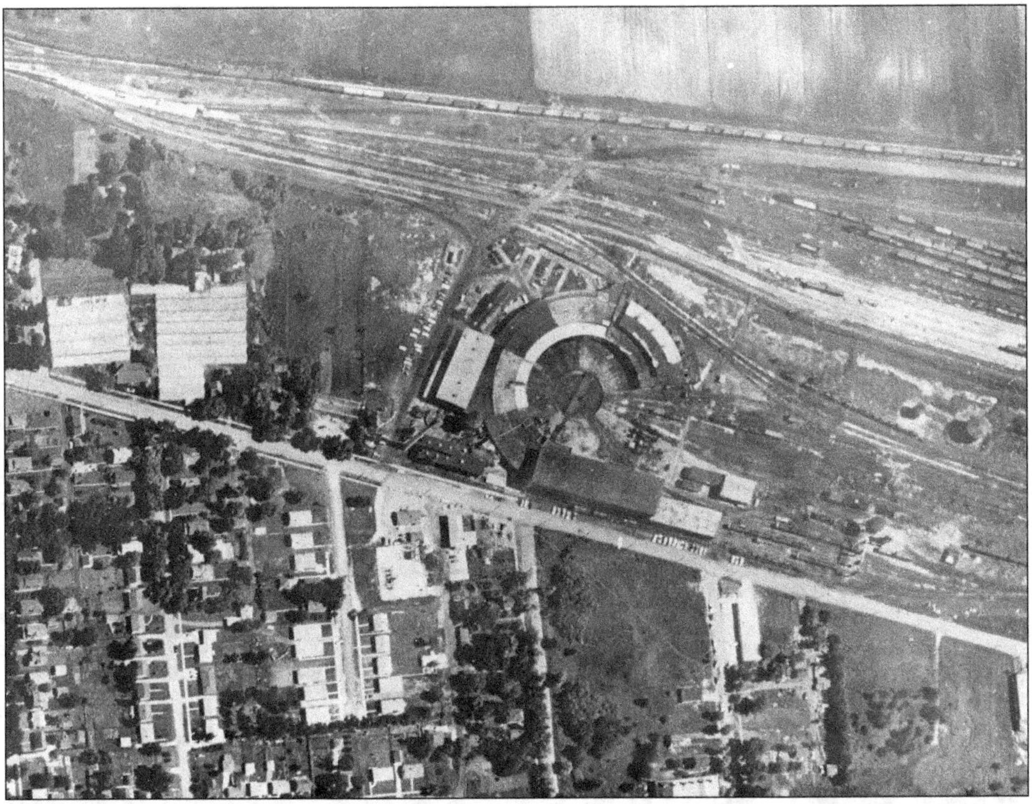

The decision was made by the Milwaukee Road to invest in what was known as Godfrey Yard. It added more tracks and a signal tower at each end. The name was also changed to the Bensenville Yard. It would change the nature of the town and its demographics.

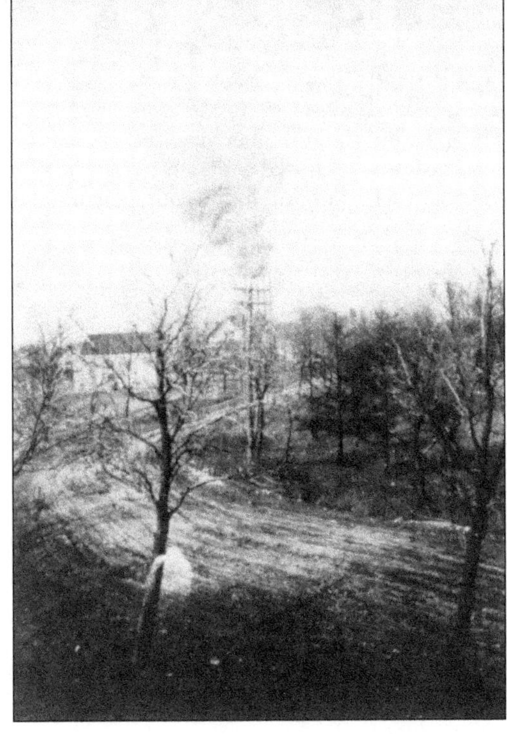

On the east side of the village, on land belonging to the Korthauers, was a favorite picnic spot. It was called Horseshoe Bend. Residents brought food and played games. The rail yard had its own coal-fired power plant, and the exhaust had a devastating effect on the tall pines in the grove. Park and Evergreen Streets along with Pine Avenue demarcate what was once Horseshoe Bend.

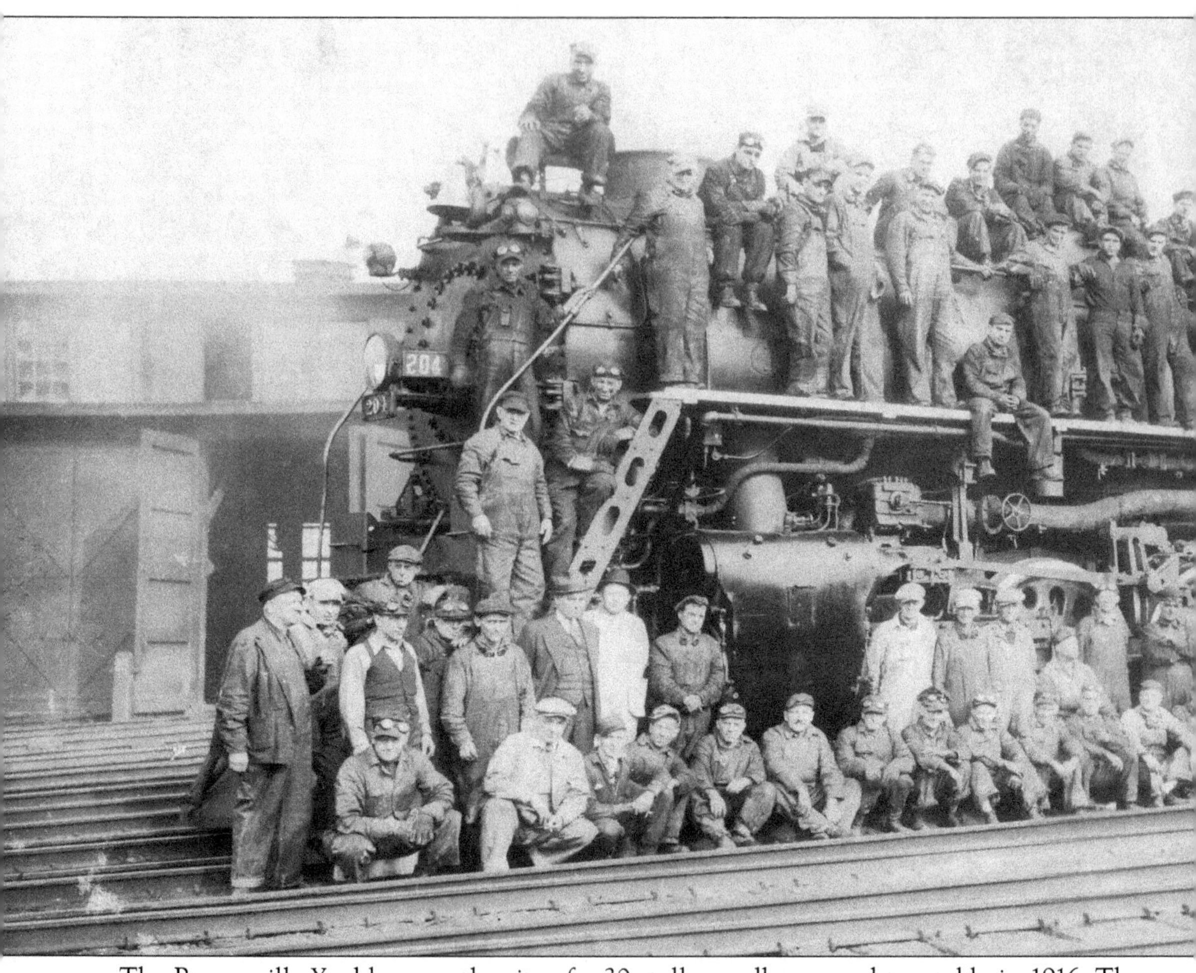

The Bensenville Yard became the site of a 30-stall roundhouse and turntable in 1916. The entrance of the United States into World War I in April 1917 increased rail traffic throughout the county. Repair and maintenance work of all types was done to the steam and then, later on,

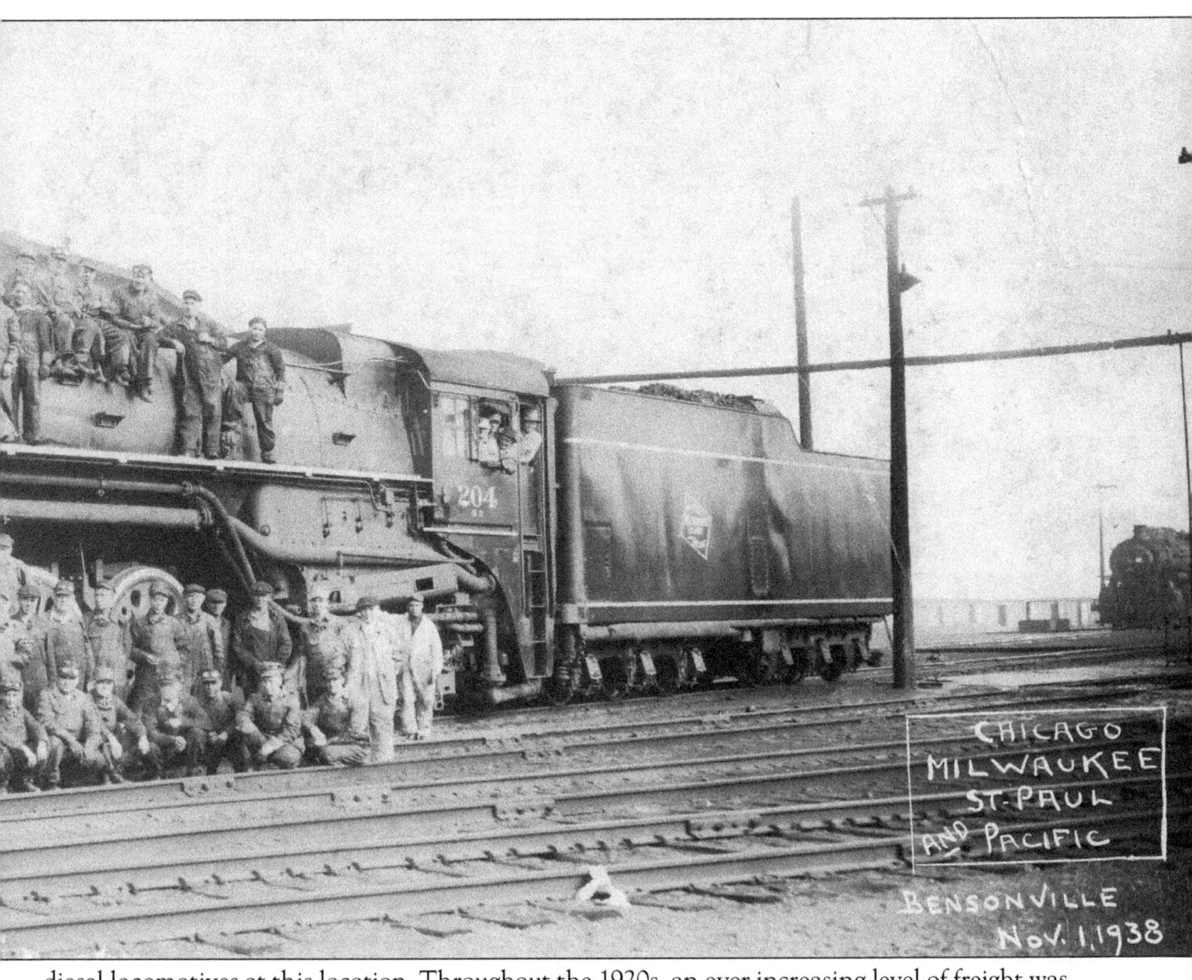

diesel locomotives at this location. Throughout the 1920s, an ever-increasing level of freight was moved through the Bensenville Yard.

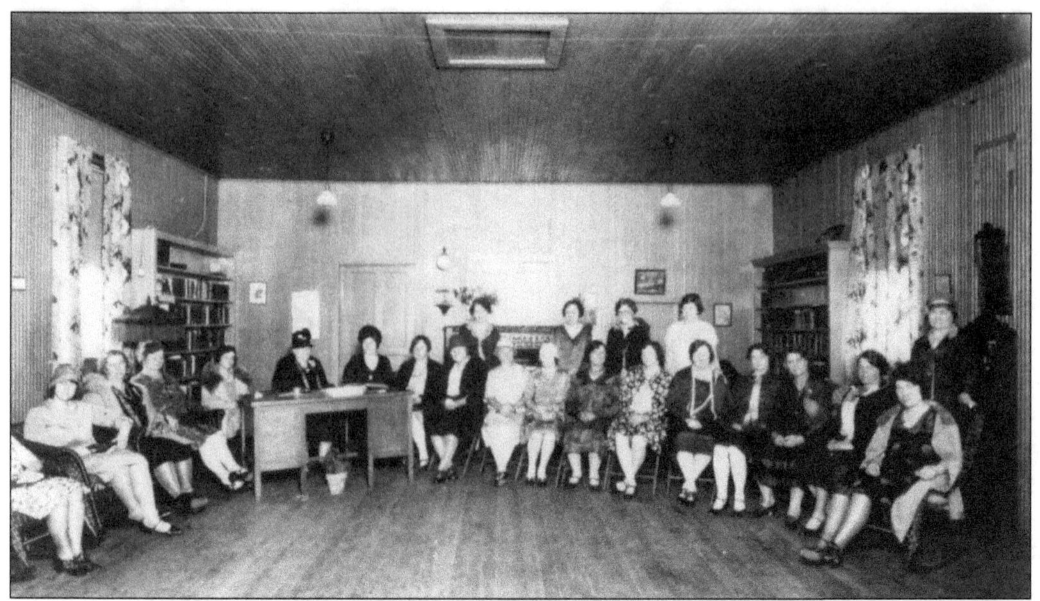

Just to the east of the depot, between York and Center Streets, two boxcars were pushed together to create a meeting place for chapter no. 3 of the Milwaukee Woman's Club. Membership was open to the wives, daughters, or sisters of the men employed by the Milwaukee Road. The Woman's Club was a philanthropic and social organization seeking to help local families that were struggling during the Depression. The structure was torn down in the late 1960s, and this chapter ceased to exist shortly after that.

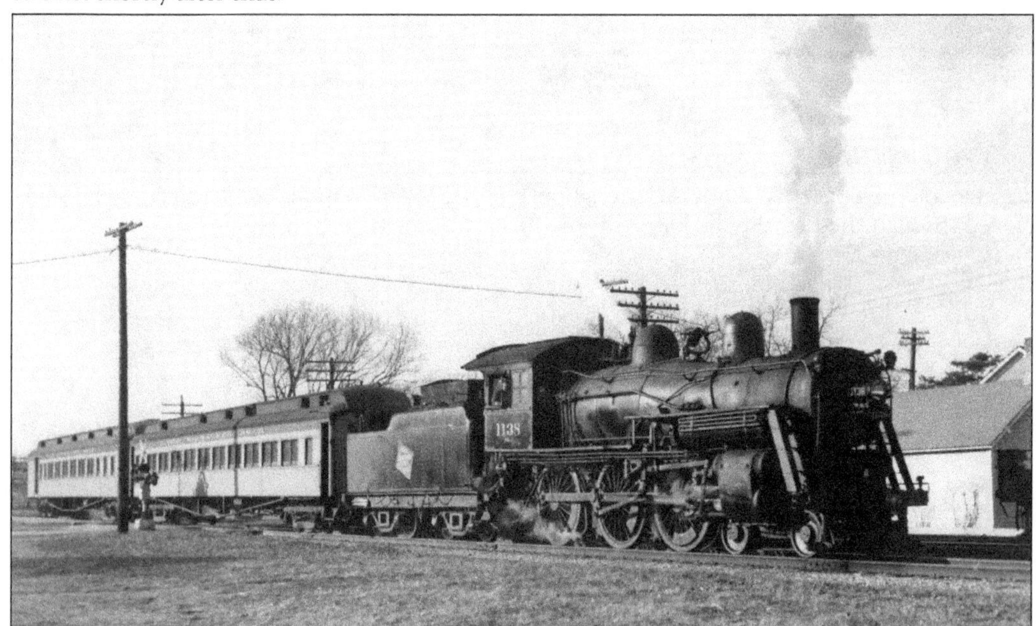

Some workers lived in Chicago and lacked transportation to work. In 1918, the company began providing a train that ran out to Bensenville and back every two hours around the clock. Some non-employees took advantage of this and efforts were put in place to control this. Other employees, especially those who had families, moved to Bensenville. Others began to rent rooms in one of the hotels in Bensenville.

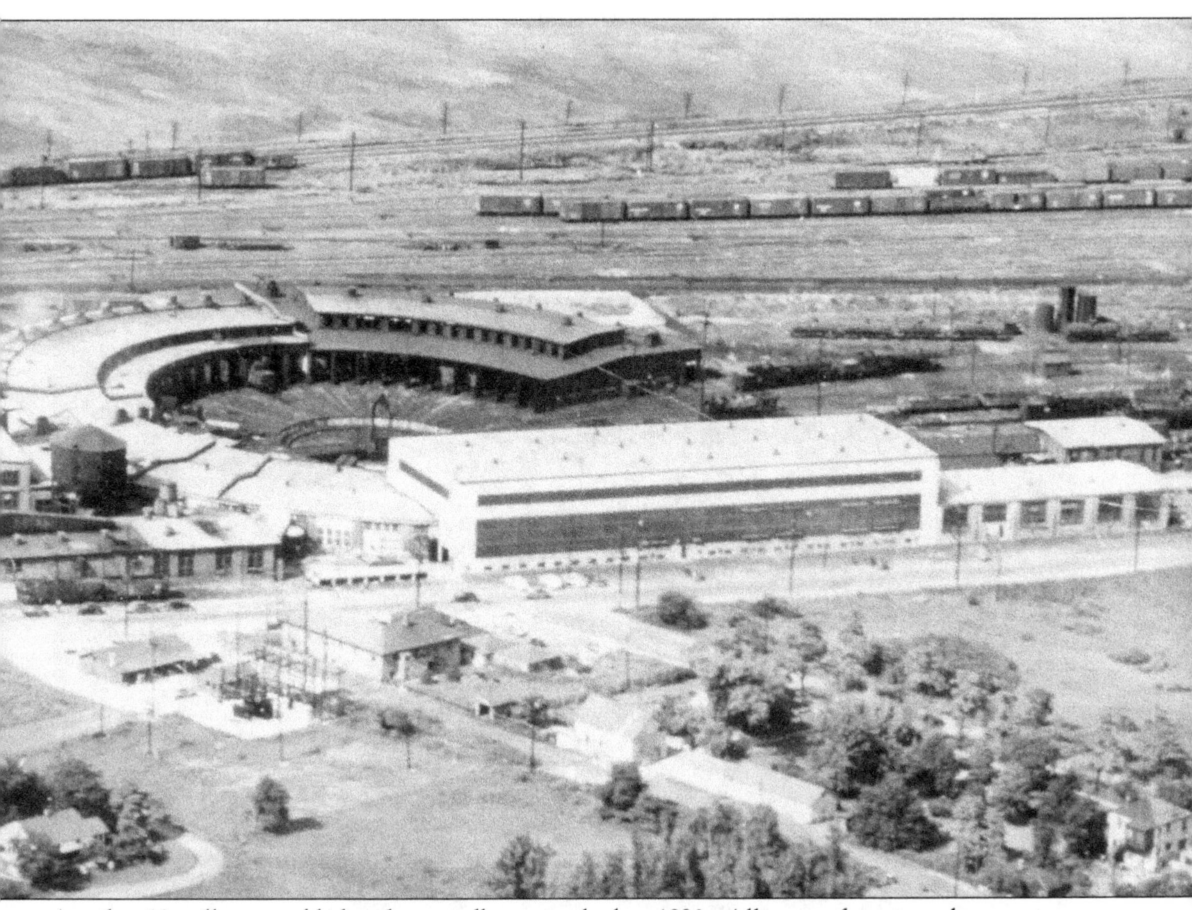

Another 10 stalls were added to the roundhouse in the late 1930s. All types of repairs to locomotives were performed as well as disassembly and assembly of trains destined to all parts of the country. By 1945, it had a capacity of 8,323 cars. In 1953, the Milwaukee Road made the yard state-of-the-art by installing electronic switches and switchboards.

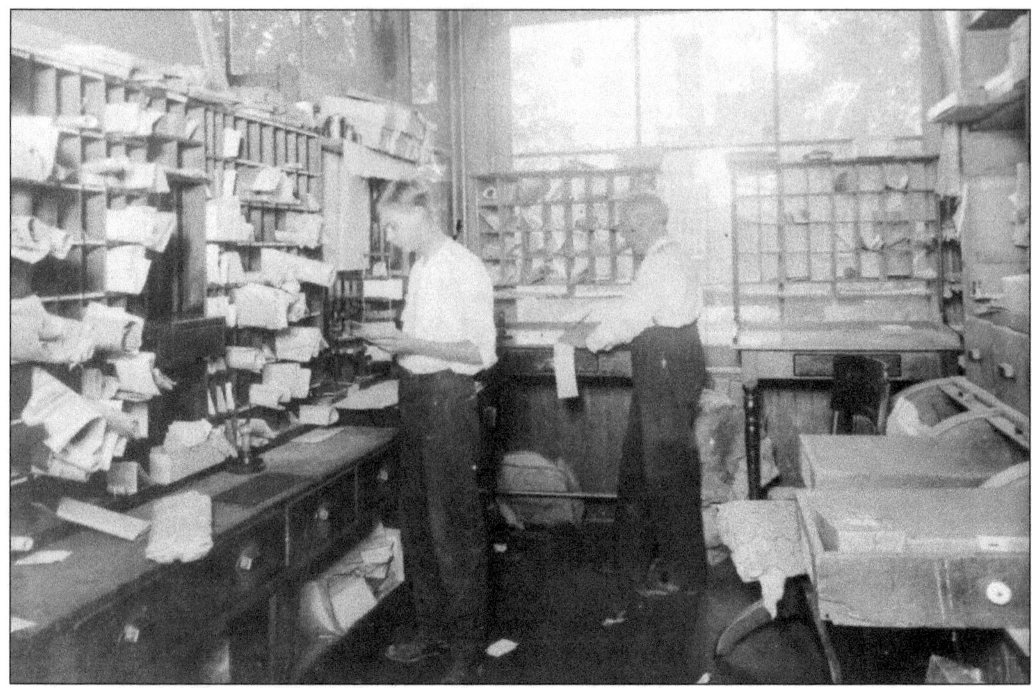

The post office for the village of Bensenville was originally established on the north side of Main Street between Center and Addison Streets. In 1890, the post office was moved into Frederick Elfring's store, which was built that same year. This was located north of Main Street on the east side of Center Street. The residents of the village as well as nearby farmers came to buy groceries and pick up their mail.

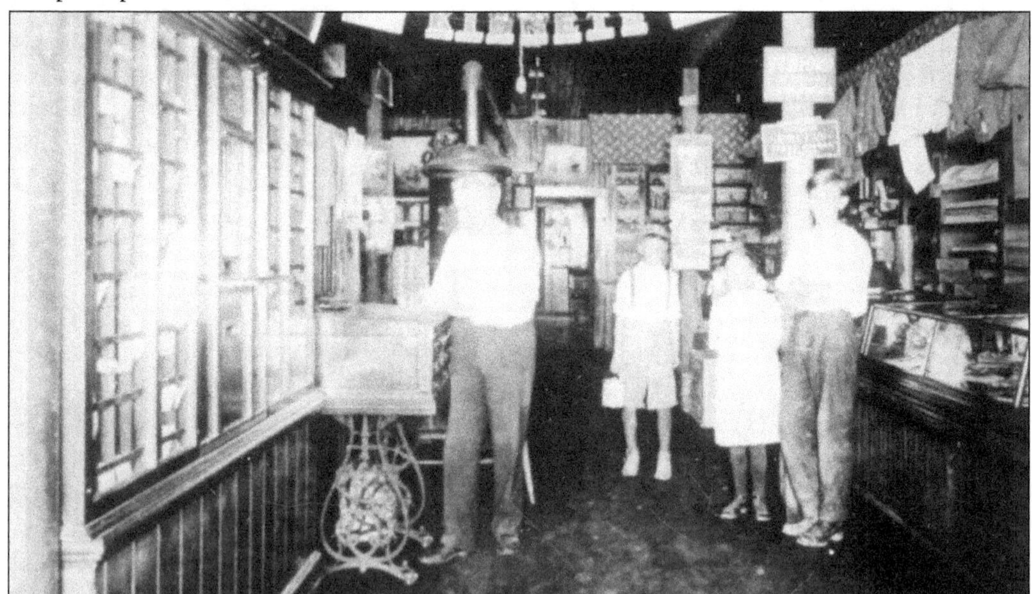

Shown here is the other side of the mailbox slots, where the residents picked up the mail. Items for sale can be seen in the background and to the right. Here, Elfring can be seen along with some Bensenville children who have stopped in the store. The building remained until 1978, when it was torn down.

Henry Thiemann and his wife operated a hotel across Center Street just east of the train station. Henry bought the hotel in 1895 and joined the volunteer fire department that same year. Evidently serving well, he earned the respect of the rest of the department and was elected assistant fire chief in 1898.

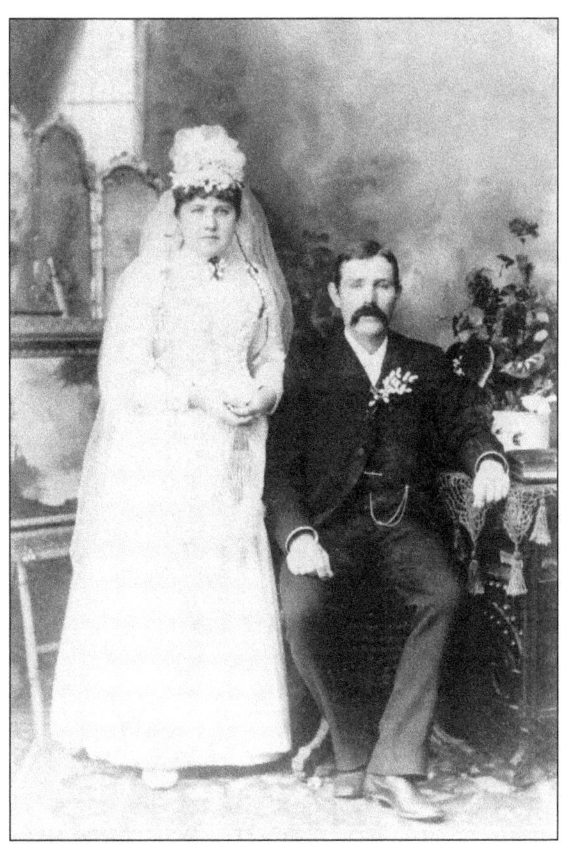

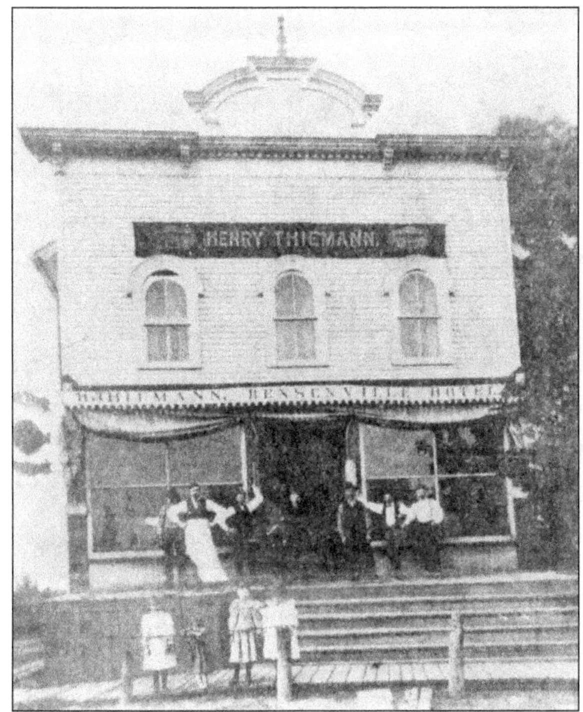

Henry Thiemann, proprietor of the hotel, is shown wearing an apron and with his hands on his hips. The hotel was built in 1875 by Herman Koch, who sold it to Henry Lagerhausen, who sold it to Thiemann. Also pictured here are, from left to right, Fred Schoo, Thiemann, Fred Laurence, town blacksmith, and "two strangers." On the boardwalk are, from left to right, Edna Ernsting, Emma Thiemann, Hulda Luehring, and Frieda Thiemann.

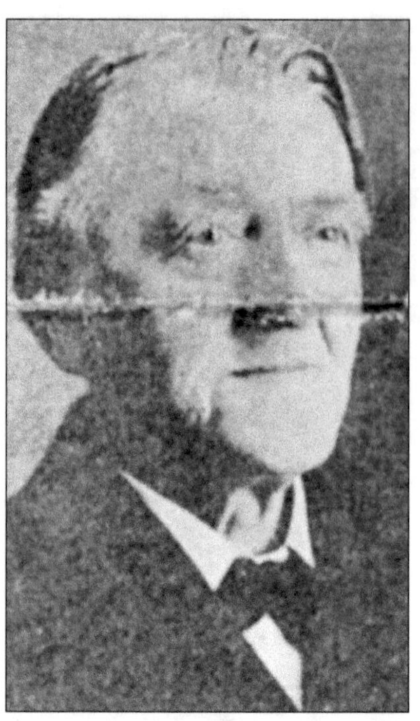

P.T. Tiedemann was Bensenville's enterprising entrepreneur. He had started out in Chicago in 1853 working for Marshall Field's. Tiedemann learned to speak English, and he learned to do business. He opened his own store in Chicago and then decided to reach a new market in Bensenville. Tiedemann lived to be 95, passing away in 1929.

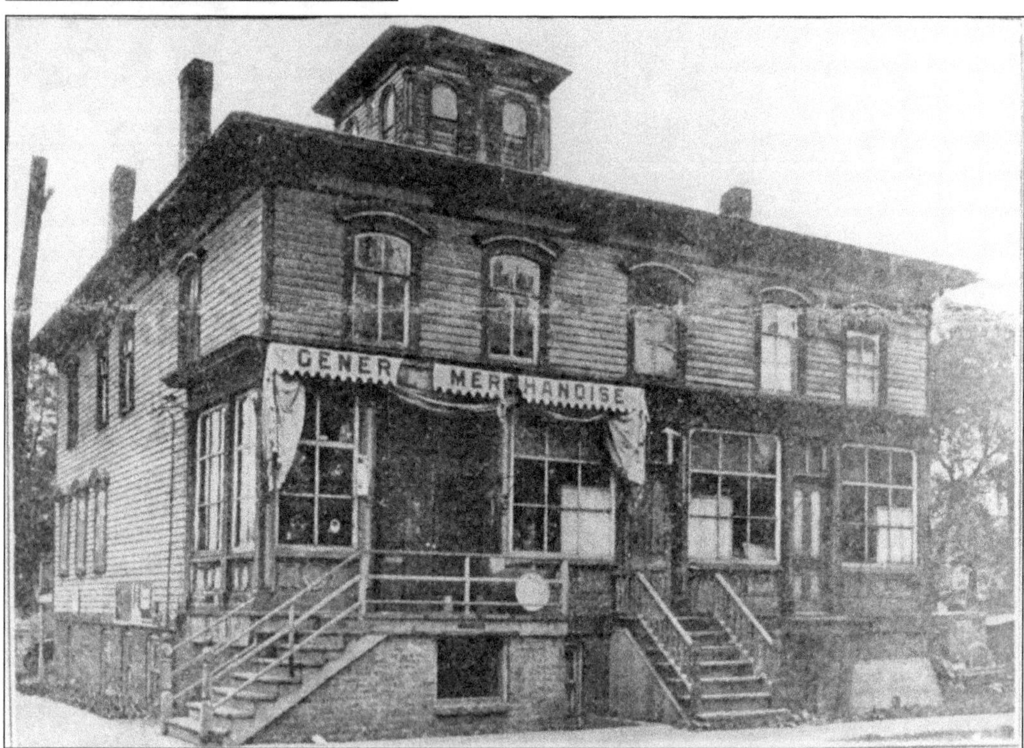

At the heart of Bensenville was this imposing structure, with the pilothouse on top. The Store of General Merchandise, seen here, was operated by P.T. Tiedemann. It had originally been located at Milwaukee Avenue and Carpenter Road on the near North Side of Chicago. In 1877, he moved it to Bensenville and set up shop right next to the depot.

Here, in 1929, Tiedemann lets his great-granddaughter May help herself to the Kellogg's breakfast cereal. P.T. Tiedemann's Store of General Merchandise, with its crowded shelves, brought a little bit of Chicago to Bensenville. He tried to keep it stocked with everything from groceries to crockery to fabric. Additionally, there were Red Cross noodles, Kellogg's Corn Flakes, Quaker Puffed Wheat, Cream of Wheat, and several others food items.

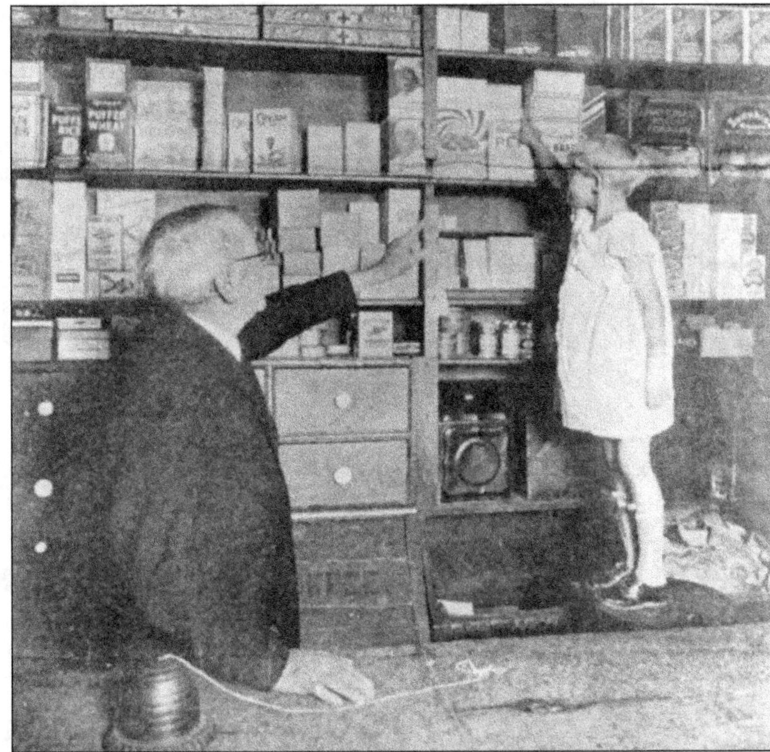

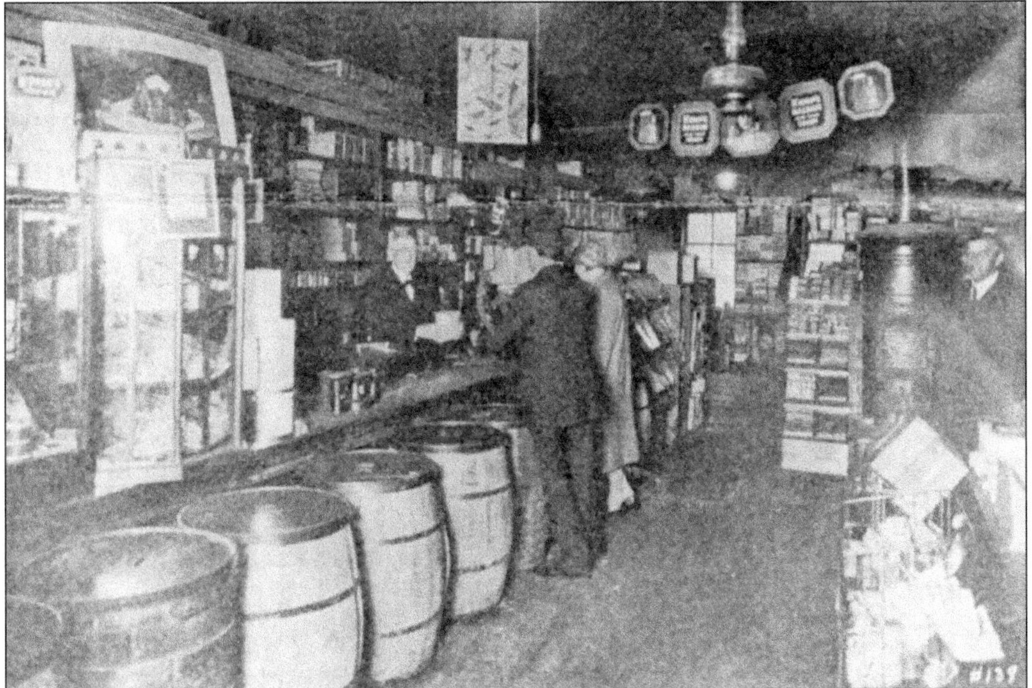

P.T. Tiedemann worked until the end of his life. This picture was taken in early 1929. He is still serving his customers. From cards to calendars, to ribbons, to bolts of fabric, to balsam to sooth one's cuts, there is something for every need. Tiedemann also served the village as its first treasurer.

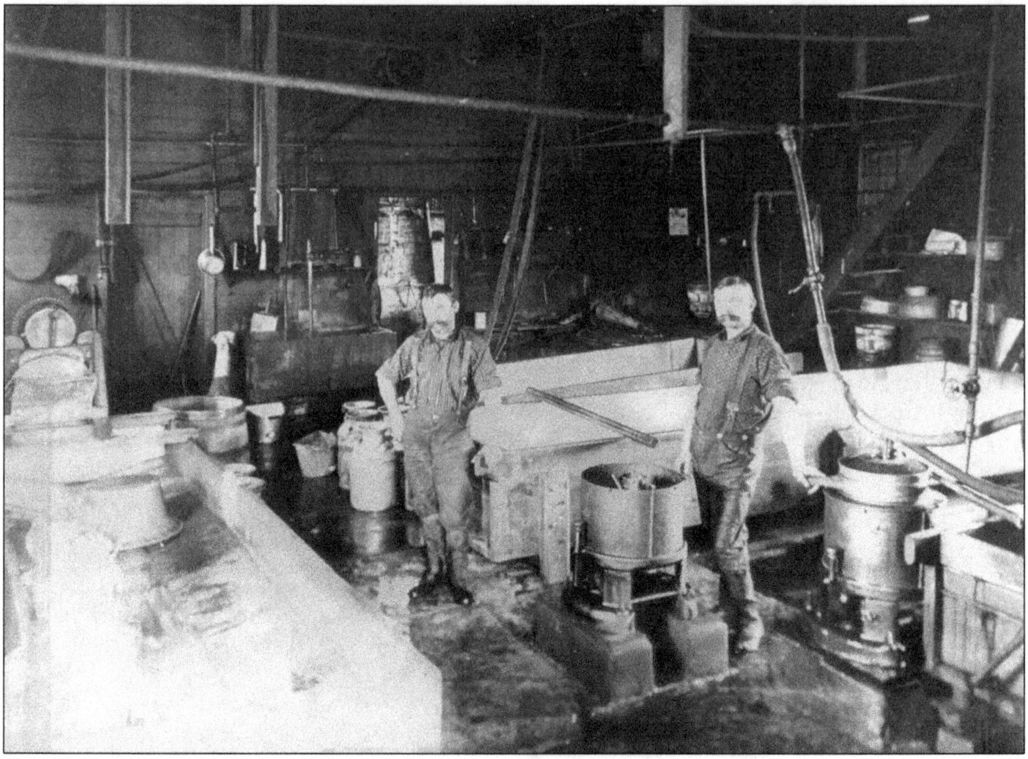

Born on March 19, 1850, near what would become Villa Park, August Asche moved to Bensenville and built a house on York Road. Just to the north of the tracks on the east side of York Road, Asche built and operated a cheese factory. He was elected village president in 1891. In 1910, Asche moved to Chicago, where he passed away on April 2, 1936.

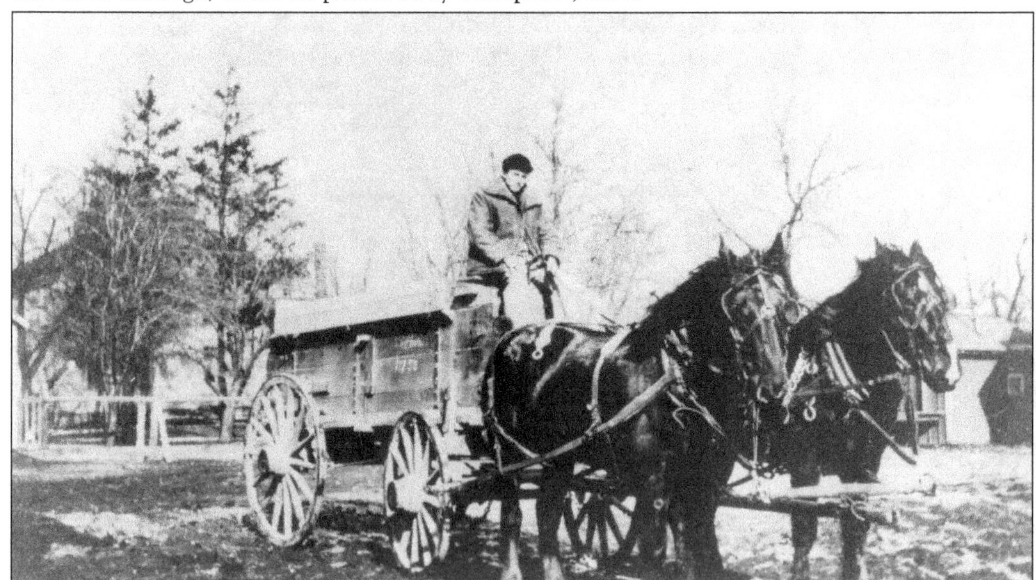

The Schultz family had originally claimed this land in the late 1830s. Now, with the marriage of Martha Franzen, granddaughter of John and Maria's younger brother Bernard, to Albert Schultz, the two these two families were related. The farm stretched over 240 acres of land.

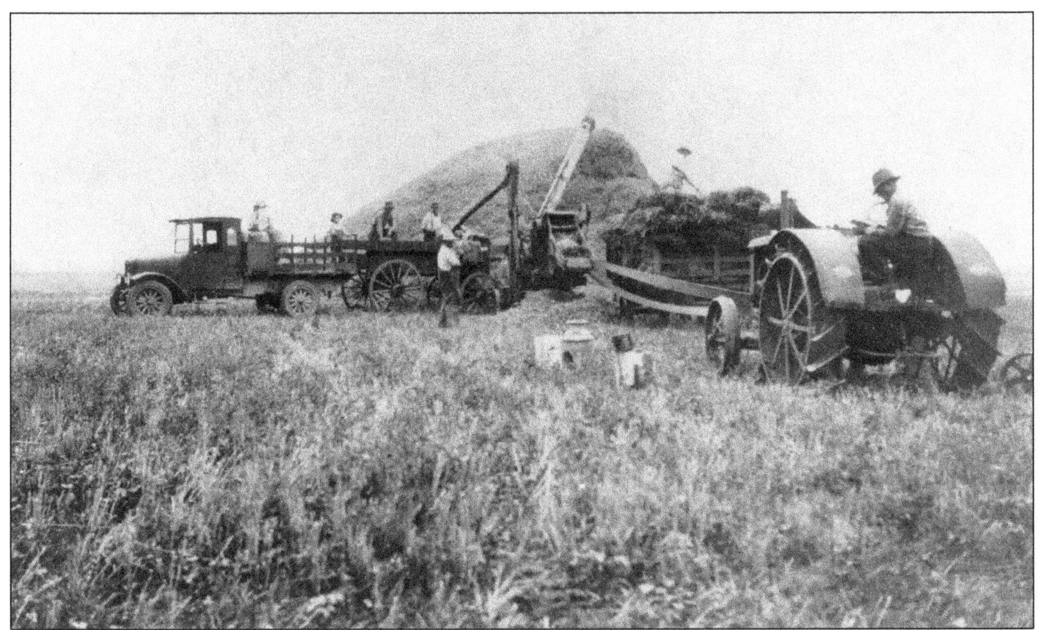

Threshing is the process of separating the seed of the grain from its husk. It had been done by hand, flailing the crop, or using horses to trample it. The first mechanical thresher was patented in 1837. Even after machines were introduced, threshing wheat and oats still took time and several hands to do it.

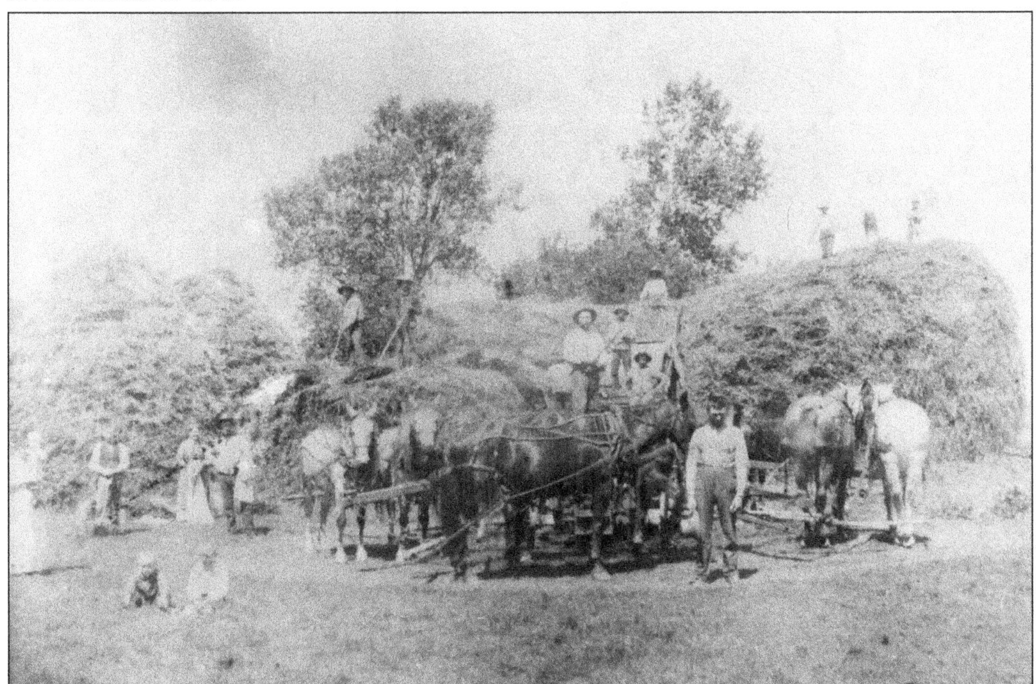

Cutting hay was still done by hand until the 1860s. The first of the mechanical reapers became available during the Civil War. Farmers looked to replace manpower that had departed to the battlefront with machines. New and bigger models continued to be developed in the last quarter of the 19th century. Here, the hay cut on Franzen-Schultz farm is being loaded onto a wagon.

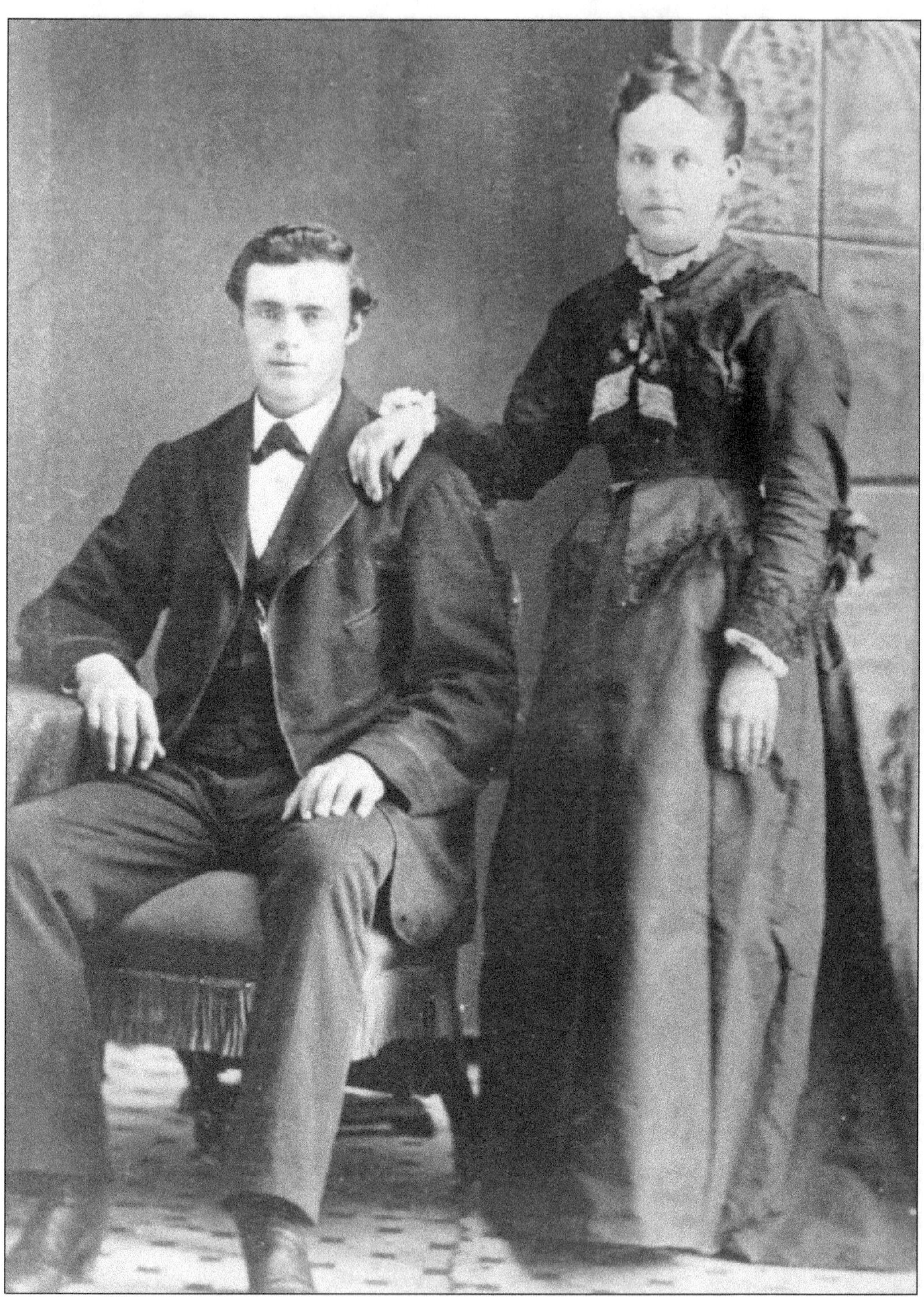

One of John Henry Franzen's sons, Charles Franzen married Mary Heuer. He had developed the property on the northeast corner of Addison and Main Streets into a lumberyard. The yard stayed busy, as the railroad continued to draw business into Bensenville. Railroad workers with families looked to move to Bensenville, which spurred the development of housing.

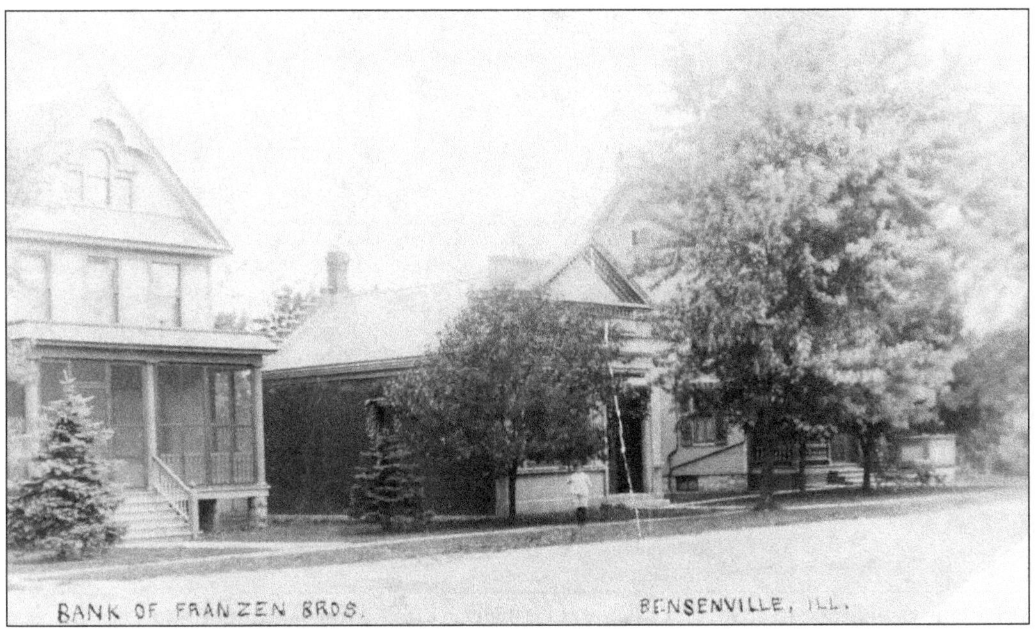

In 1900, Charles Franzen joined two of his brothers, William F. and A.W. Franzen, in opening the Bank of Franzen Brothers. This was built next to Charles Franzen's house on the north side of Main Street between Addison and Center Streets, and the lumber warehouse was moved to the west side of Addison. The name was changed to the First State Bank of Bensenville in 1911.

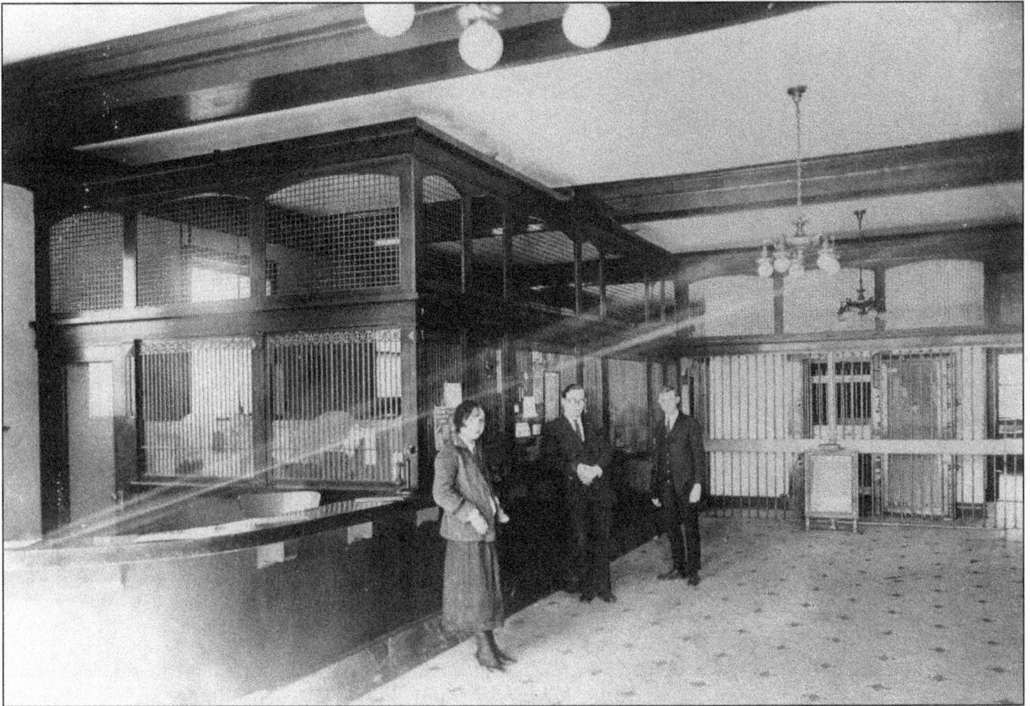

Hardworking residents of Bensenville were quickly attracted to the bank. Charles Franzen served as president of the institution from its founding until after it became a state bank. He also helped to start other local banks and served terms on their boards of directors.

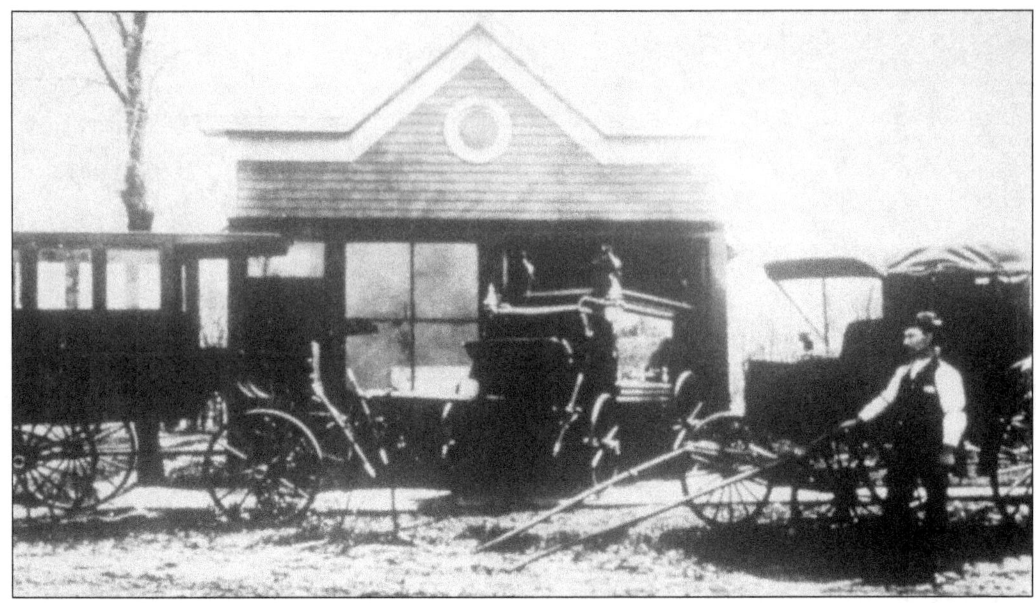

Originally established in 1898, Geils Funeral Home was located near Lawrence and Mt. Prospect Roads. The family moved the business to Bensenville in 1922. It still operates and is still owned by family. This image shows the pallbearers wagon at left, the hearse in the center, and the mourners' carriage on the right. The family also started the Geils Funeral Home Ambulance Service. It continues today as Superior Ambulance.

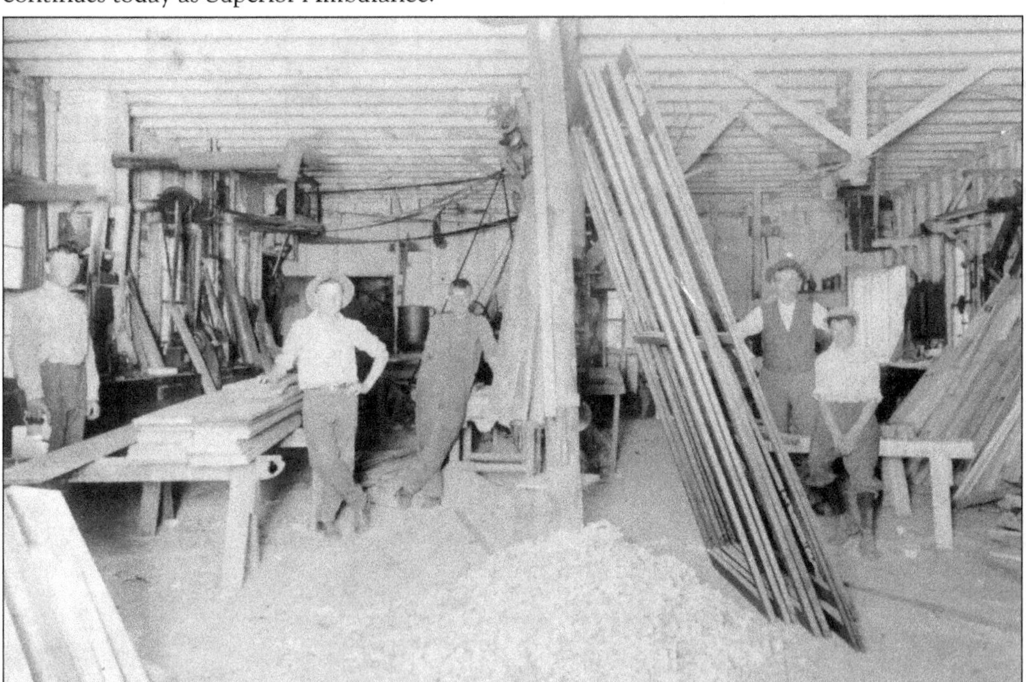

There was another lumberyard on the east side of town. Herman Geils had married Martha Landmeier. They built a house on the east side of York just south of the tracks. Next door, Herman Geils opened his lumberyard. It was located on the east side of York Road between the railroad tracks and Lincoln Street. Later, this became Hill Behan Lumber Co.

Their son, Irving Geils, continued to operate the lumberyard. Later, he became a stationary engineer. Irving married Mille Thiemann and moved to a house on May Street. Their sons—Robert, born in 1921, and Lawrence, born in 1923—both went on to serve in World War II. Robert passed away in 1998, and Lawrence followed in 2010.

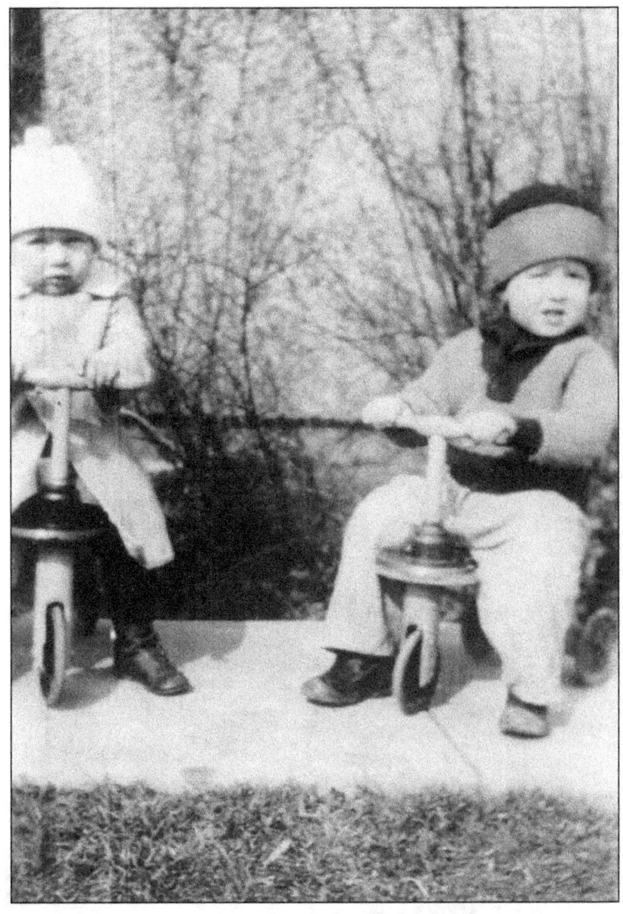

The Korthauer family had arrived in Addison Township in 1838 and staked out a claim east of York Road and south of Green Street. They first constructed a simple log home. That house was later dragged to the south and additions were made. Herman built his own home, pictured here, just to the west in 1910. Horseshoe Bend, though it would lose pine trees, served as access to the Korthauer residence.

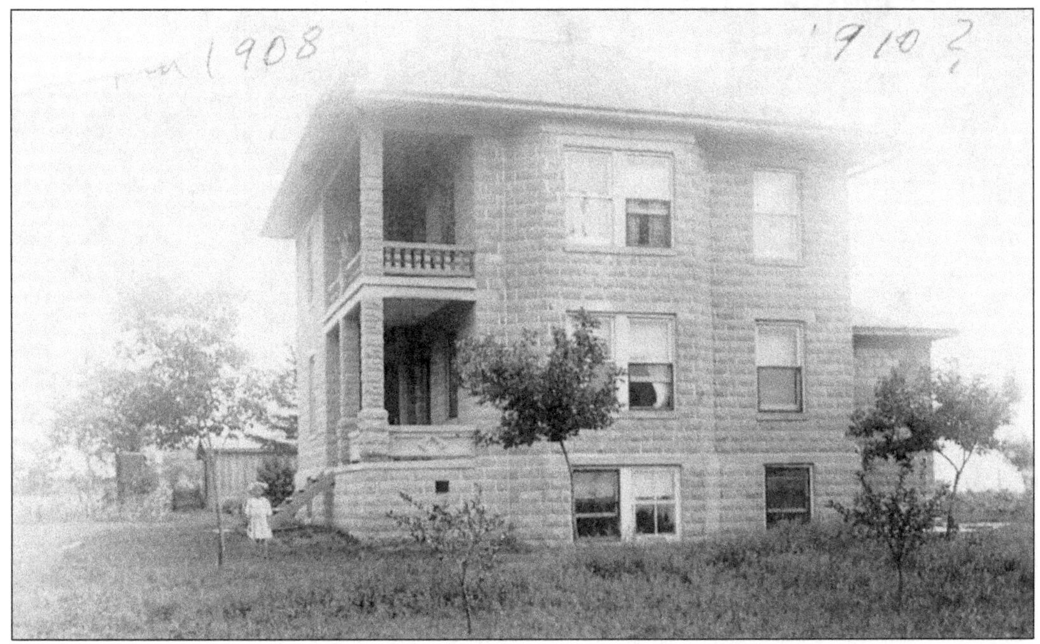

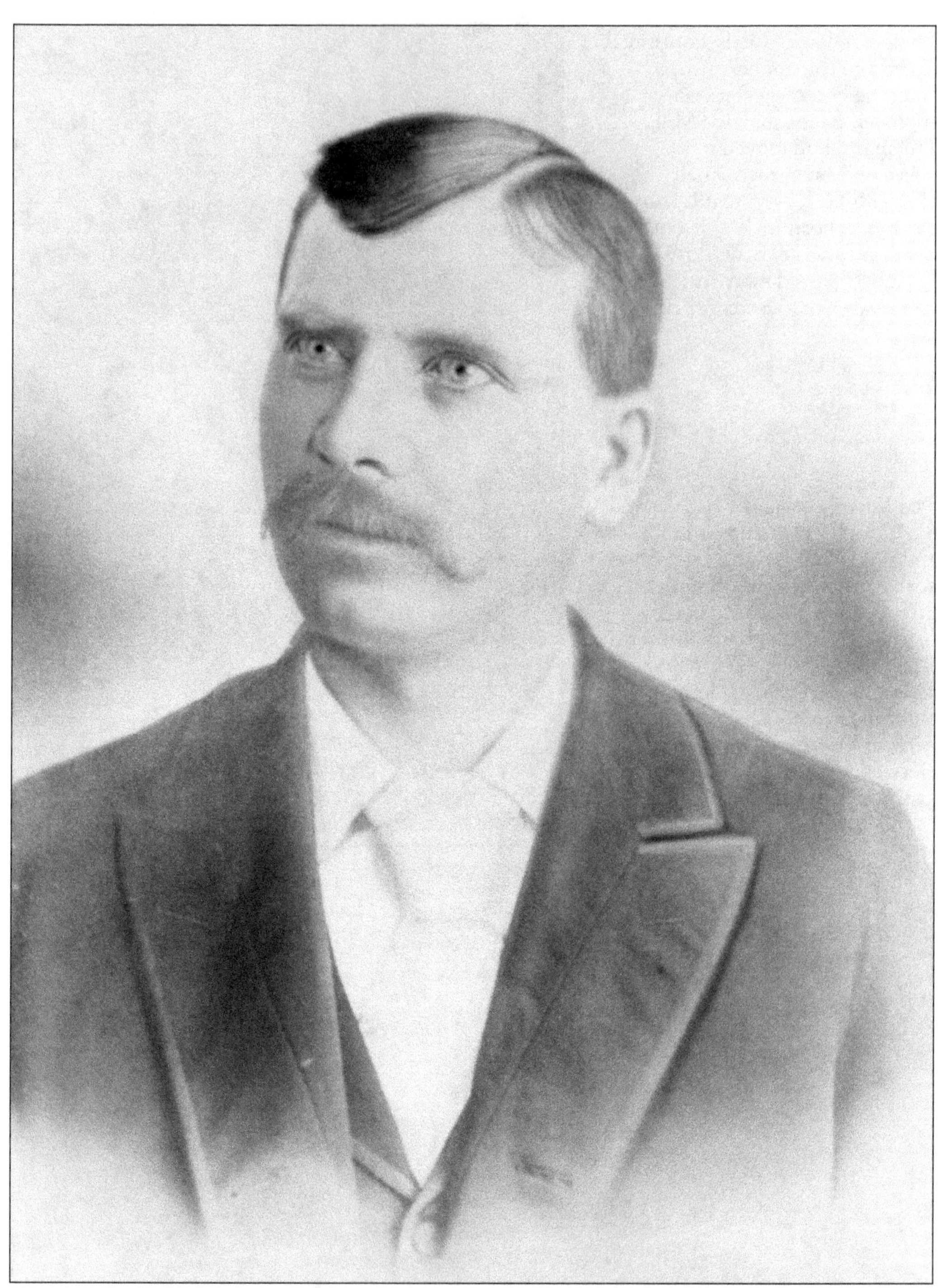

Herman Korthauer, like the other early settlers, was concerned about the development of the community as a whole. That concern extended to the education of the children. The village did not have a school of its own and it was a mile and a half to the Churchville School, originally called Fischer Schoolhouse. In April 1884, a poll was taken to determine thoughts on incorporation and the building of a school.

Herman Korthauer offered the use of his store as location for a public meeting on these issues. On April 12, he reported that the responses had been positive on both issues. In light of this, a petition for incorporation was filed at the DuPage County courthouse the next Saturday, April 19. The vote on incorporation, held on Saturday, May 10, passed 42 to 7.

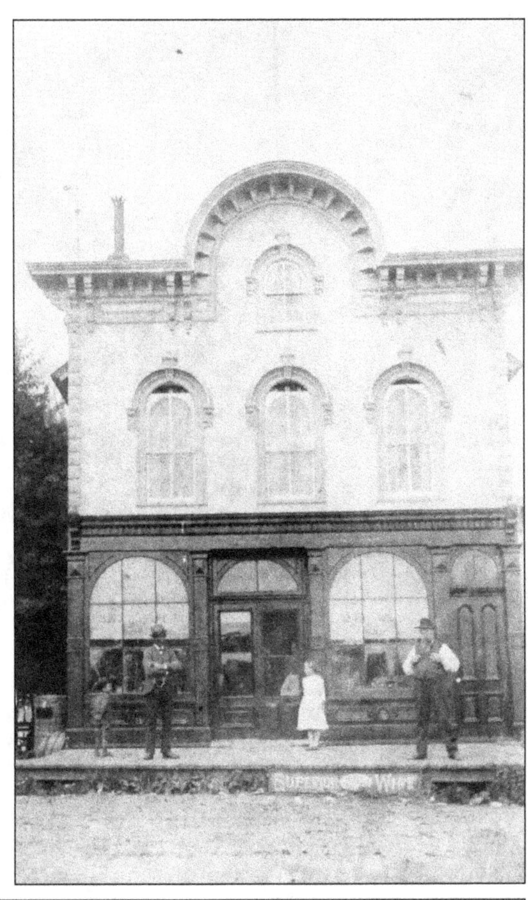

With incorporation came the need for formal government. A village president, clerk, treasurer, and four trustees were chosen to constitute the first village board. These were unpaid positions for the first three years. Then it was decided to compensate village officials by paying the clerk $50 per year, the treasurer $15 per year, and the president and trustees $1 per meeting. The village hall was built in 1909.

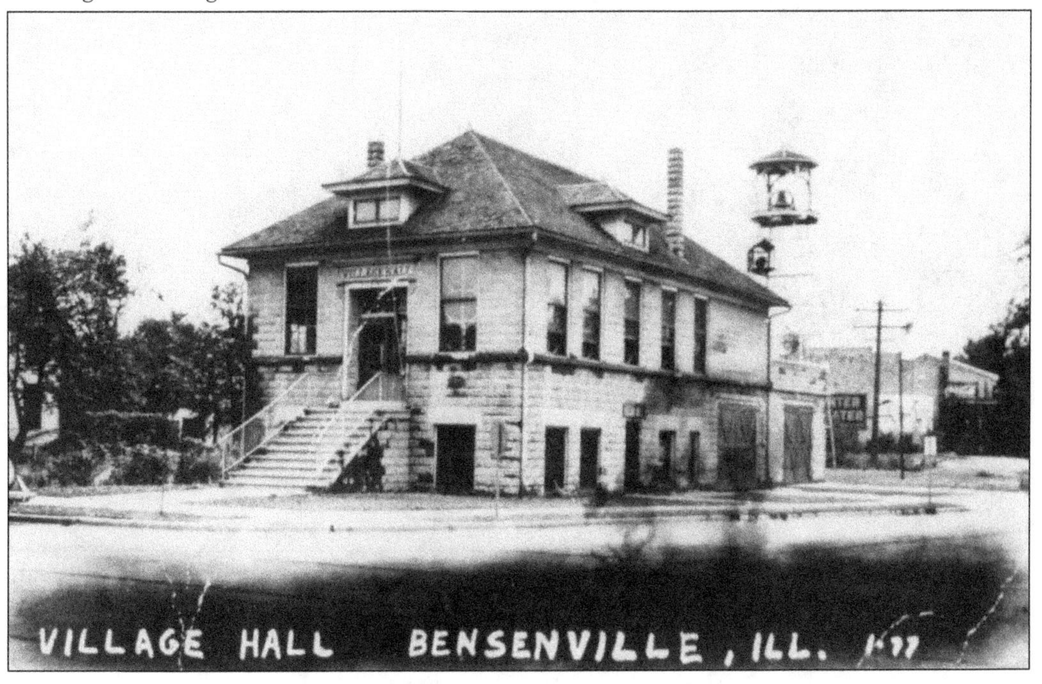

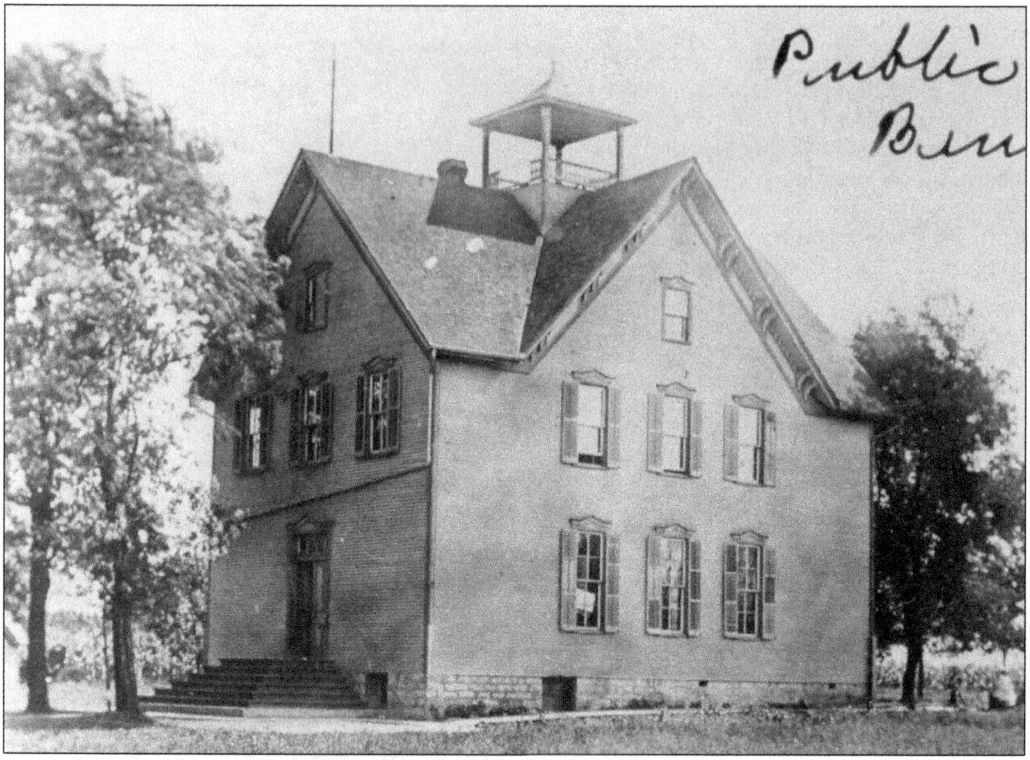

The village board immediately set to work creating a school district, which was officially recognized by the state as District 2 in April 1885. Construction of the school began forthwith on the north side of Green Street one block east of York Road. This Green Street School opened in October 1886 and housed kindergarten through high school.

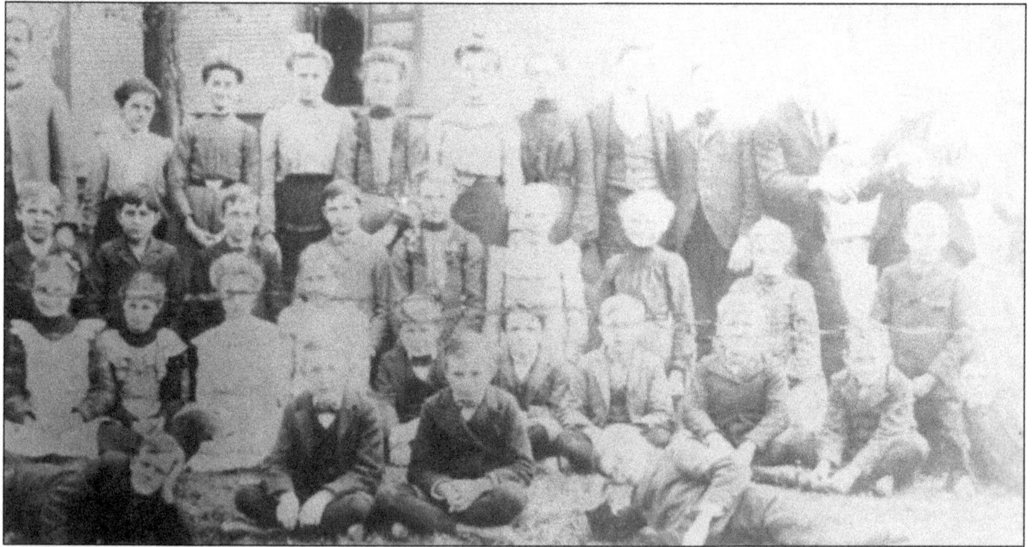

The population of the village had surpassed 325 residents in 1880 and continued to grow through the end of the century. In the early 20th century, the demographics of the village began to change. Mexican families began to arrive. Later, those from other Latin American countries and some from eastern Europe would come.

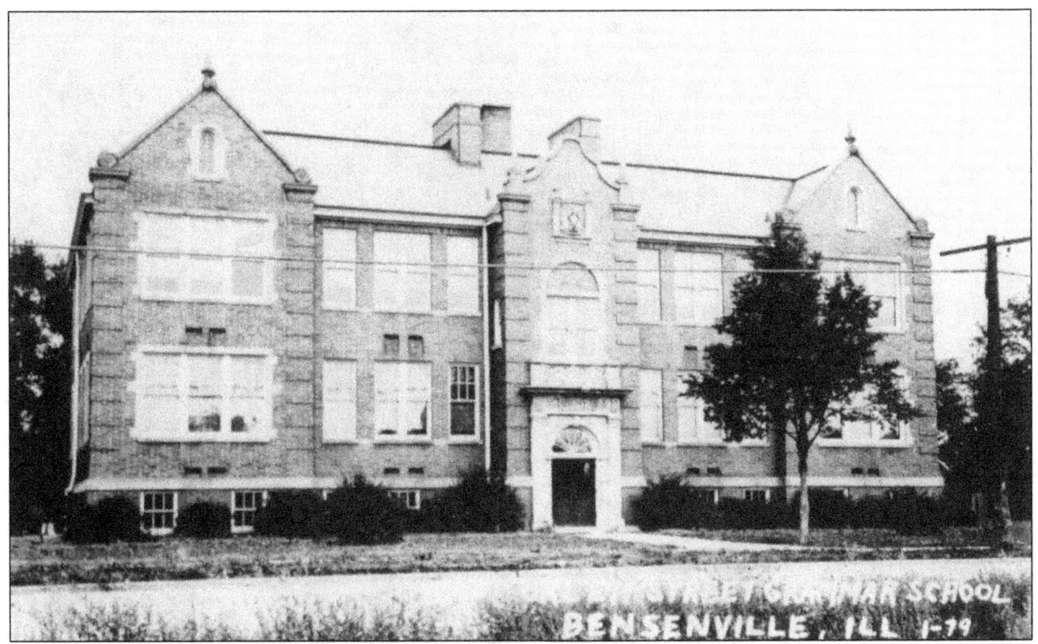

The school operated for 30 years. By the early 20th century, the population of Bensenville had increased to 650. As employment at the Milwaukee Road Bensenville Yard increased, more people moved into the village. Housing was in demand. Some families had to live in boxcars until homes were built.

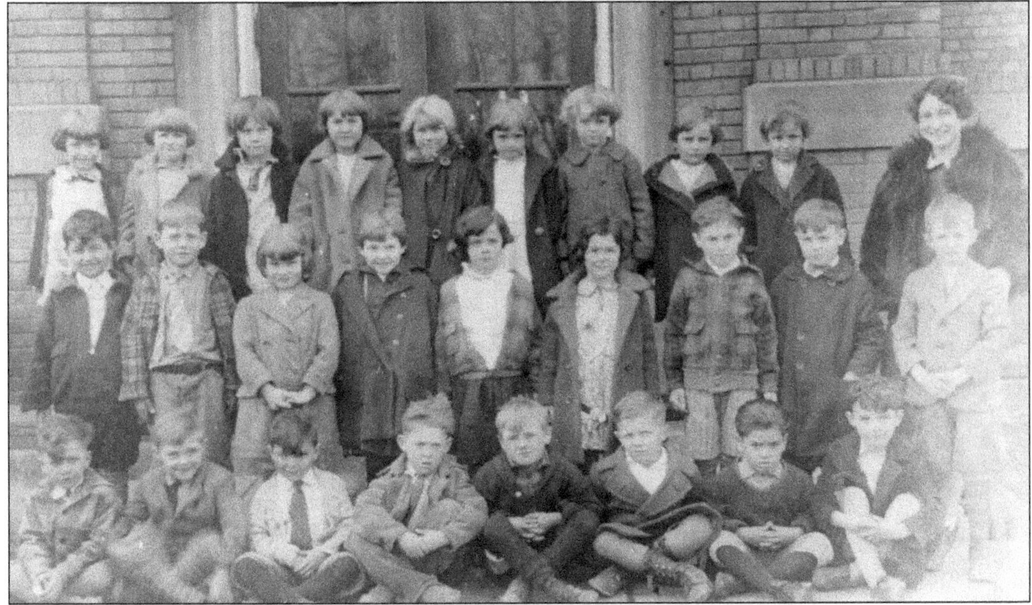

Meeting the demands of a larger student body, the village sold the school building and constructed a new building on the same property. This was an all-brick structure that survives today. Currently, it houses an art gallery and business offices. The original school was moved and remodeled into a private home.

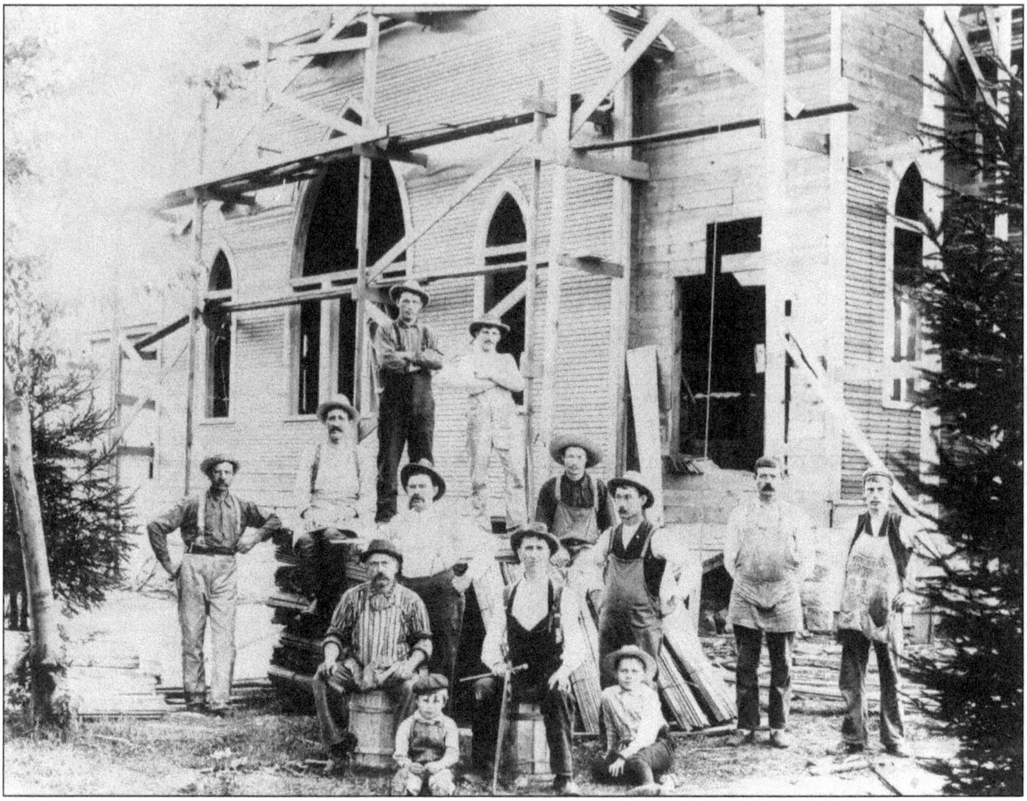

Peace Church was constructed in 1903. Some of those who had attended St. John's Reformed Church and some who had attended Friedans Church left their respective congregations and joined together to create a new church.

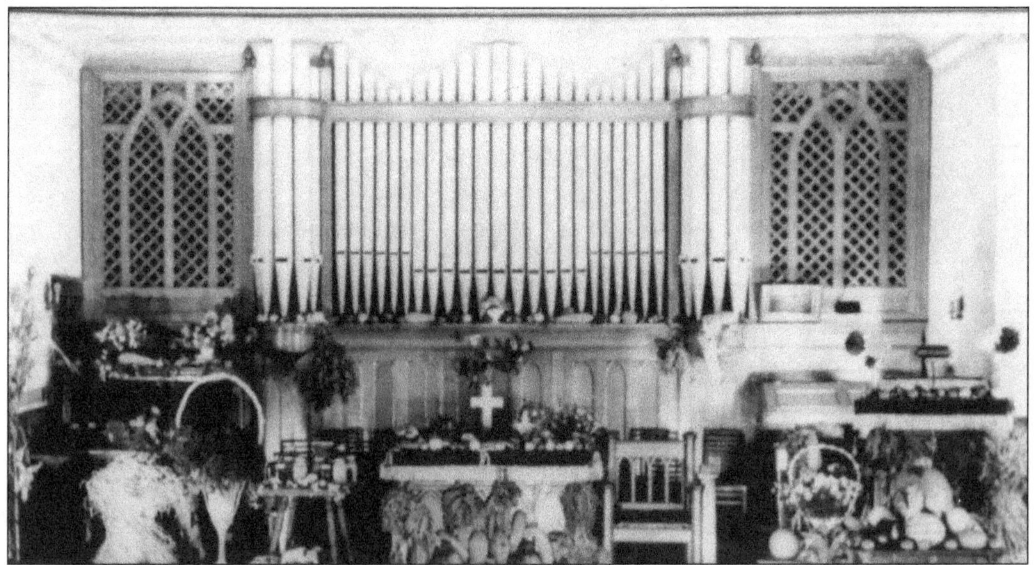

The interior of the completed church is shown here. The sanctuary is decorated for a harvest festival. Agriculture was still central to the village. The families were thankful for all that had been provided over the course of the past year.

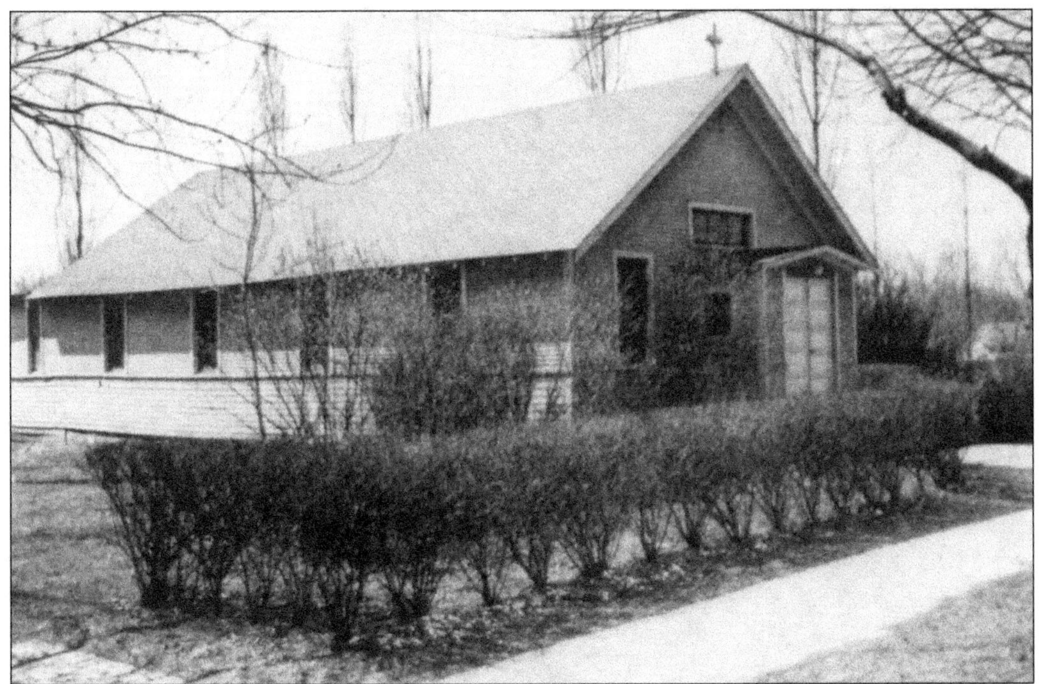

There were a handful of residents who practiced their Christianity in the Catholic tradition. Mexican families moving into Bensenville often shared this faith. In 1921, the first Catholic services were held in the village hall. A church was built in 1926 at Rose and Wood Streets with the name St. Alexis. The congregation continued to meet at this location until 1949, when property at Wood and Barron Streets was acquired.

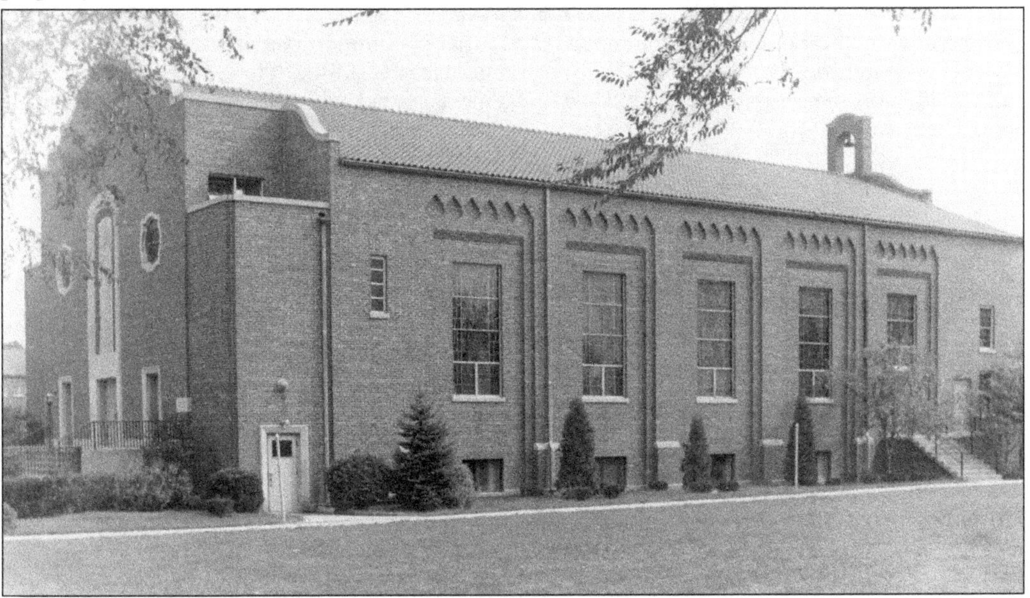

This property had been the site of the Franzen flaxseed mill. The mill was gone by the early 1920s. There was a pony farm that reached as far west as Church Road. The St. Alexis congregation bought a parcel of this property and constructed a school building with the sanctuary in the basement. In 1957, a separate church building was built just to the west of the school.

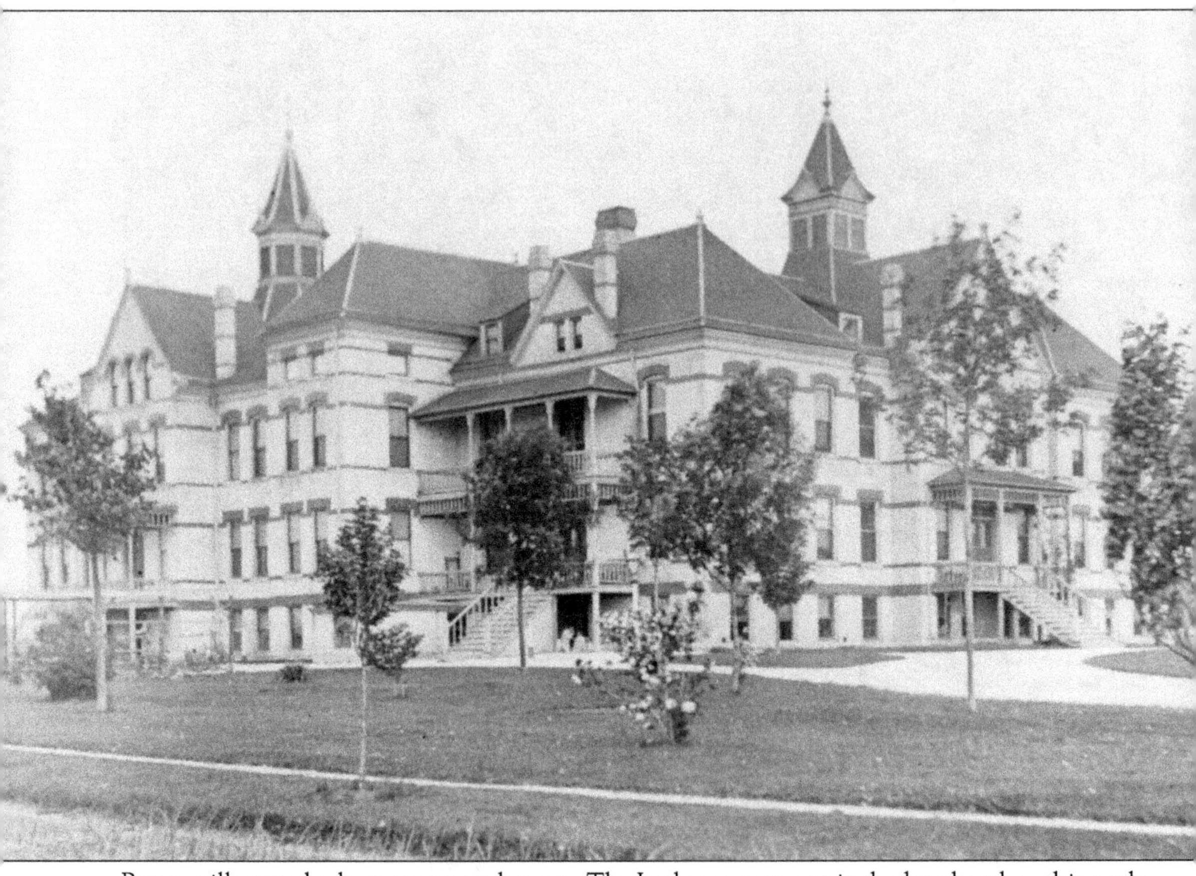

Bensenville was also home to an orphanage. The Lutheran community had undertaken this work in other communities including the neighboring village of Addison. Here, the orphanage was built in 1895 on the east side of York Road at Memorial Road. As many as 85 orphans resided here. They attended the Green Street School.

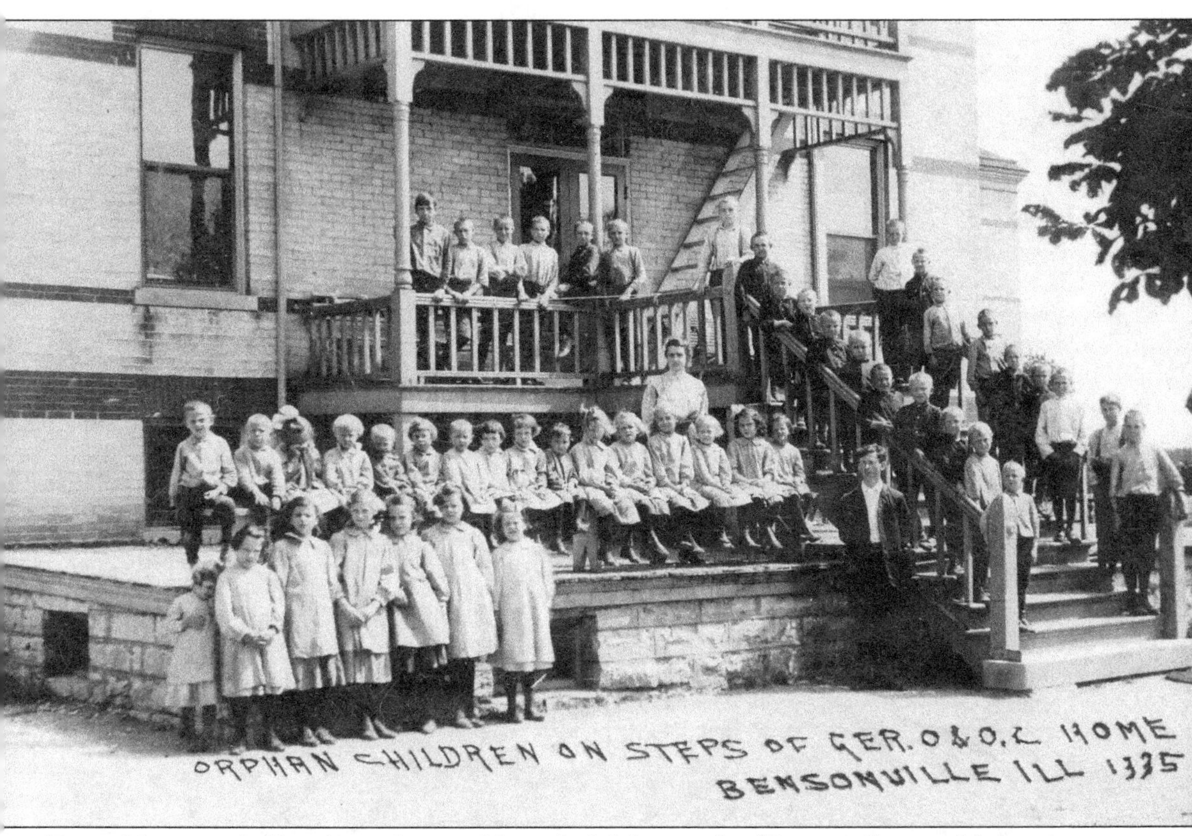

Festival days were held at the orphanage. Not only did the people of Bensenville attend, but some residents of Chicago also came on special trains run for the occasions. The typical festival day consisted of games and picnics. The 30 acres around the building were used to grow foodstuffs for the orphans.

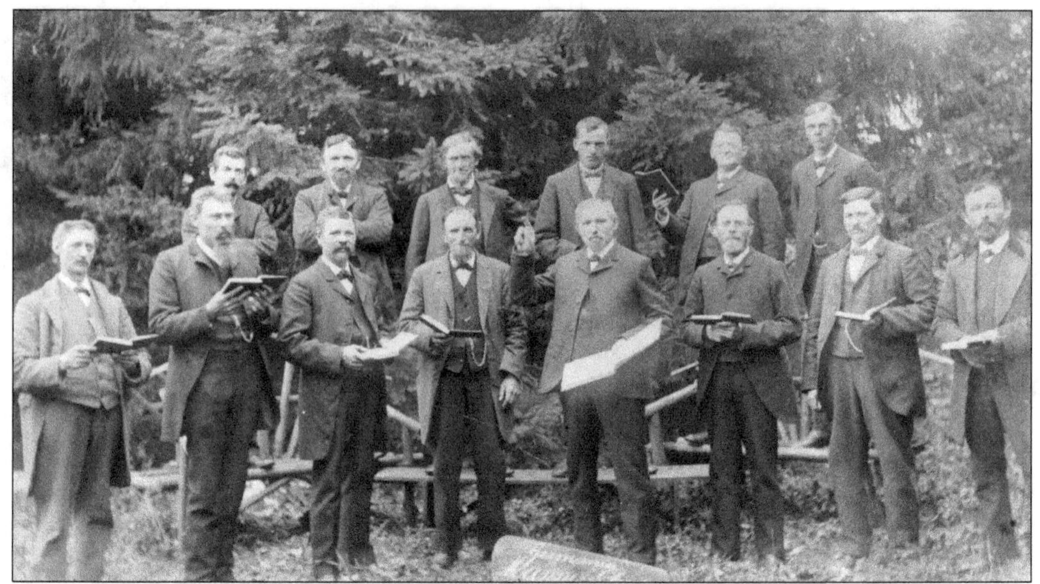

The area bordered by Pine and Evergreen Streets and Pine Avenue was called Horseshoe Bend. Here, on land belonging to the Korthauers, the families of Bensenville gathered for picnics. They would spend the day playing games and listening to music. The manor choir would perform concerts for the enjoyment of relatives and friends.

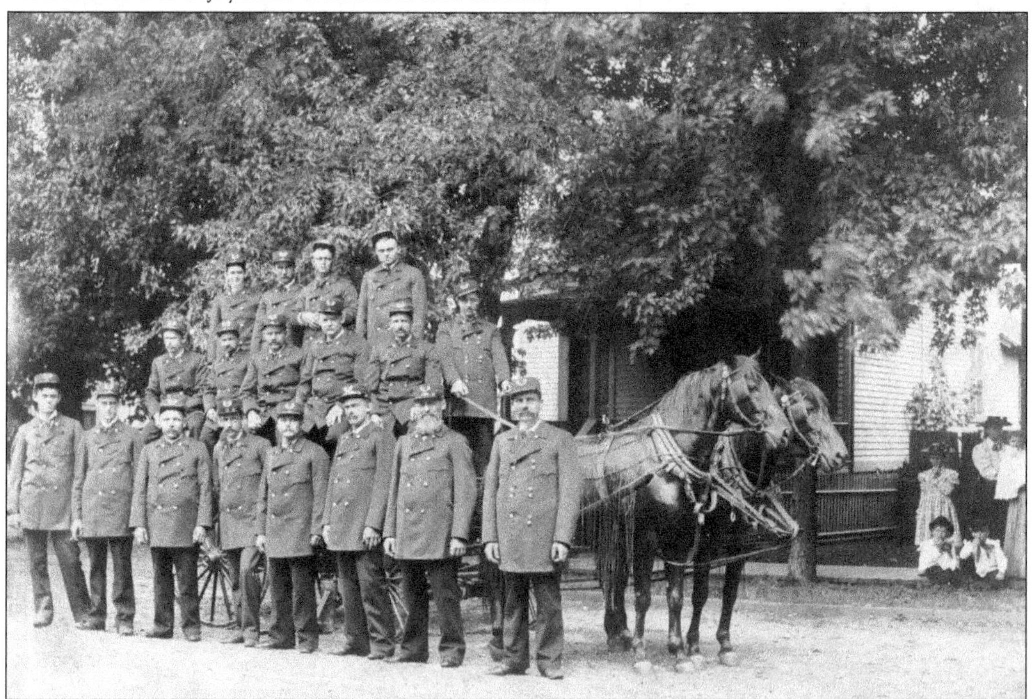

At one of the picnics in 1891, money was raised to purchase a small hand pumper to fight fires. The residents also recognized the need for an organized fire department. It was formed on August 27, 1894, and consisted of 21 members. Herman Korthauer was the fire chief, and his younger brother William was the secretary. In September, a picnic was held to raise money for additional equipment.

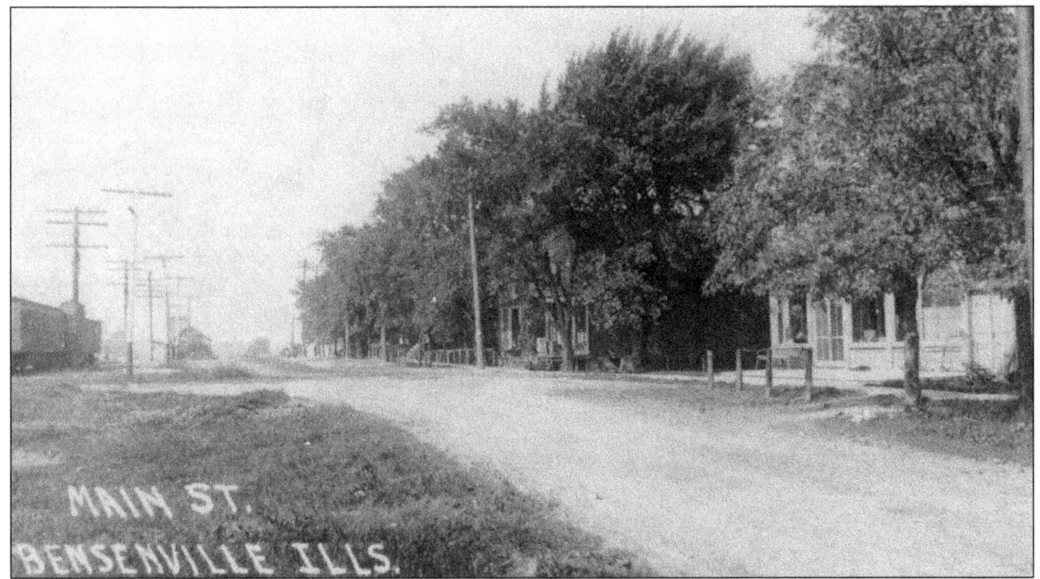

Bensenville still felt like a country town. A photographer snapped this picture in 1910. In this view looking west from Center Street, a train can be seen at the Bensenville depot. At right, part of Herman Korthauer's hardware store is visible. Herman passed away in 1939. The store survived until July 5, 1963, when it burned.

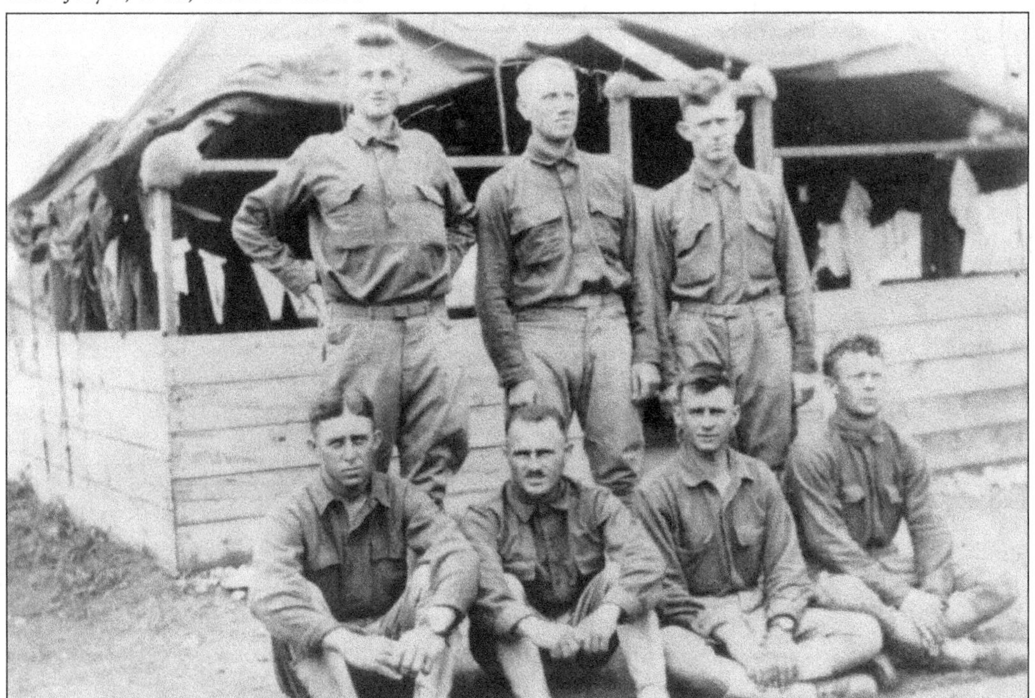

In April 1917, the United States entered the world war on the side of the Allies. While German traditions were strong, that did not stop men and women from serving; however, names of clubs, organizations, and buildings were often changed to demonstrate patriotism. From left to right are (first row) Otto Herr, Herman Miller, George Korthauer, and Richard Andorf; (second row) Owen Kindby, Frank Koebbeman, and Pat Murphy.

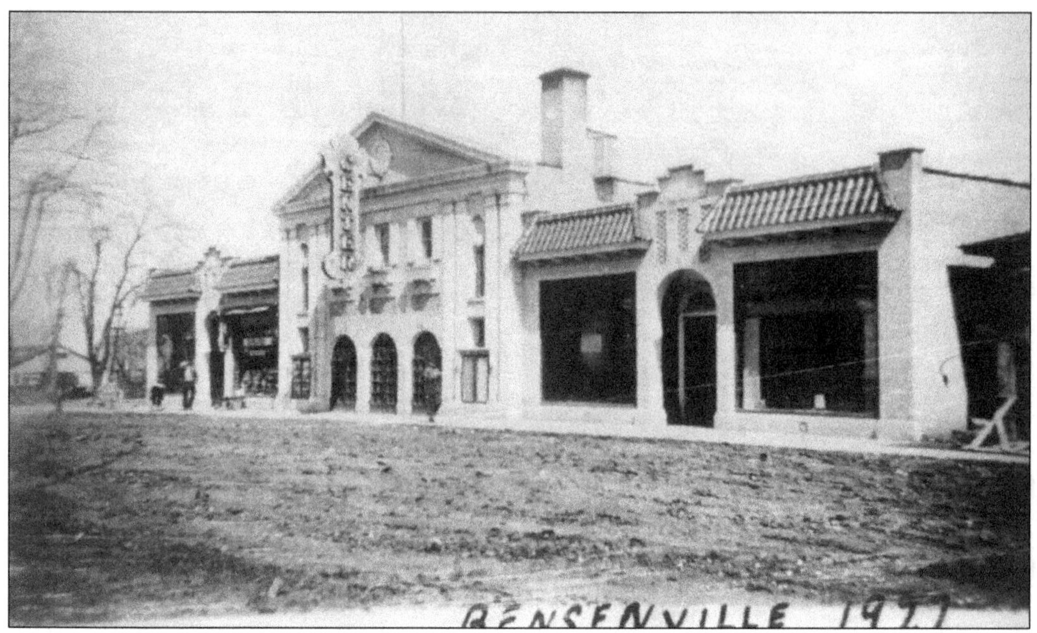

The town began to look different. In 1927, the theater was built on Center Street. Tiedemann's and Elfring's were no longer the only stores in town. Two new shops opened on either side of the theater. An apartment building was constructed. A water main system was installed for the village. Frank Koebbeman, home from the war, opened an ice-cream shop.

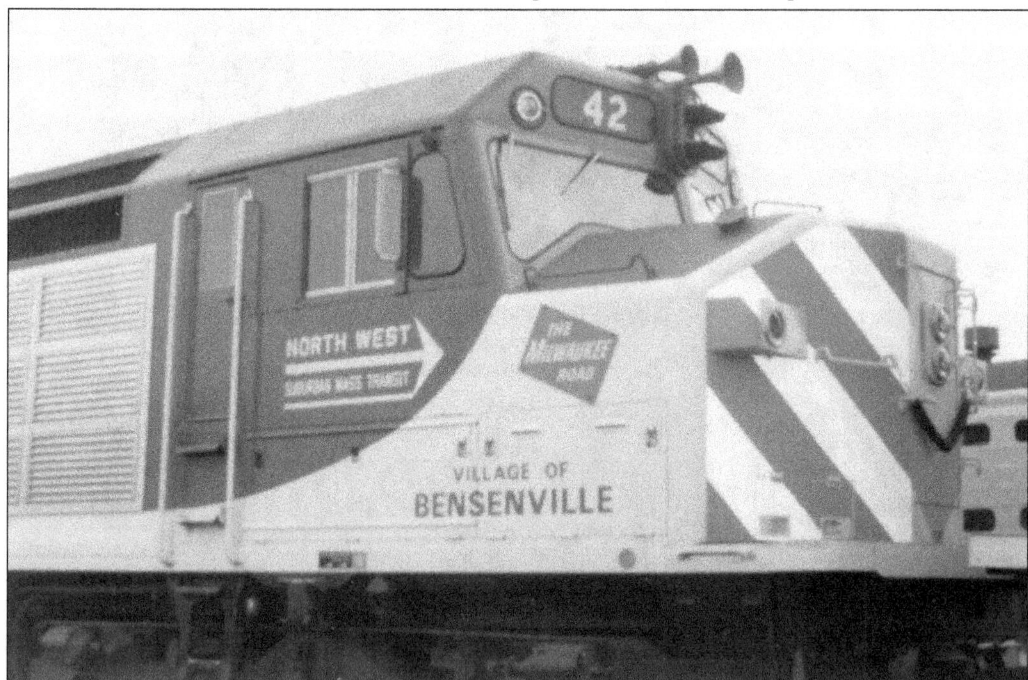

The village of Bensenville was turning into a suburb of Chicago. By the 1930s, it did not look like the same little country crossroads it had even 30 years earlier. Soon, residents of Bensenville would find their way to work in the city of Chicago. Freight trains would share space with passenger trains.

Three

O'Hare

The country village was not to last forever. The theater was built in 1927 on Center Street. It was later flanked by the post office, two stores, and apartments. The Franzens diversified into banking, opening the First State Bank of Bensenville on the northeast corner of Addison and Main Streets. They sold their lumberyard just northwest of Addison and Main Streets, and a shopping area developed. The gravel of downtown streets gave way to pavement.

In June 1942, the US Army Air Corps condemned and purchased 1,300 acres of land immediately west of Mannheim Road and north of Irving Park Road. With the United States' entry into World War II, the military began looking for sites for aircraft manufacturing facilities. A three-man committee from the Air Corps arrived in Chicago on April 23, 1942, and began an inspection of nine sites, ultimately selecting a location just northeast of Bensenville known as Orchard Place.

The Douglas Aircraft Company was having a factory built in Oklahoma City for the production of C-54 Skymaster and C-47 Dakota cargo planes. In order to keep up with the demand, the company decided to construct only the C-47 Dakota planes at that plant and to move the C-54 Skymaster production site to Chicago. Workers started clearing the ground in June, and construction of the first building began on June 30. Production launched a year later, with the completion of the first plane on July 30, 1943. Ultimately, 655 planes would be constructed here.

Chicago city officials had been looking for alternate property to expand the aircraft industry, even though the American Society of Planning Officials had declared that Municipal Airport, now Midway Airport, was capable of handling current and future demands of air traffic. The City of Chicago purchased the property in 1946 and converted it into a commercial airport, which opened in 1955. O'Hare Airport continues to directly impact the village of Bensenville. Necessary expansion was made possible by securing land to the west across the county line in DuPage and even in the village of Bensenville. Industry continued to be developed in Bensenville, spreading as far north as Devon, where the northern border of the village has since been moved.

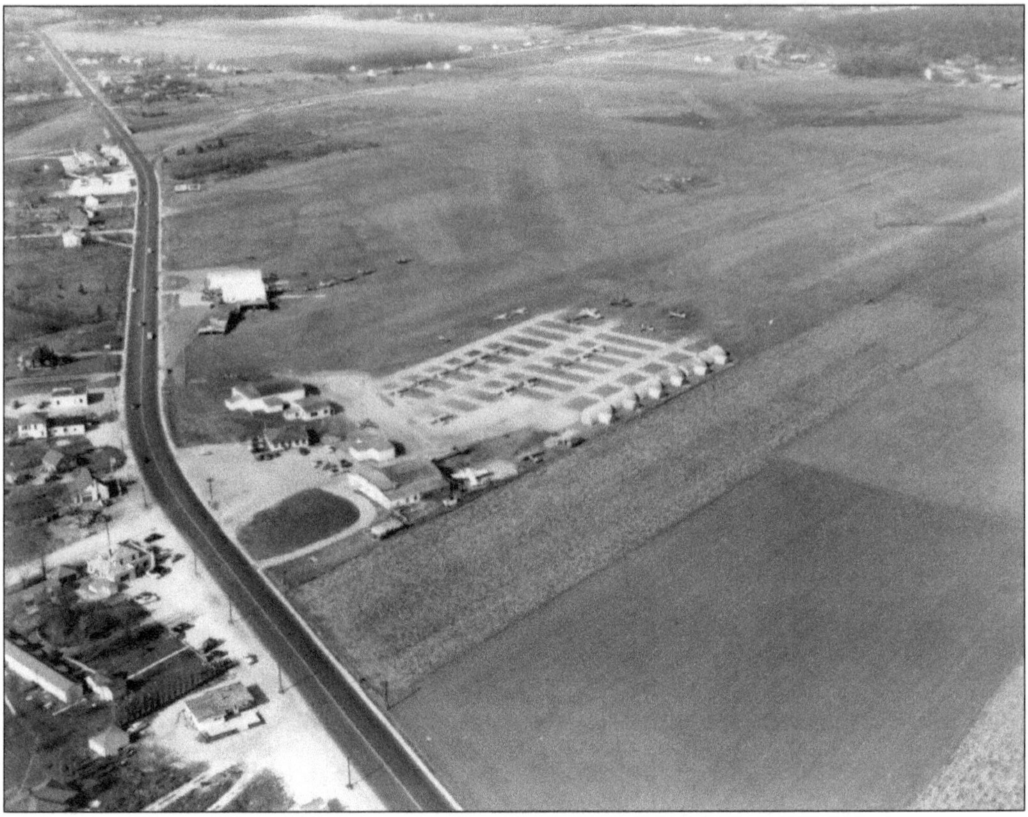

One early airfield in the area was located in Churchville on the southwestern part of the Fischers' land. Fred Bouchard and Joe James leased the land from Alvina Fischer. Its official name was Elmhurst-Chicago Airport, but many referred to it as Fischer Field. In 1929, Alonzo Fischer, nephew of Alvina, became the owner of the property. Alonzo was the president of the First National Bank of Elmhurst. (Courtesy of Elmhurst History Museum.)

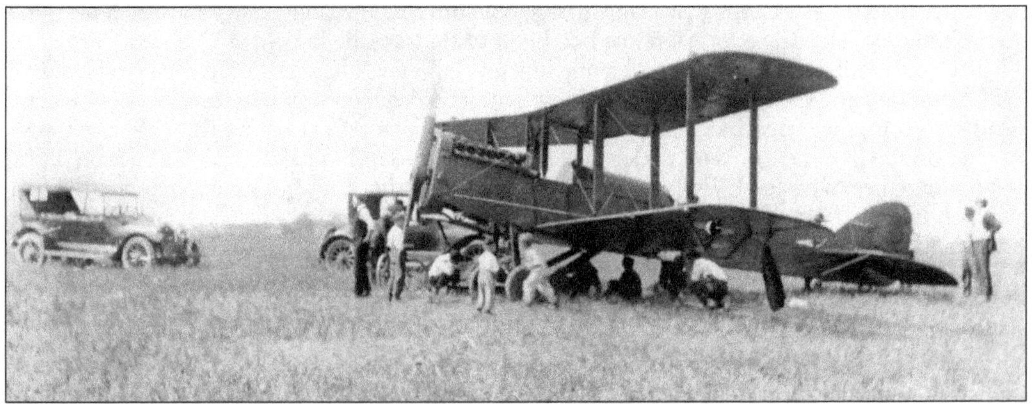

Immediately to the west, Greer School of Aviation was established on land belonging to George Fischer. Edwin Greer operated the flying school and offered flying circuses. In 1939, Elmhurst-Chicago Airport closed, and the two airfields were consolidated under the name Elmhurst Airport. The airport experienced a brief revival after World War II, and some improvements were made to the runways. Ultimately, on December 31, 1956, the airport closed. (Courtesy of Elmhurst History Museum.)

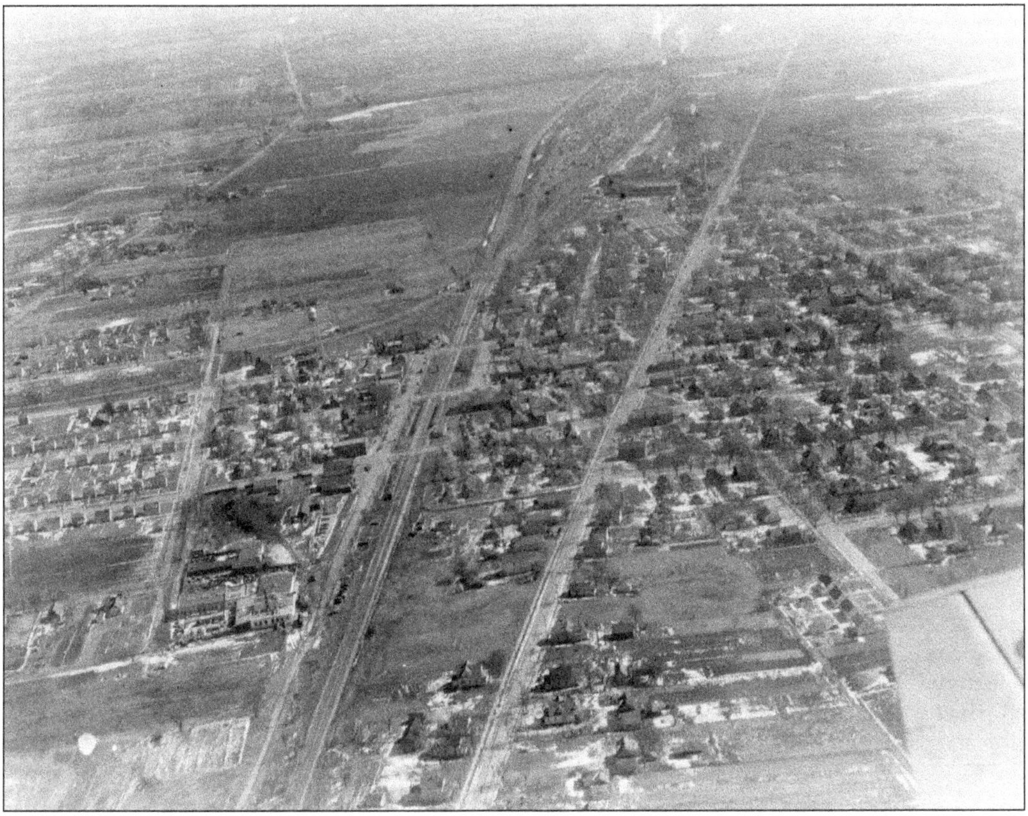

Nearly three miles to the northeast, another airport would take shape. This land was the site of St. John's Reformed Church. This church was the result of a separation of the original congregation of Zion Lutheran Church. This separation by those of the reformed tradition took place in 1848, and they built a church of their own at the intersection of Lawrence Avenue and Mount Prospect Road.

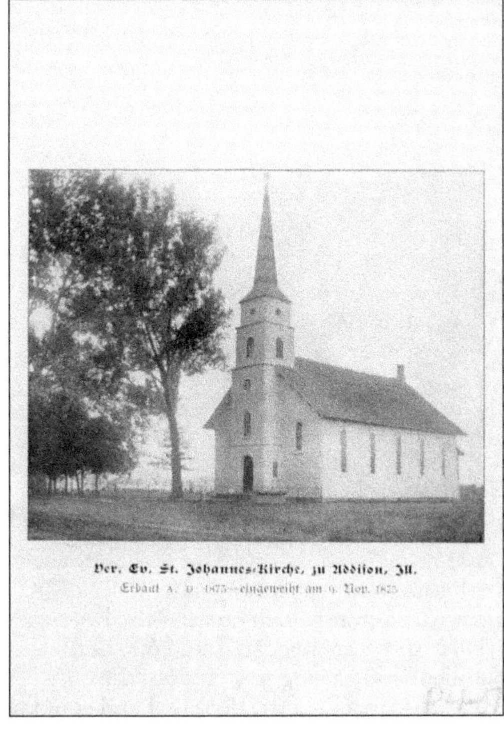

The congregation met here until 1954. Then, with what would prove to be only the first major expansion of O'Hare Airport, the congregation moved to Route 83 and Foster Avenue. The church closed in April 2009, and then it and Immanuel United Church of Christ, which had also been the result of a separation from Zion Lutheran, merged with Peace Church. The name was changed to Faith Community United Church of Christ Bensenville.

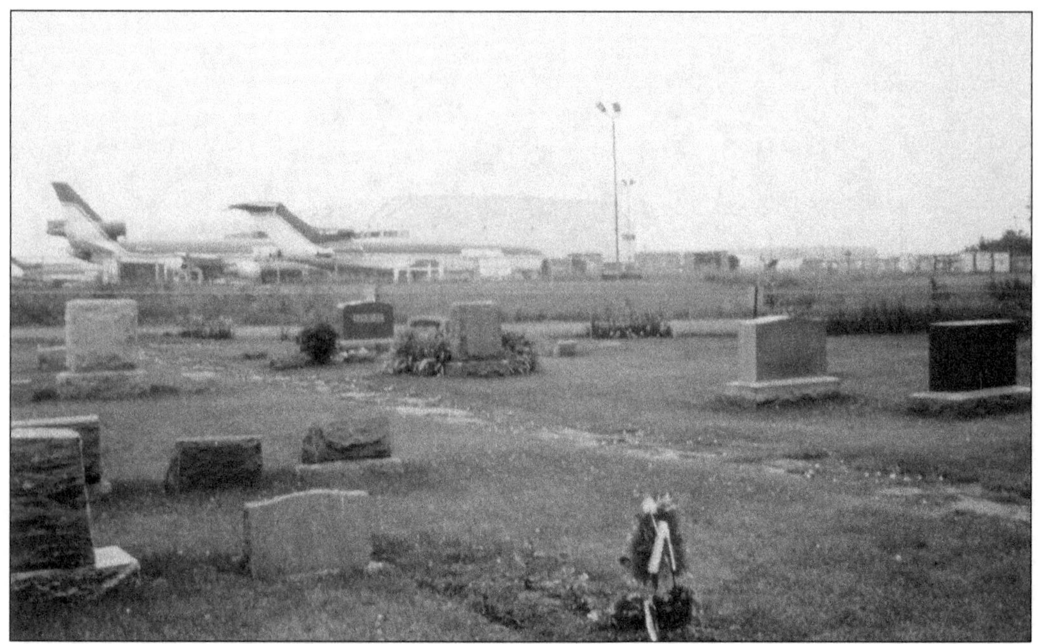

The cemetery was laid out near the church, with the first burials taking place in 1849. The cemetery continued to be in use into the 2000s. Plans to expand the airport included the land on which the cemetery was located. Ultimately, the case was settled in court, with the City of Chicago paying for the land.

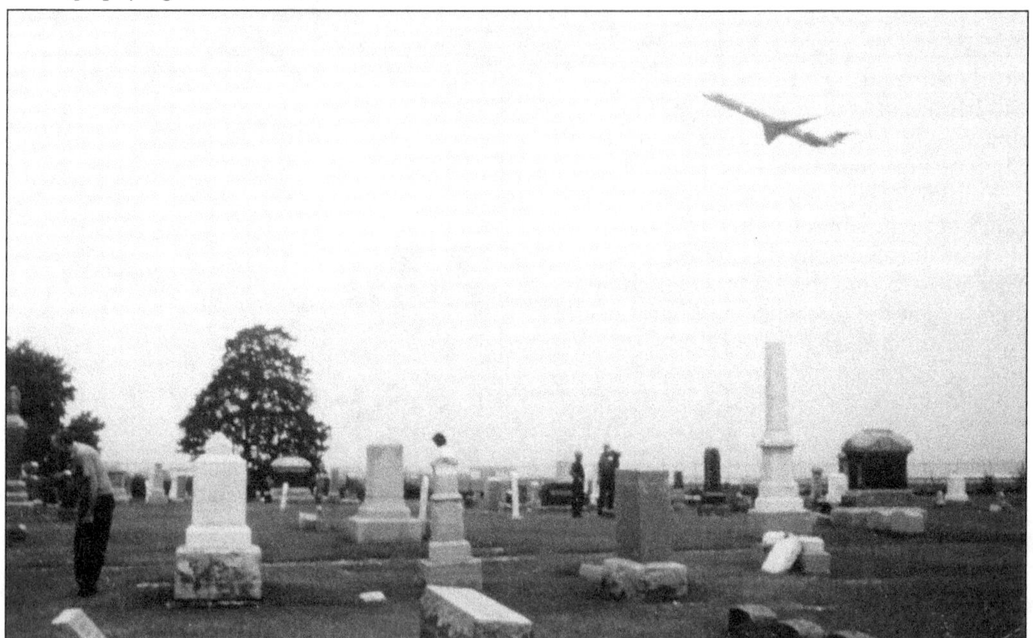

With the airport expansion under way in 2010, family members of the deceased were contacted in order to remove the remains and the headstones to cemeteries of the families' choice. A total of 1,494 bodies were relocated, and 600 of these were reburied at Eden Memorial Park Cemetery in Schiller Park. During this process, the City of Chicago called the author, who explained he was not related to any of the deceased and could not stipulate where the remains should be moved.

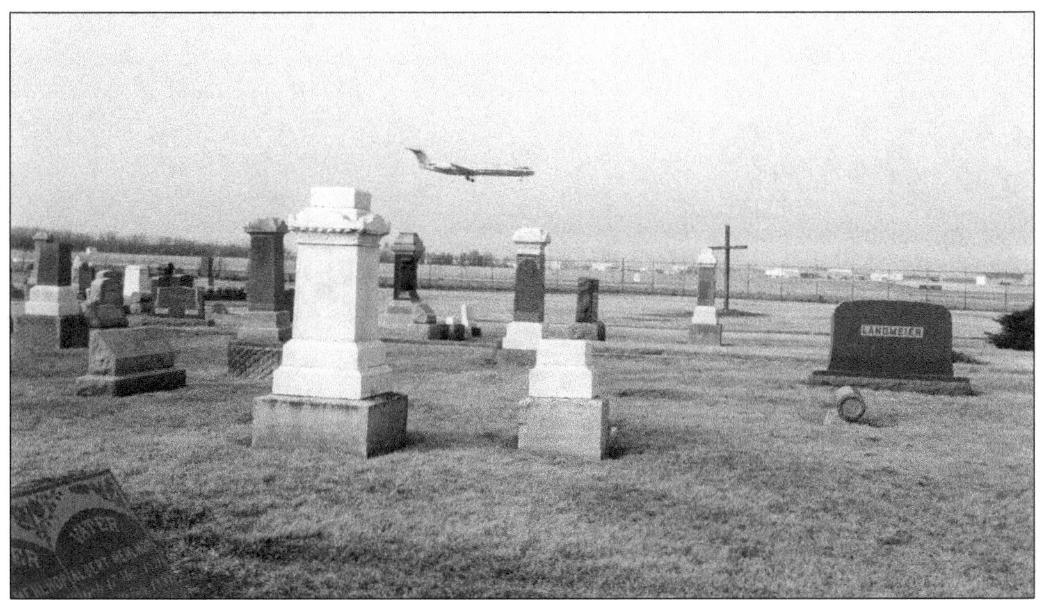

Historical artifacts uncovered in the process of removing the graves and excavating to build the runway were bagged and given to the Village of Bensenville per agreement with the City of Chicago. Through an intergovernmental agreement with the Bensenville Park District, the artifacts were placed at Fisher Farm. St. Johannes was not, however, the only cemetery on what had become airport land.

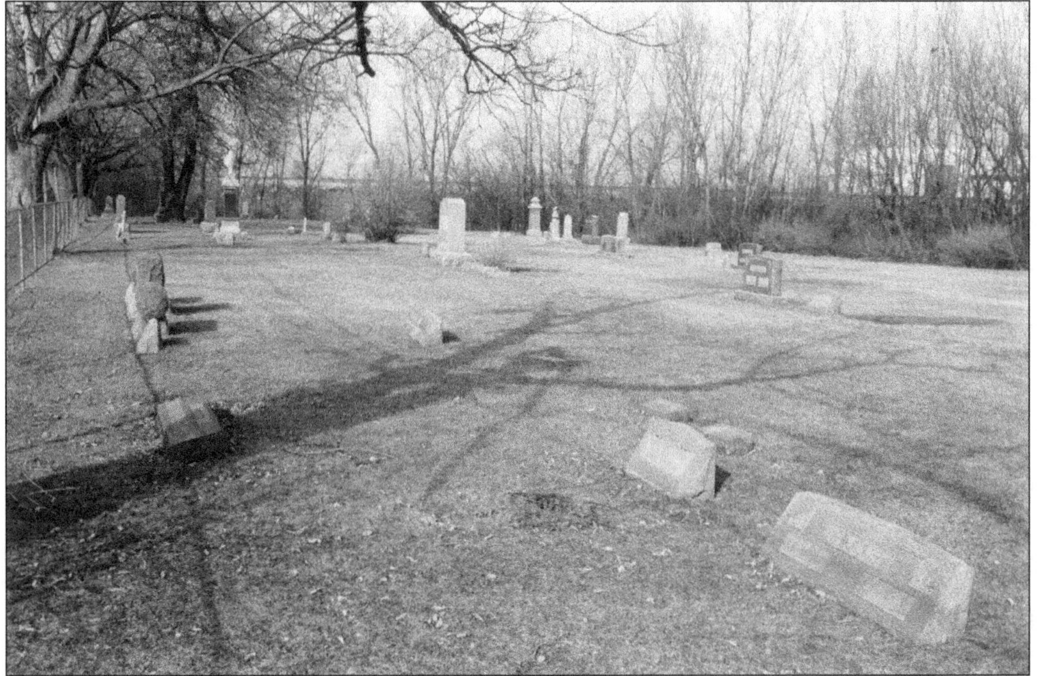

Resthaven Cemetery also dates to the 1840s. This little cemetery survived the modernization program and still rests inside the airport property. The names are familiar to those of the area. There is a Franzen. The Elfrings, including Frederick, who operated his store in Bensenville, were buried here as well. There are Biesterfields, who settled just to the north.

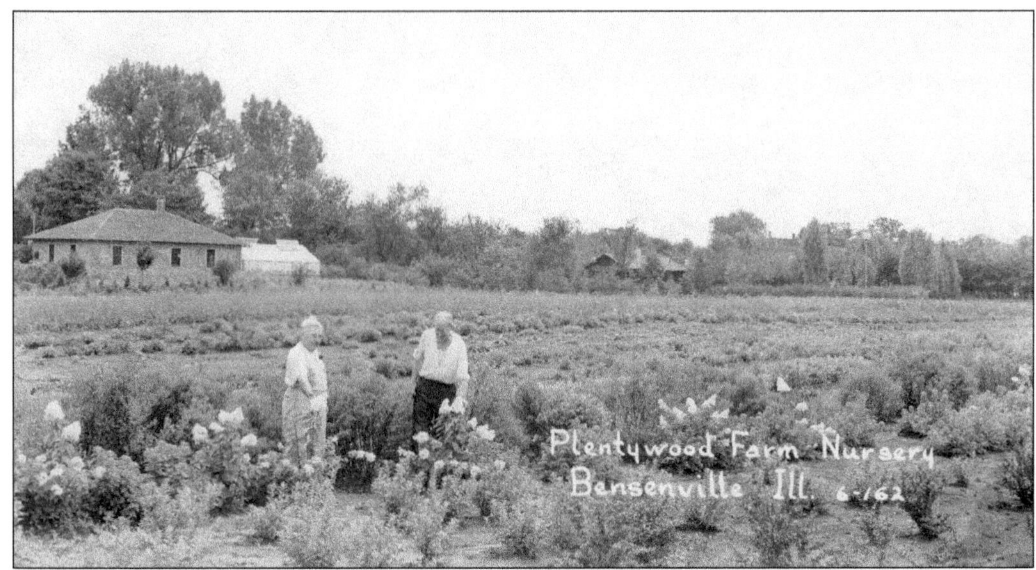

The Howell family purchased land east of Route 83 and north of Green Street. Soon, they started serving meals. Local people struggling during the Depression were allowed to pick flowers on the property and sell them for a little income. Eventually, the meal service was turned into a full-scale restaurant and operated until 1998. Clarence Howell, who operated Plentywood Farm, passed away on January 25, 2017.

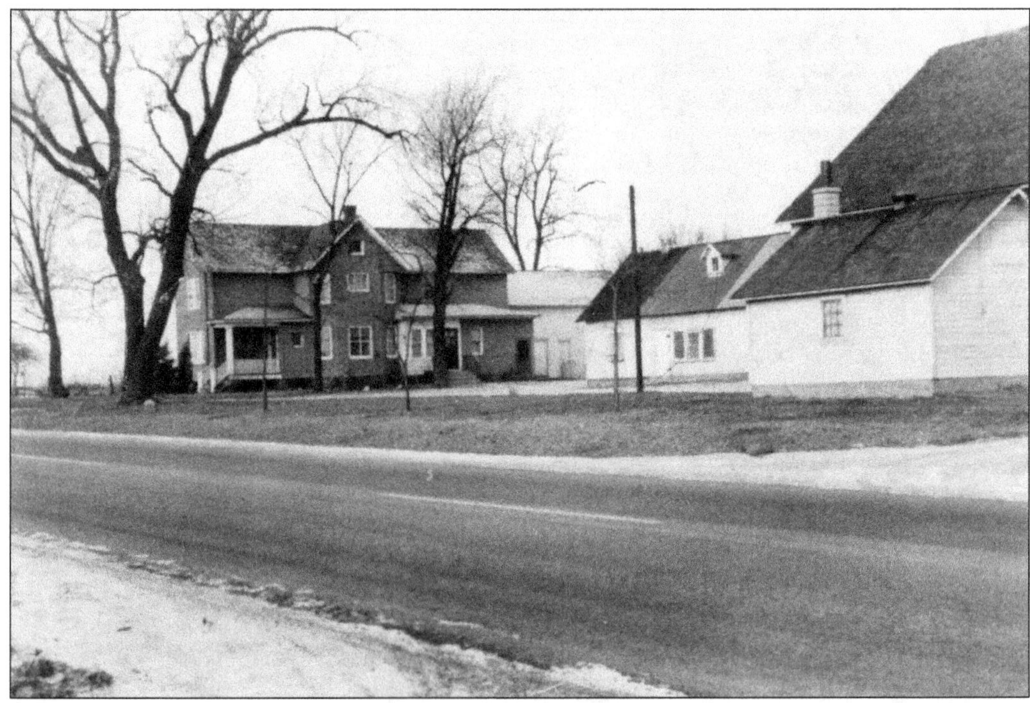

To the southeast of the village, the Fischer family had also sold off the property north of Grand Avenue and east of York Road. The Luessenhop family settled here and began farming. The property was eventually developed with the River Forest Country Club and then the St. Charles Borromeo Catholic Church and School. The farmhouse was renovated and used as the rectory.

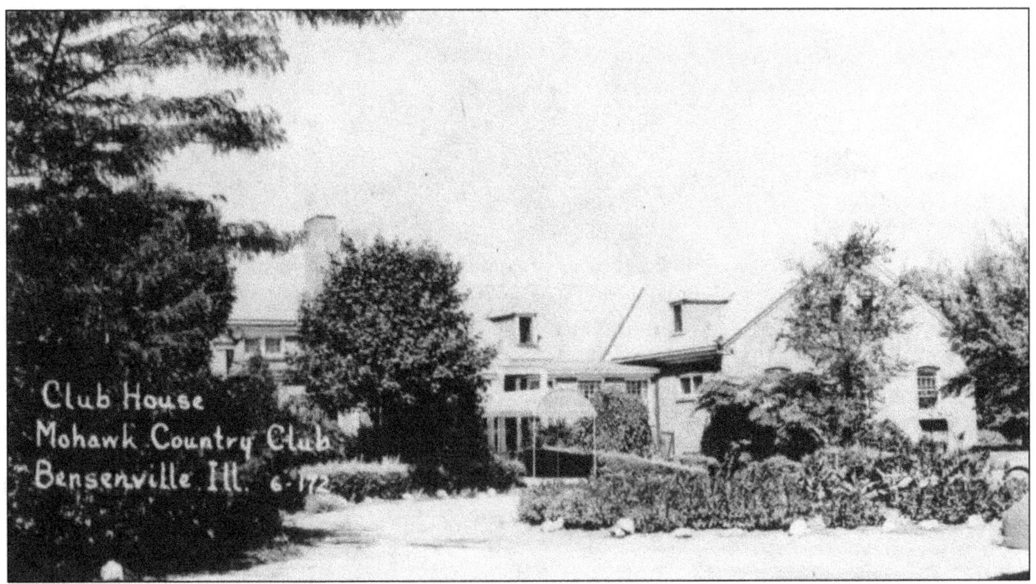

Land to the north of the village was also being developed. The Mohawk Country Club was created in 1929 and encompassed 190 acres of land. On the southern part of the property, just north of Irving Park, was a nine-hole course for women. By 1931, the club had 450 members.

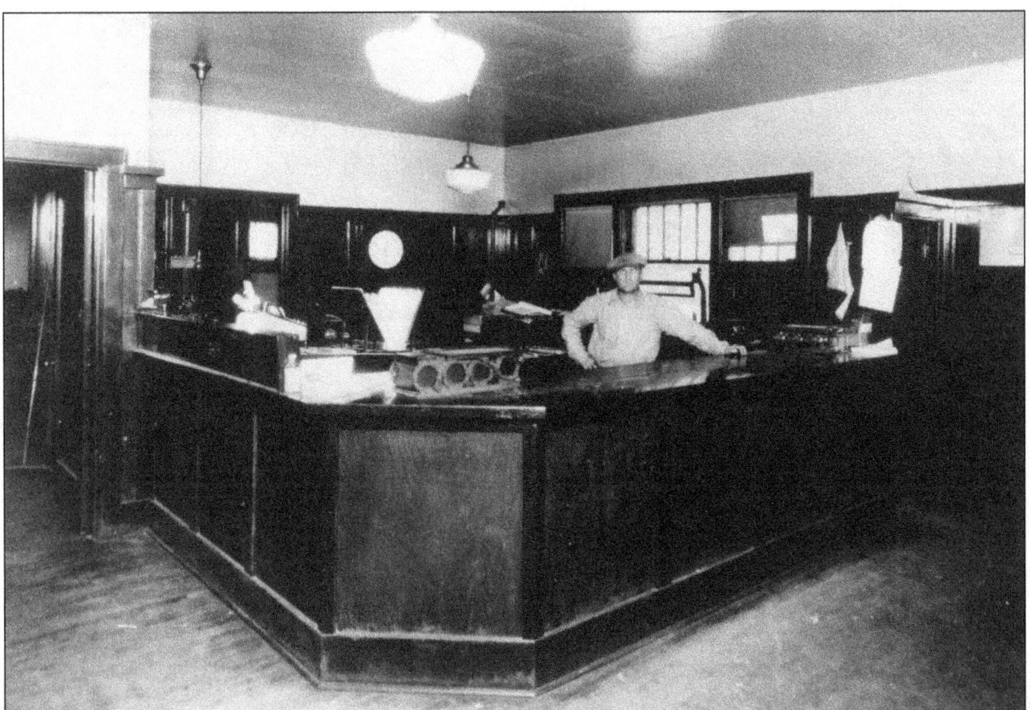

The first part to be sold was the southern 40 acres in 1946, with houses constructed over the course of the next two years. In 1955, investors purchased the option to buy the rest of the course and some surrounding property. This happened in 1960. It took six years for plans to be drawn up. The last season was 1971. In December, ground was broken for the industrial park.

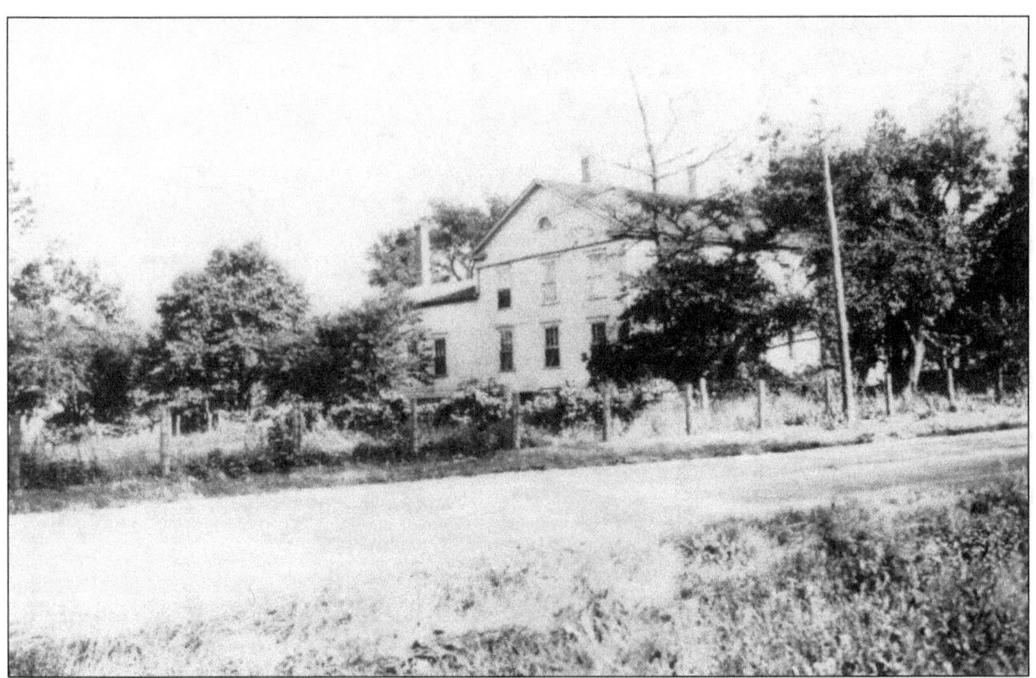

On the other side of the village, just to the south, was the Franzen-Schultz Farm. The 240-acre farm remained into the early 20th century. Albert and Martha raised six sons and one daughter. Shortly after the birth of their youngest son, who would serve in the navy in World War II, they sold the farm.

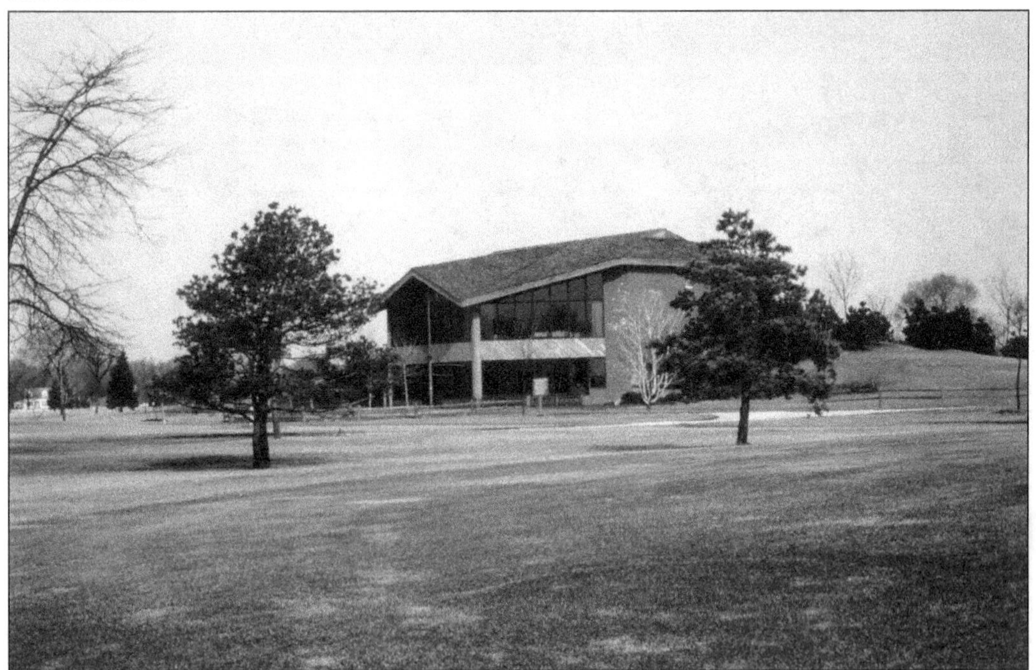

New uses would be found for the land. It became the White Pines Golf Course in 1928. A second course was added the next year. The farmhouse was converted into the clubhouse for the course and opened in April 1939. It operated as a private course until 1967.

The Milwaukee Road passenger service began in 1886. Two trains ran between Chicago and Elgin and one additional train ran between Chicago and Itasca. A third round-trip was added in 1893. The first nonstop train between Elgin and Chicago ran in 1915. Commuter service in Chicagoland has since come under Metra, which is part of the RTA (Regional Transit Authority). Now, there are 23 inbound trains and 24 outbound trains during the week.

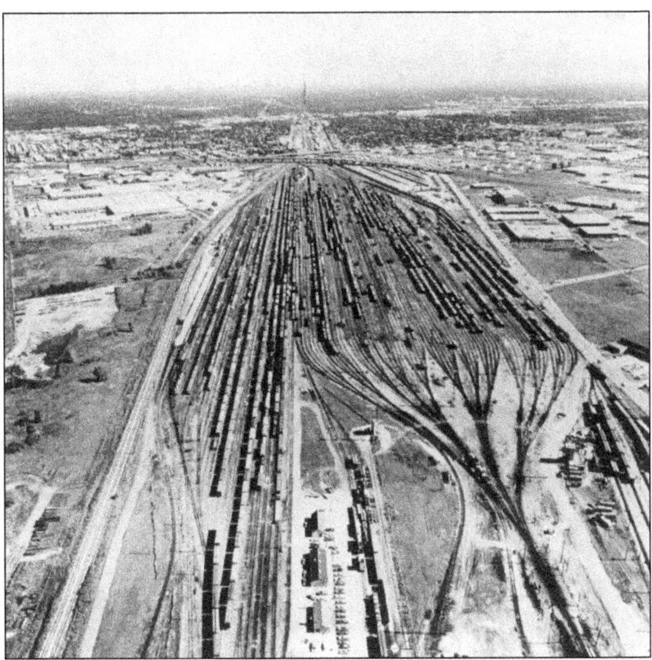

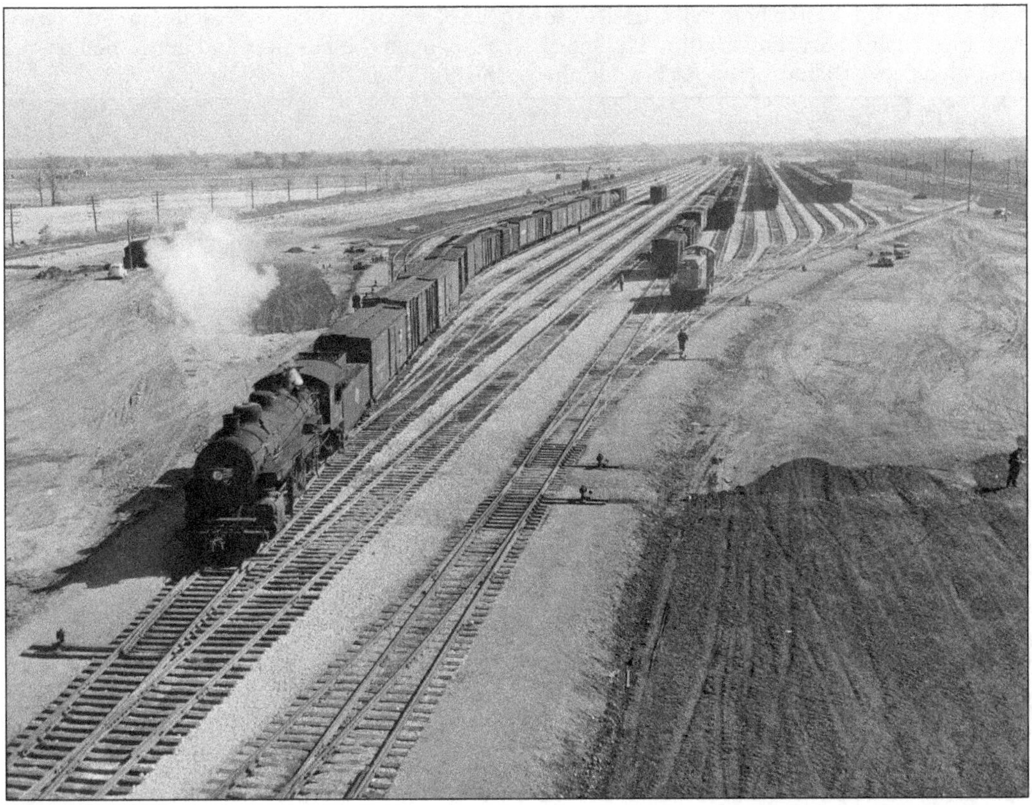

The Milwaukee Road's freight operations were bought out by other railroads before it went bankrupt in 1982. In northern Illinois, the Canadian Pacific bought tracks as well as the Bensenville Yard. Here, trains are assembled as well as off-loaded or loaded from the intermodal trucking facility.

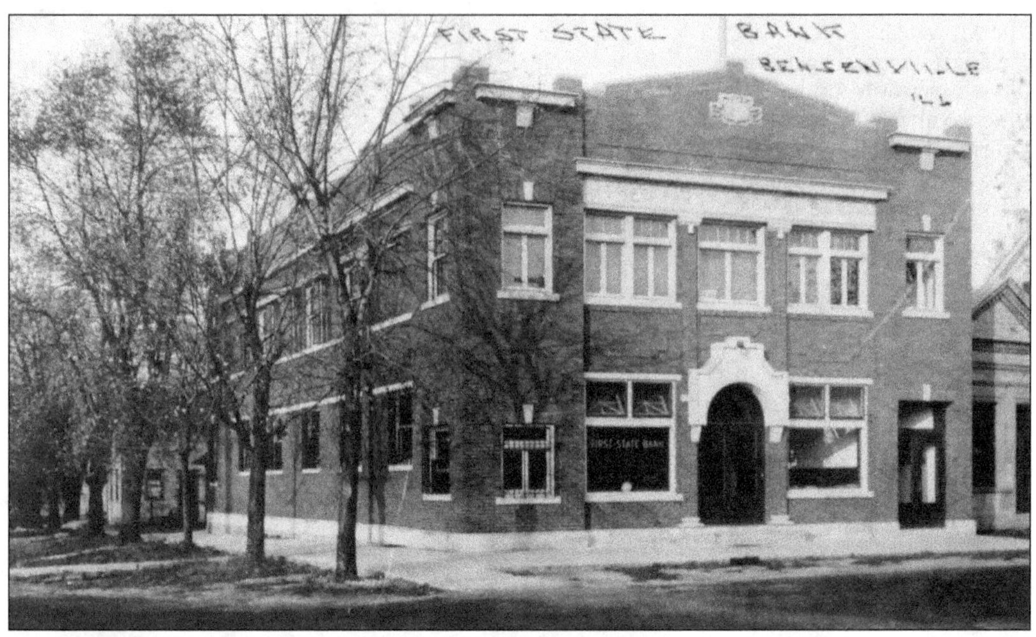

The Franzen Bank became the First State Bank of Bensenville in 1911. It failed, as did many other banks, in 1933. Chester Franzen, Charles's son, opened an insurance, real estate, and currency exchange business in the building. His son Richard bought the business and continued to sell insurance. Now, Richard's son Rick works out of the building.

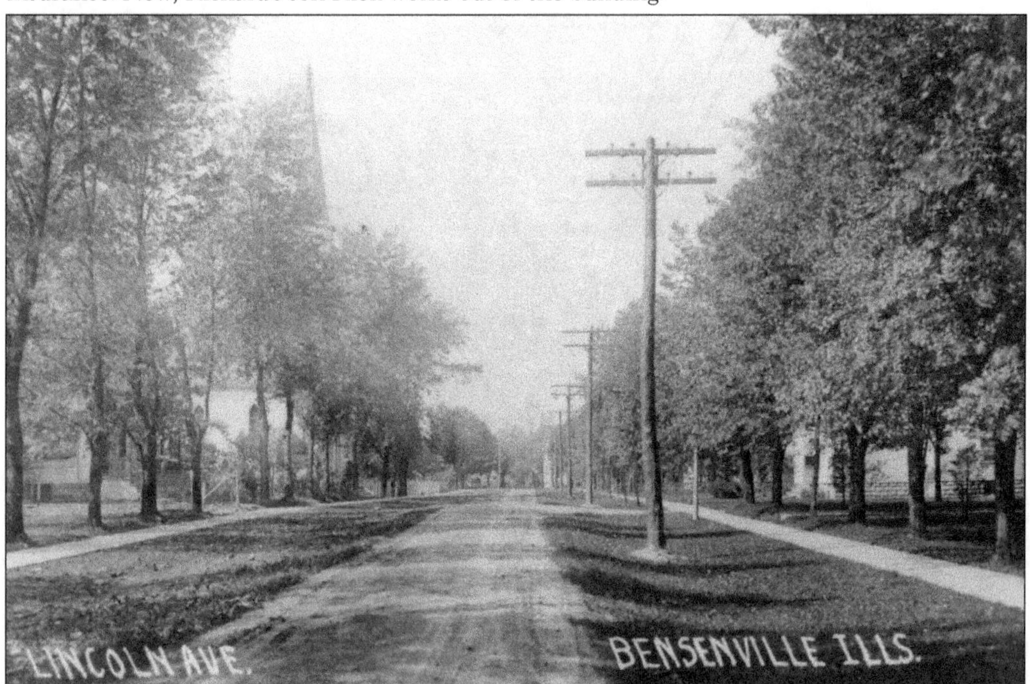

One area of Bensenville that has been significantly changed is pictured here. This was Lincoln Street in 1910. There is no street there now. The Green Street School building, the post office, and the police station face Green Street to the south and back up to this location. Immediately to the north is the Bensenville Railroad Yard.

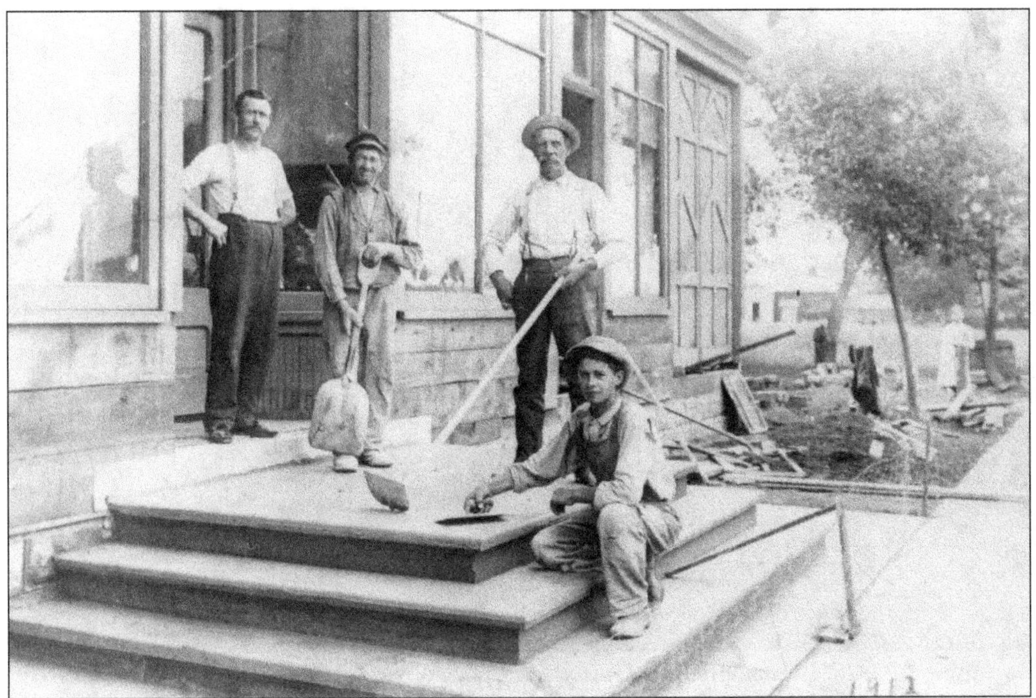

The businesses in Bensenville continued to diversify. Fred Mess opened a furniture store that doubled as a mortuary. This store stood on Green Street. Here, Mess (left) observes the finishing touches to the new concrete steps leading into his shop. To the right, Herman Korthauer stands above his son George. The man second from left is unidentified.

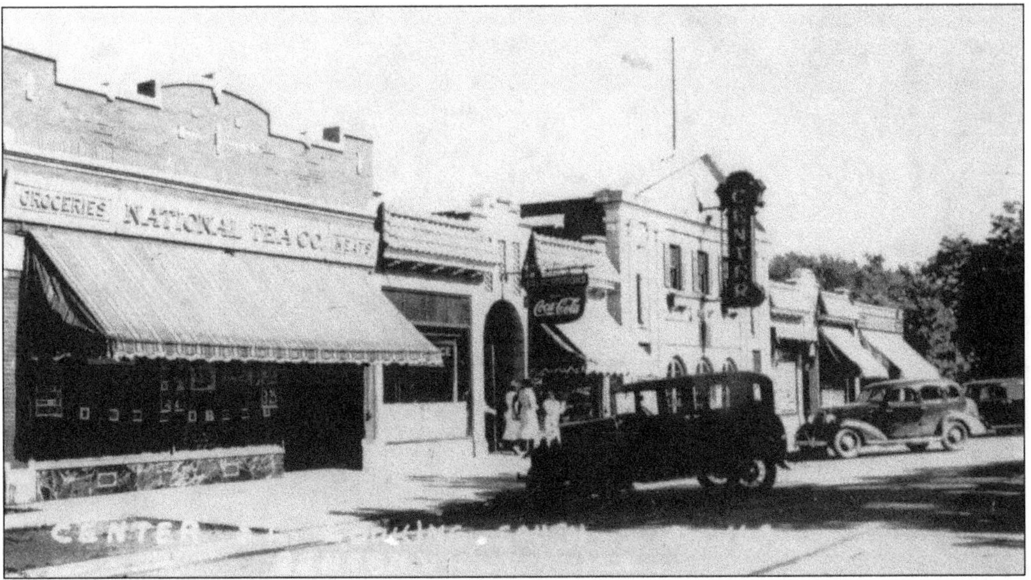

Center Street was now fully developed. The theater remained the focal point and was increasingly popular. Even in the Depression, Americans could still afford to see a movie. This image, taken in 1937, shows that street parking has been added. Shoppers are making their way into the store. Also, a new larger grocery store of a national chain, National Tea Co., has arrived in Bensenville. The old general stores would not last.

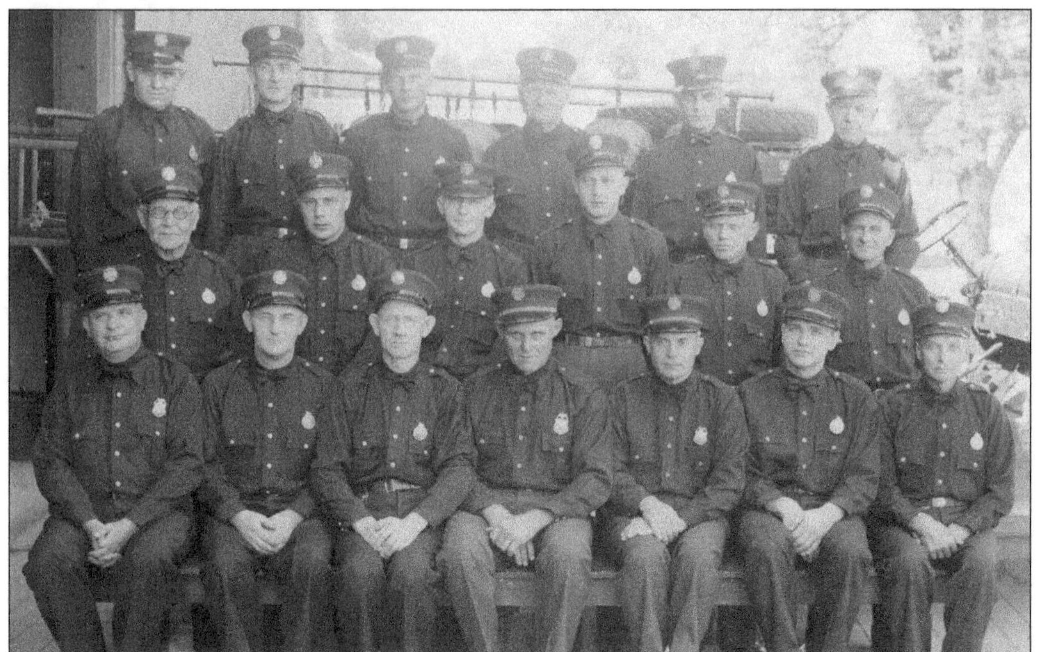

Beginning in 1926, Bensenville firemen received pay consisting of $2 per drill and $2 for the first hour of a fire and $1 for each succeeding hour. In 1937, the village board decided that the fire department should not report to fires outside of village limits. This decision brought the creation of a rural fire protection district. Picnics and carnivals were held to raise money for these organizations.

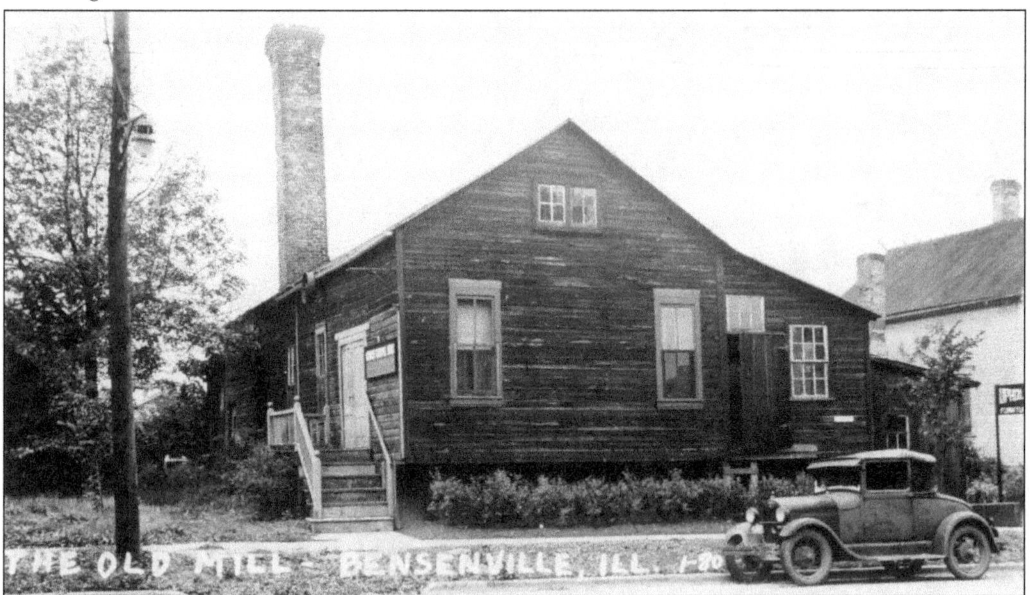

During this same decade, another group began meeting for prayer and Bible study sometimes at the village hall, sometimes in the theater. On October 6, 1935, sixteen charter members moved into a building on the west side of Center Street north of the tracks that had originally operated as mill. In 1950, the congregation broke ground on a new building at York and Memorial Roads and took the name Bensenville Bible Church.

After church on spring, summer, and fall afternoons, many Bensenville residents could be found at one of the local baseball diamonds either watching or playing. No sport was more popular than baseball. The games were competitive, and the players took pride in their team and their community. Most of the surrounding towns had teams, so there was no shortage of games that could be played.

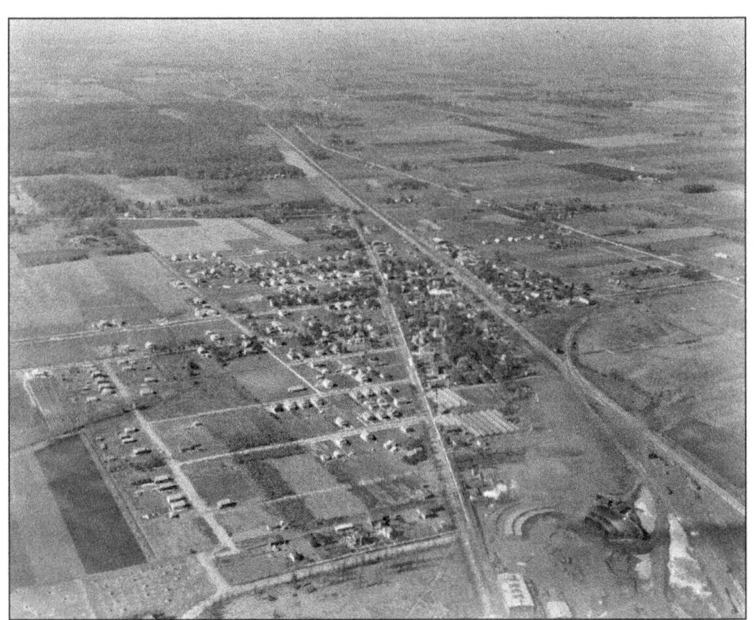

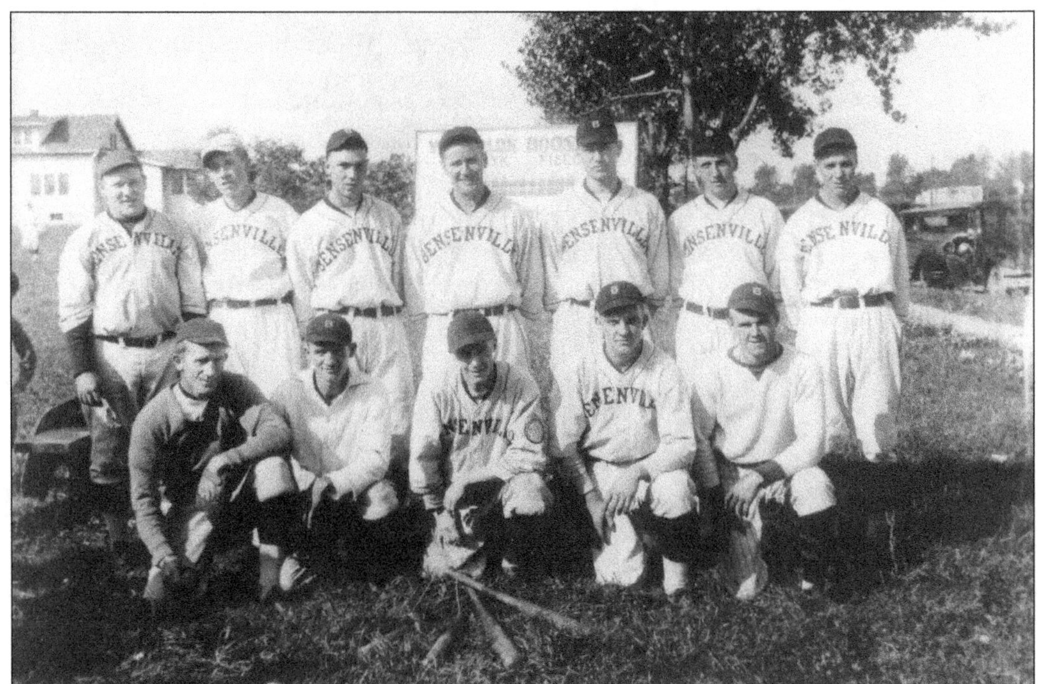

The best diamond was at Green and Mason Streets. Home plate was just southwest of the corner. People lined the sides of the field to watch the games. There was also a diamond on the northwest corner of Church Road and Main Street and a third diamond east of York Road on the south side of Roosevelt Avenue.

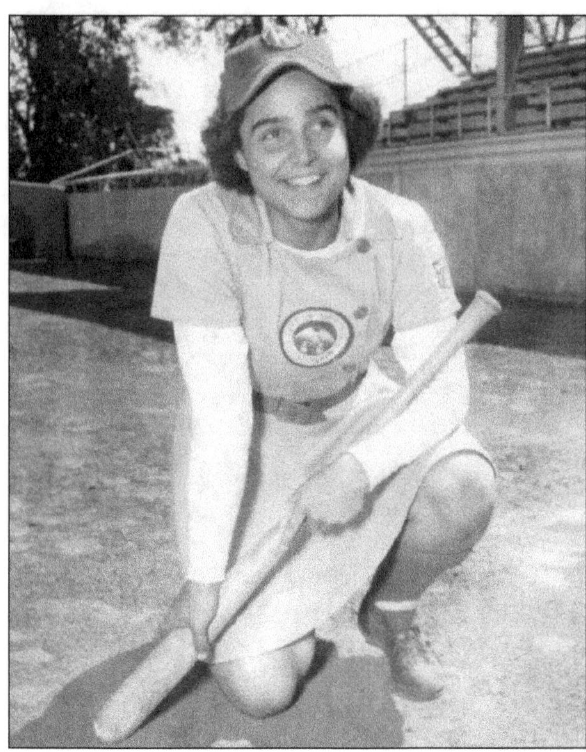

Potentially, the best baseball player to grow up in Bensenville was Audrey Wagner. Born on December 27, 1927, she played baseball as often as she could. In 1942, her family encouraged her to try out for the All-American Girls Professional Baseball League that was going to be formed for the next season. The family had to save money for her train fare. (Courtesy of George Wagner.)

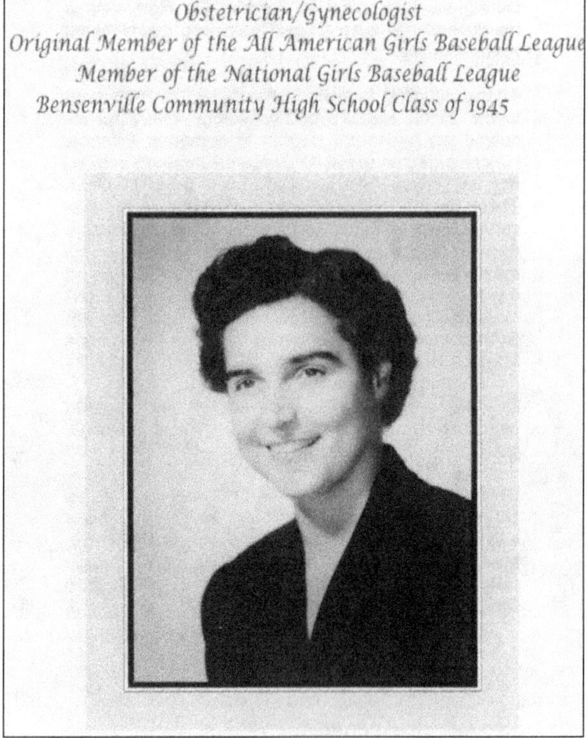

The rain started to fall before Audrey Wagner had a chance. Philip K. Wrigley was not about to end the tryouts. Under the bleachers at Wrigley Field, on the concrete surface, Cubs coaches hit her ground balls, which she managed to field perfectly. Audrey went on to be a two-time All-Star, lead the league three times in home runs and total bases and win the batting title in 1948. Later, she became an obstetrician and learned to fly. (Courtesy of George Wagner.)

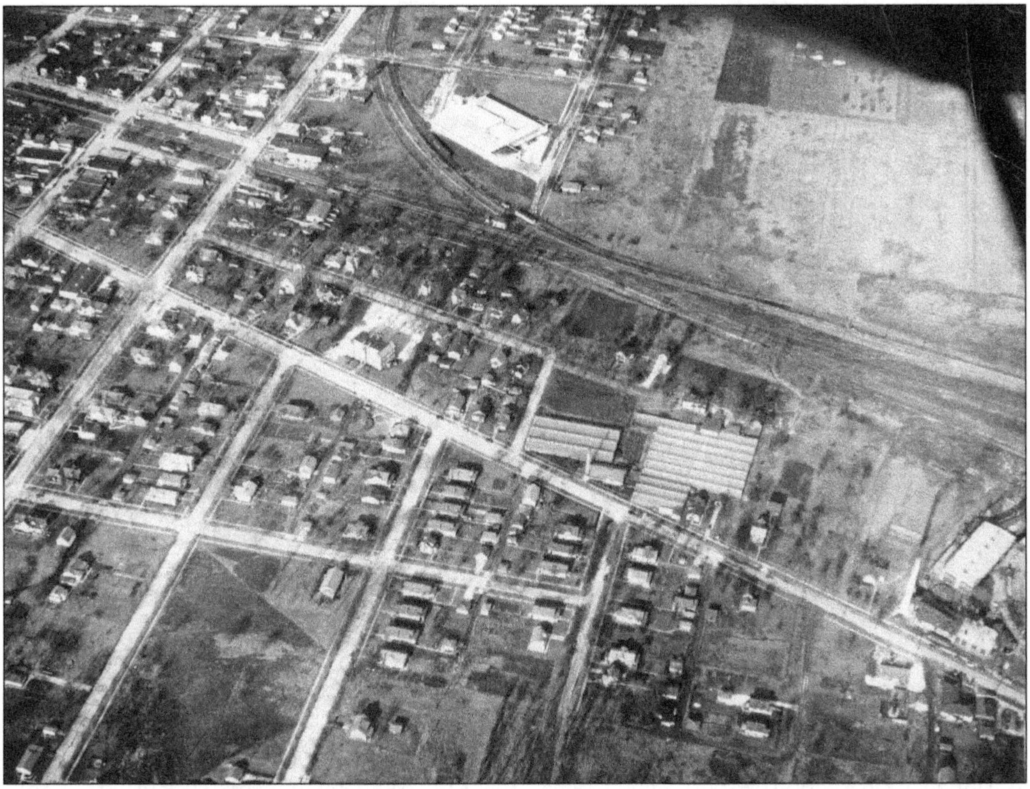

Four miles to the northeast of Bensenville, another community of German immigrants had been taking shape. It had first been referred to as Farewell. After 1887, when the Wisconsin Central Railroad laid tracks through the little town, it was called Orchard Place. The small collection of buildings extended just to the northeast of the intersection of Mannheim and Higgins Roads.

It too was an agricultural community. Centered around the orchards, which stood just to the southwest of the crossroads, the community would soon be forever changed. In late April 1942, a three-man committee from the US Army Air Corps conducted an inspection of nine locations for the construction of an aircraft manufacturing plant. Their recommendation was for the area southwest of Orchard Place.

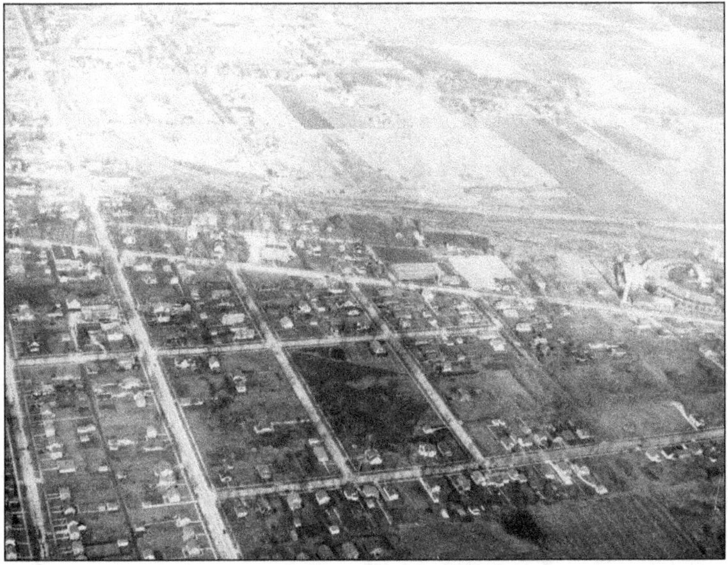

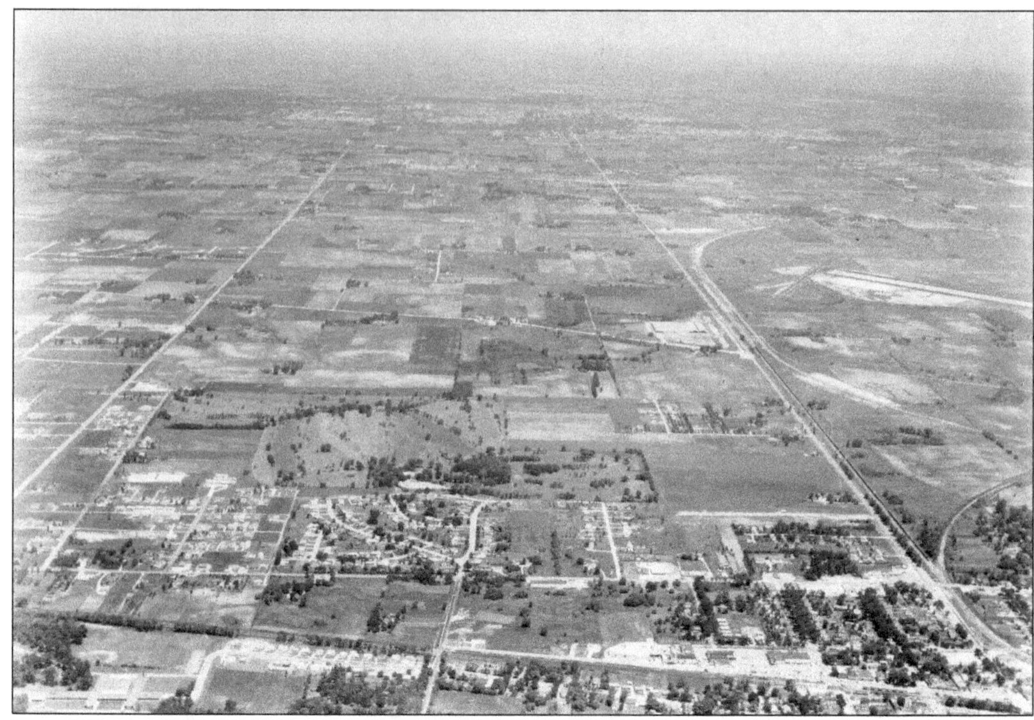

Based on the recommendation from the inspection committee, the Army Air Corps purchased 1,300 acres of land on the west side of Mannheim Road stretching from Higgins on the north to Irving Park Road on the south. The Douglas Aircraft Company immediately started clearing land and, on June 30, 1942, broke ground for the construction of the first building.

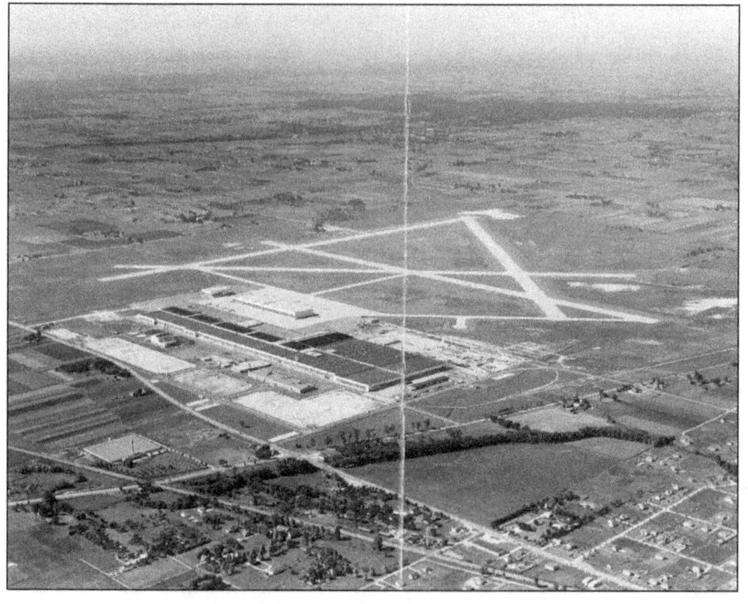

Douglas was under contract to produce both C-54 Skymaster and C-47 Dakota cargo planes. In order to keep up with demand, the company decided that only the former would be constructed at Orchard Place, with the latter being built at the factory under construction in Oklahoma City. A total of 655 planes would be built here. In 1946, the property was sold to the City of Chicago and opened to commercial traffic in 1955.

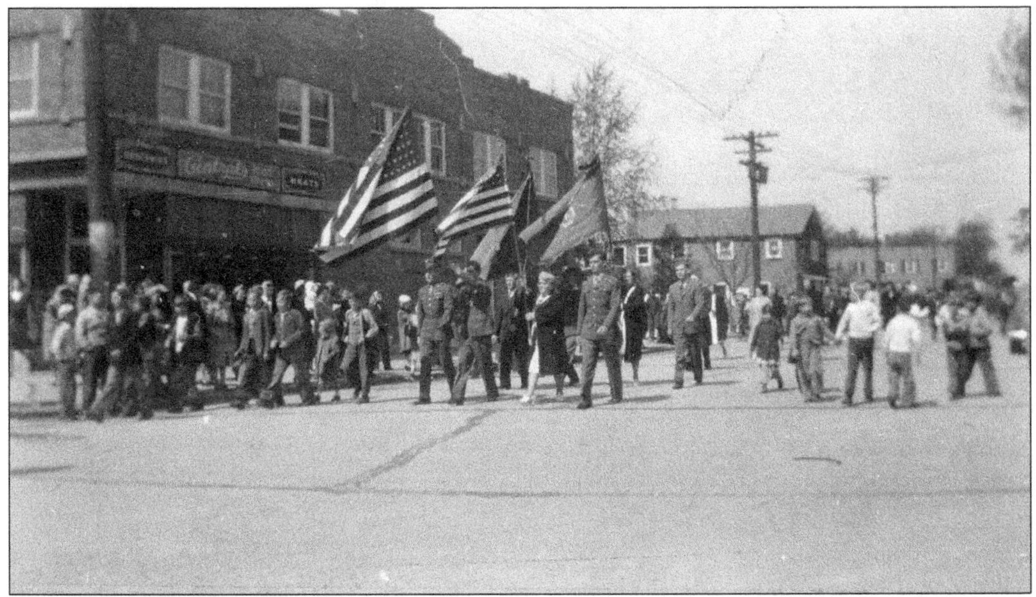

The Bensenville community had been involved in the war effort just like other communities all across the country. The residents dealt with rationing and grew what foodstuffs they could. Numerous men served overseas, including Audrey Wagner's brother George. Arthur Fischer had to hire boys between the ages of 15 and 17 to help him run the farm.

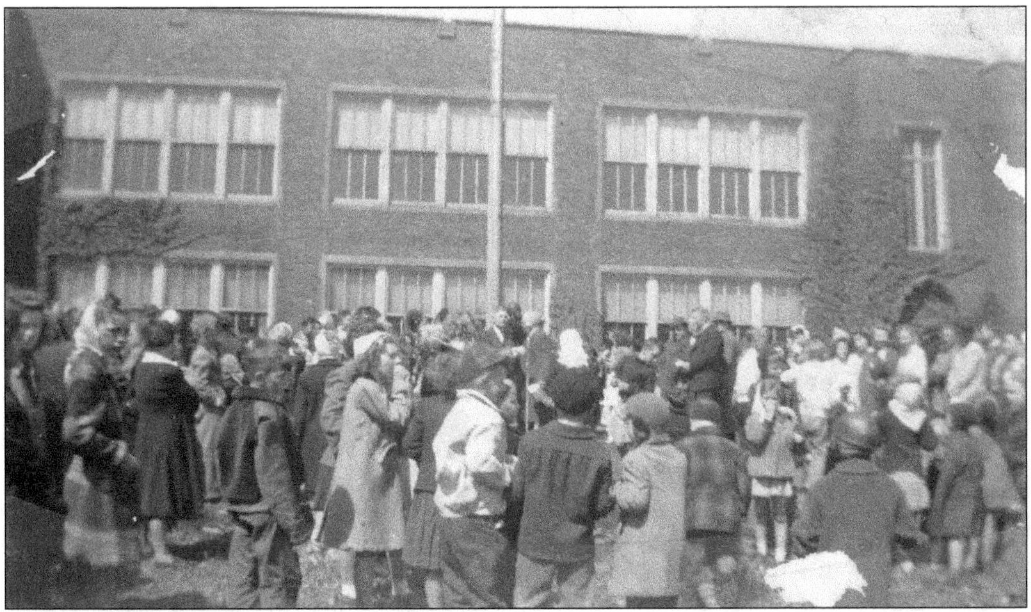

The people of Bensenville celebrated the victory of the Allies over Nazi Germany on April 30, 1945. The parade went from what had become downtown Bensenville to the high school that had been built to the south at York and Memorial Roads. There, a ceremony was held remembering the sacrifices necessary to achieve victory.

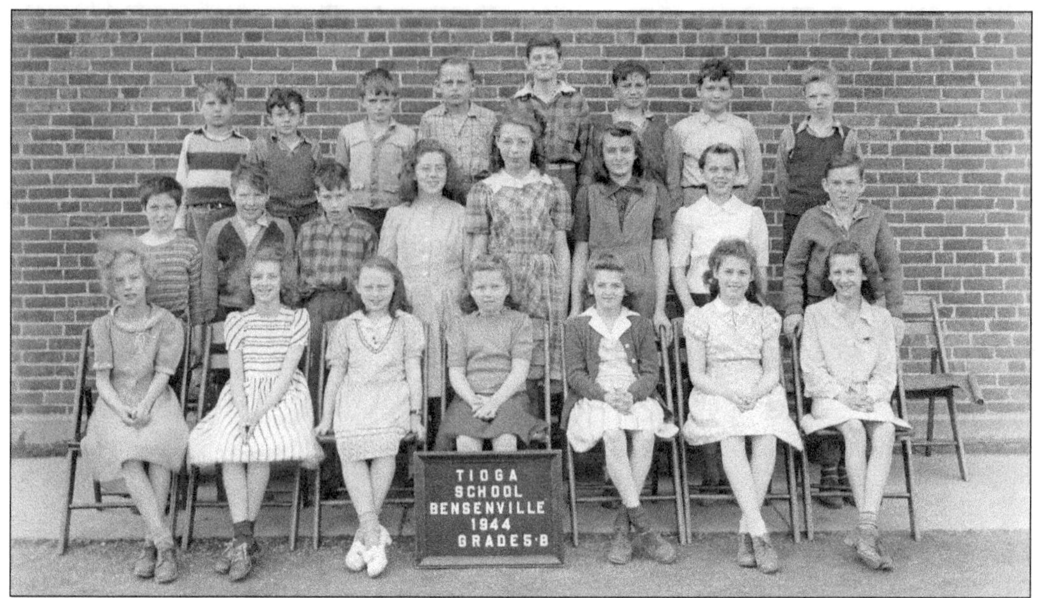

Soldiers returning home from the war as well as families looking for a suburban location raised the population from 3,700 in 1950 to 9,141 in 1960. This necessitated new school facilities. First, the high school students had been moved from Green Street School to a high school building. Then, in 1931, Tioga School was built just to the west of the high school building as a second elementary school.

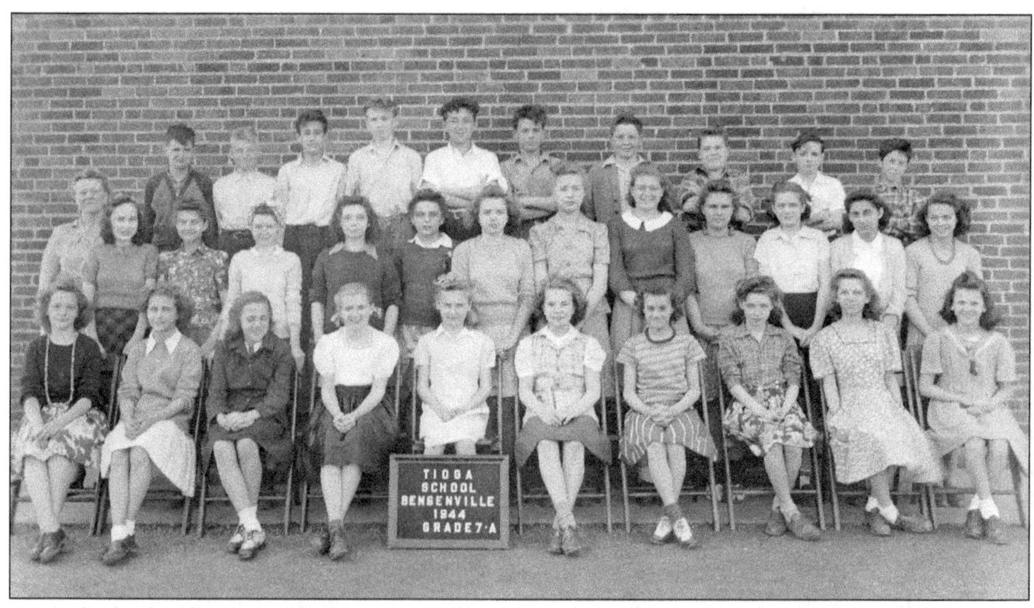

Now, the high school was slated to house the junior high classes to create more space in Green Street School. This meant that a new high school would have to be constructed. This issue was taken to the residents through a bond referendum, which passed on February 23, 1953. The next year, property on the north side of Grove Avenue and the east side of Route 83 was secured.

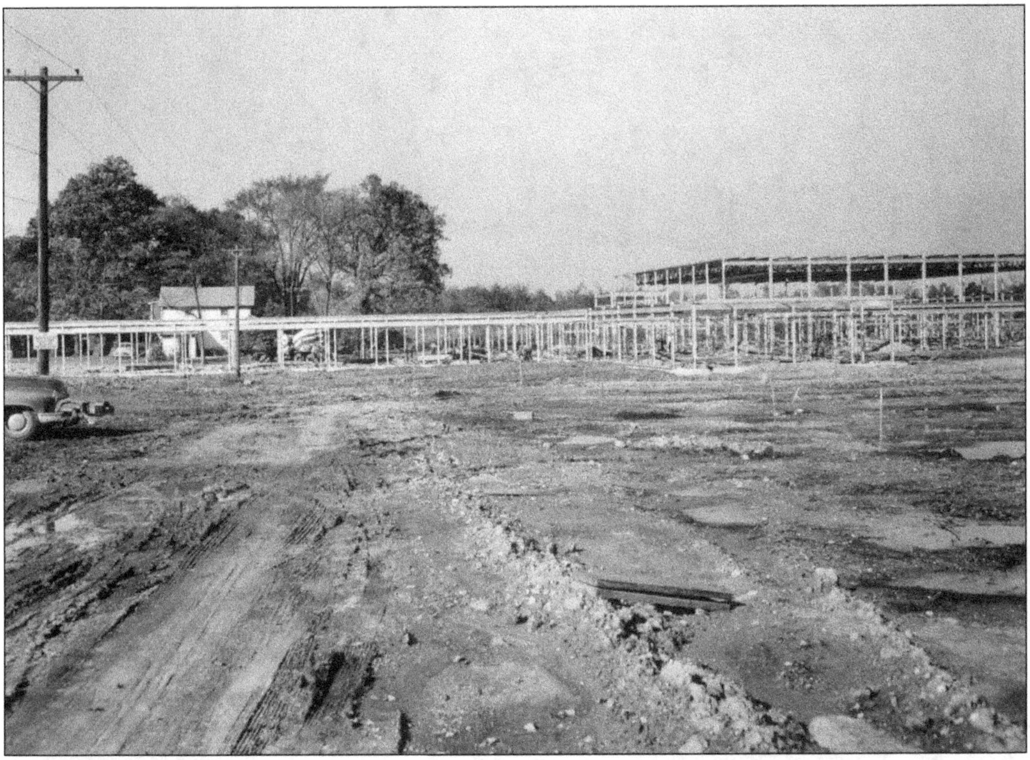

Construction began that same year with the opening of Grove Avenue onto Route 83 to make the site more accessible. The new high school building featured white brick on the exterior. This caused some debate among Bensenville residents at the time. It came to be seen, however, as an attractive building. The athletic fields were laid out to the north of the building.

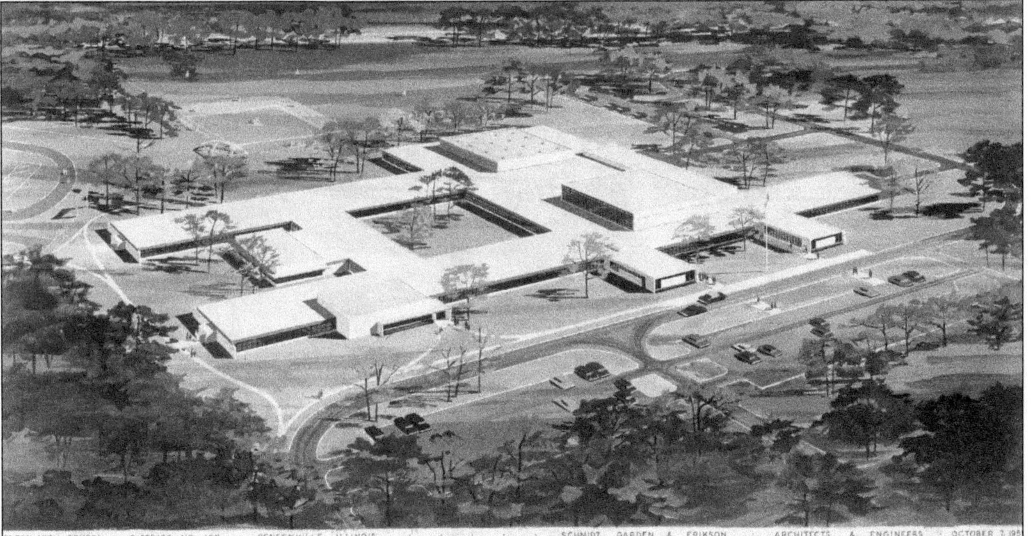

The high school students arrived in September 1955 to the newly finished building. Named after the first superintendent of District 100, Frederick C. Fenton, the school continues to serve both Bensenville and Wood Dale as a community high school district. The first additions came in 1974 and the latest in 2015.

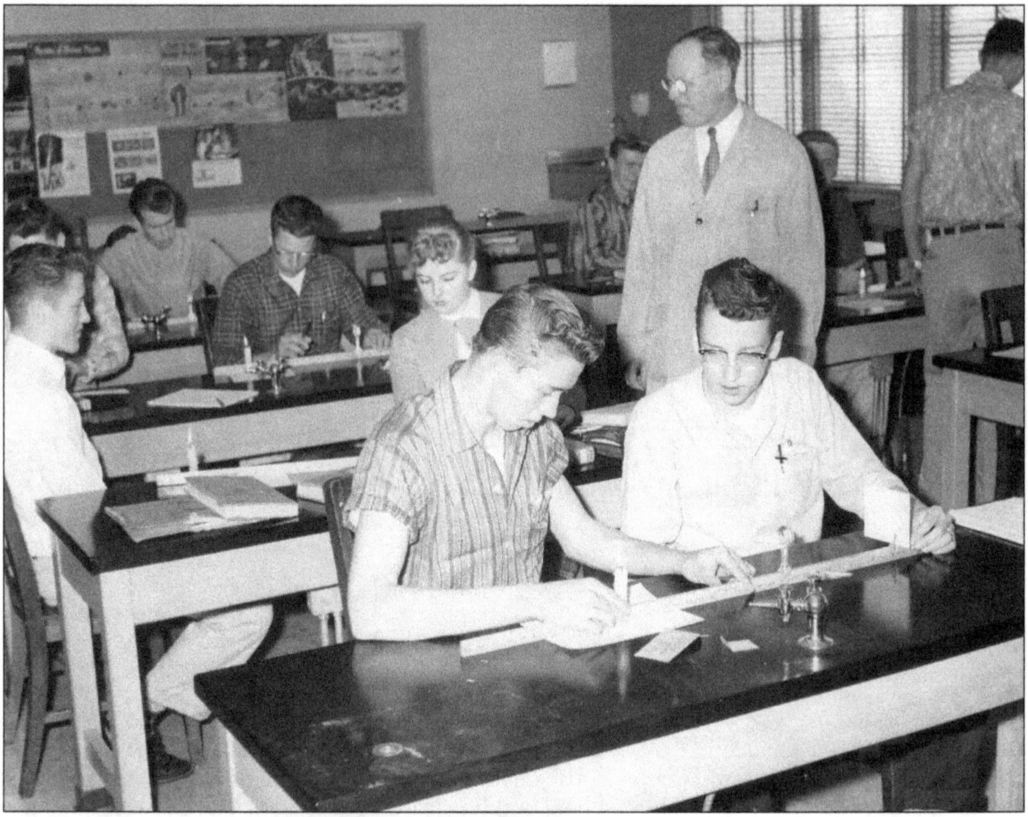

Fenton provided the latest in classroom amenities. Here, in science class, the students are using candles and magnifying glasses. Teacher Samuel Richmond observes the students as they conduct the tests. Outside of class, it was a different story. One Halloween night in the late 1950s, an outhouse was taken and put on the roof of the school building.

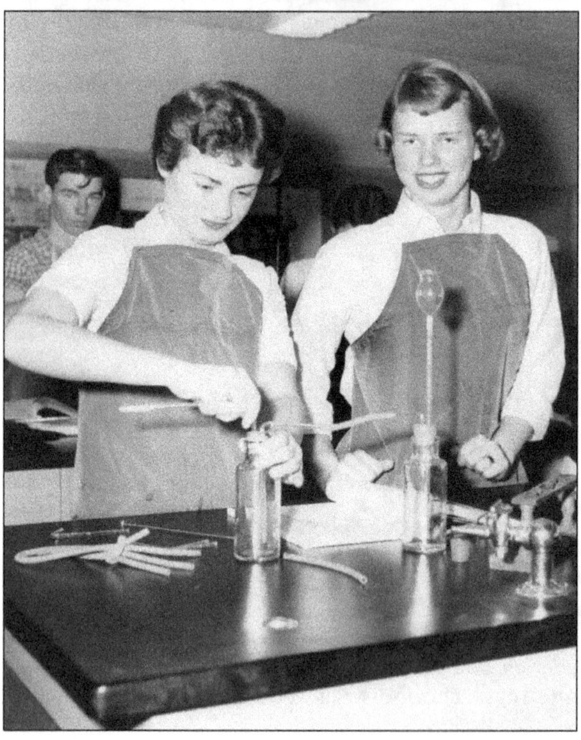

Fenton students Claudette Lauck and Ann Linden conduct an experiment in science class in 1958. Intentionally missing school was punishable with an entire letter-grade deduction. One opening day for major-league baseball in the late 1950s, two Fenton students just happened to be identified in a *Chicago Tribune* photograph of the Wrigley Field bleachers. The picture was posted on the school bulletin board the next day.

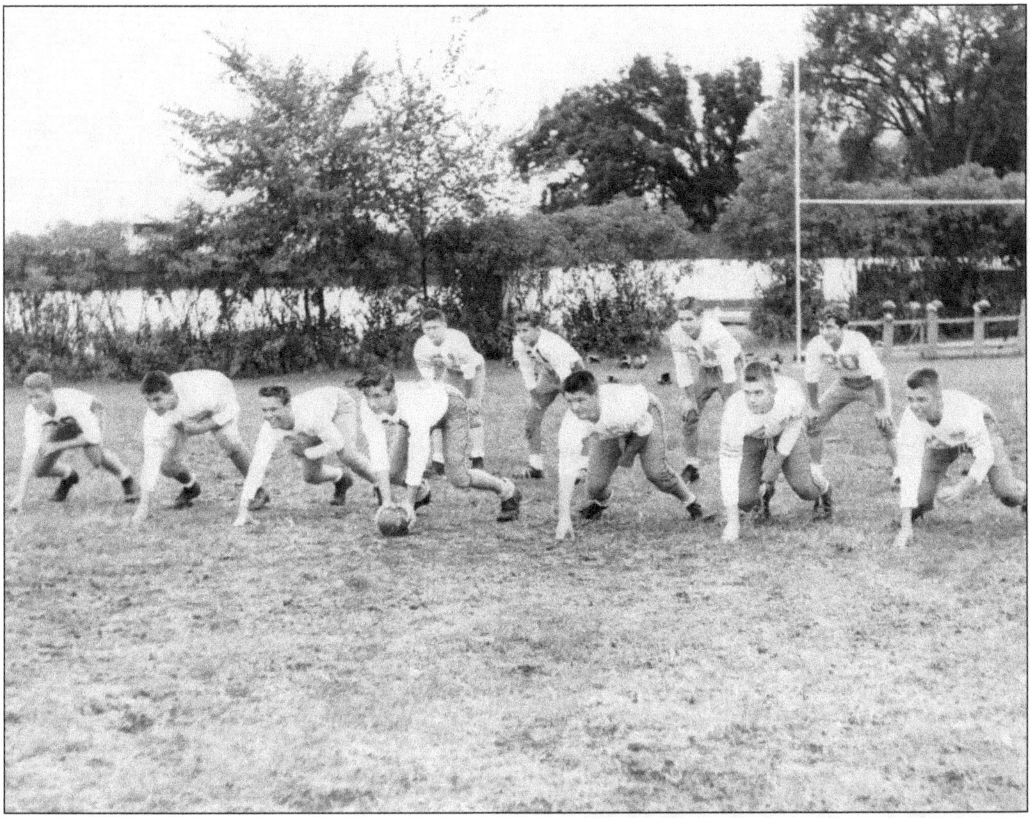

Football had been a part of the high school experience since the Bensenville Community High School opened in 1921. Wesley Johnson took the lead not only in teaching, as he also made sure that extracurricular activities were available. As friendly rivals, Fenton and Lake Park High School in Roselle competed for the Milwaukee Road Bell. The school with the most athletic victories in a given school year proudly displayed the bell over the next year.

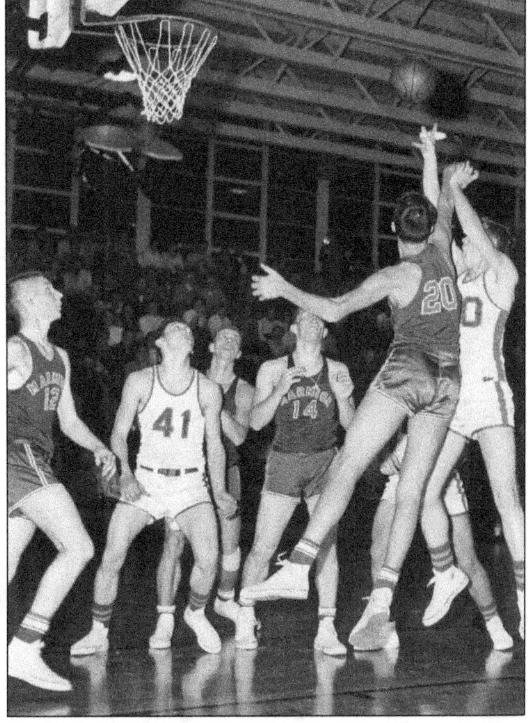

Basketball had also been a part of the high school experience. Again, it was Wesley Johnson who coached the first high school team for Bensenville as he had with football and baseball. Pictured here, Fenton battles Marmion High School in 1956.

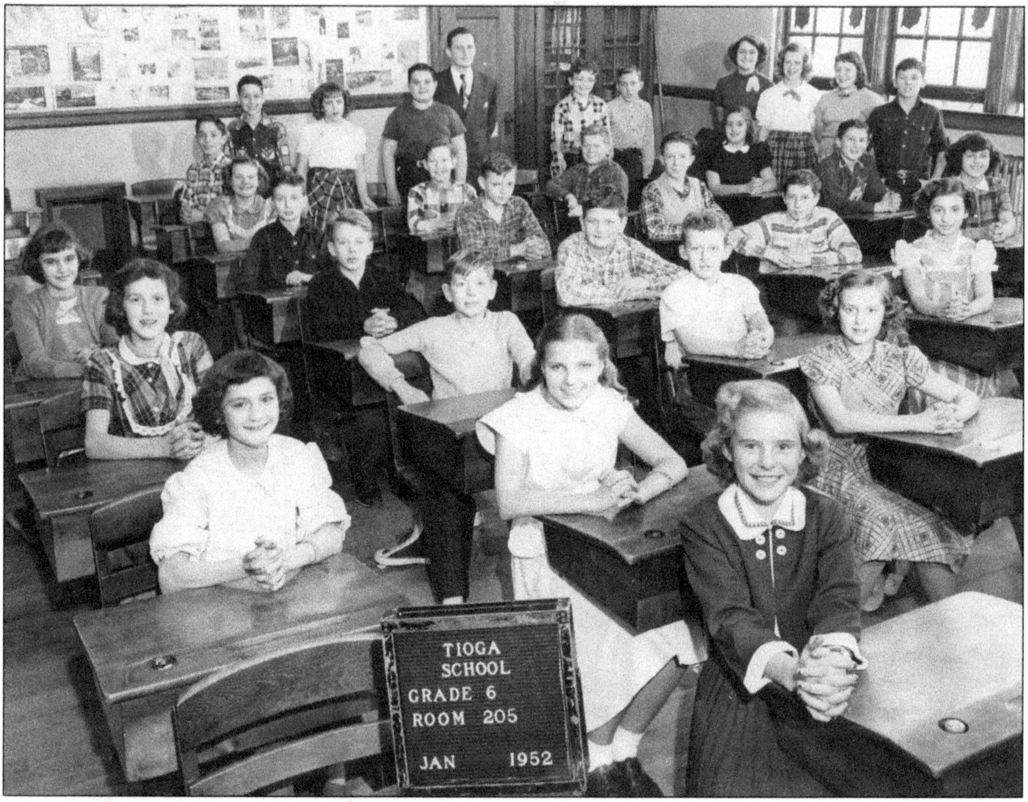

Tioga had opened in 1931 and served the elementary-age students from the southern part of Bensenville. Shown here are the eager students in 1952. After a new junior high was built, the lower grades were separated to the renamed Chippewa to the east. Tioga survived until June 2014, when it and Chippewa were torn down and a new Tioga School was constructed.

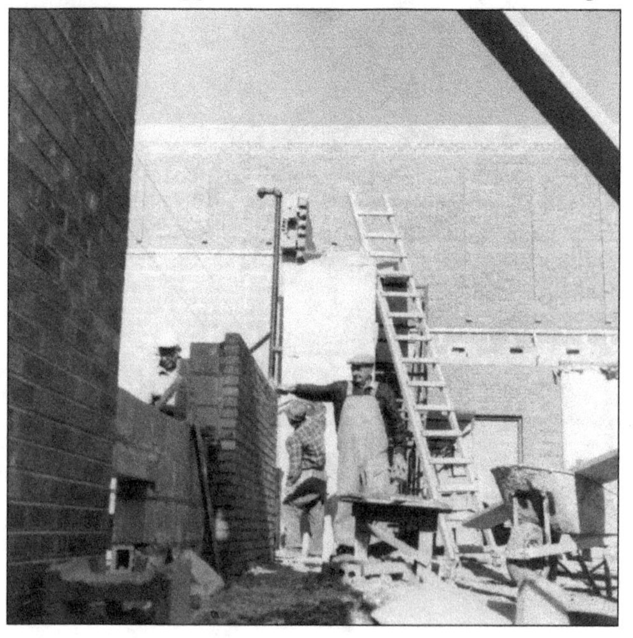

After District 2, the elementary school district for Bensenville, bought the high school building from District 100, it was used as a junior high school. It occupied this building for 10 years. Property was purchased on the west side of Church Road north of Memorial. The new Blackhawk Junior High opened in September 1965 and continues to serve the community in this capacity today.

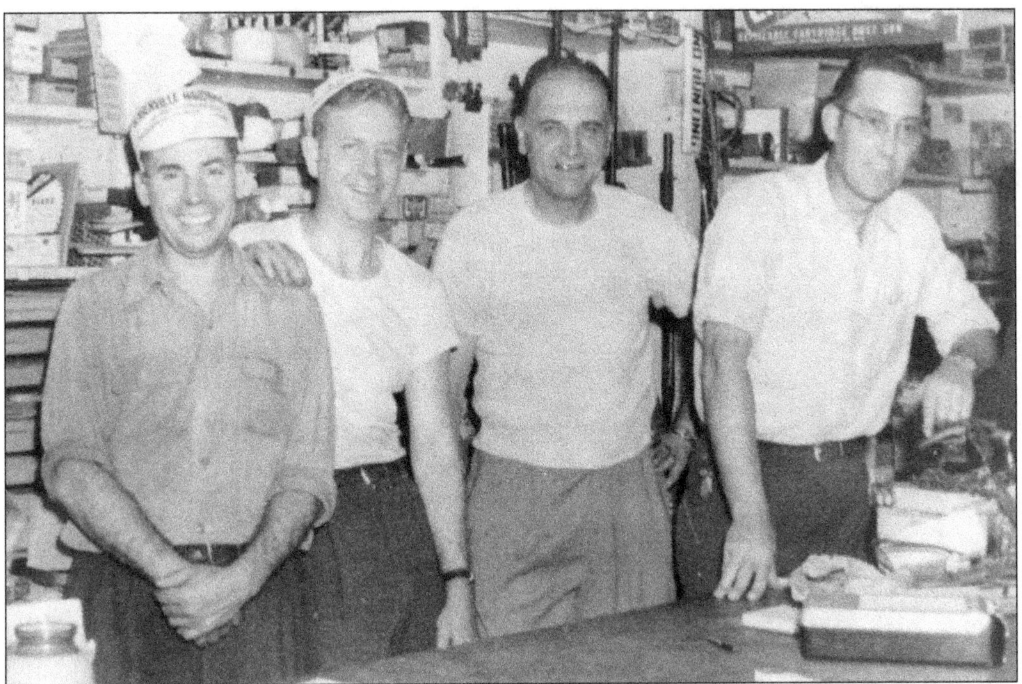

The rest of the community was changing as well. Center Street now had a hardware store operated by Chips Ortega. Ortega (far left) is joined by (from left to right) Scott Kinneman, Fred Koebbeman, and Walter Kehoe. The streets were being paved. The vacant lots were being filled in.

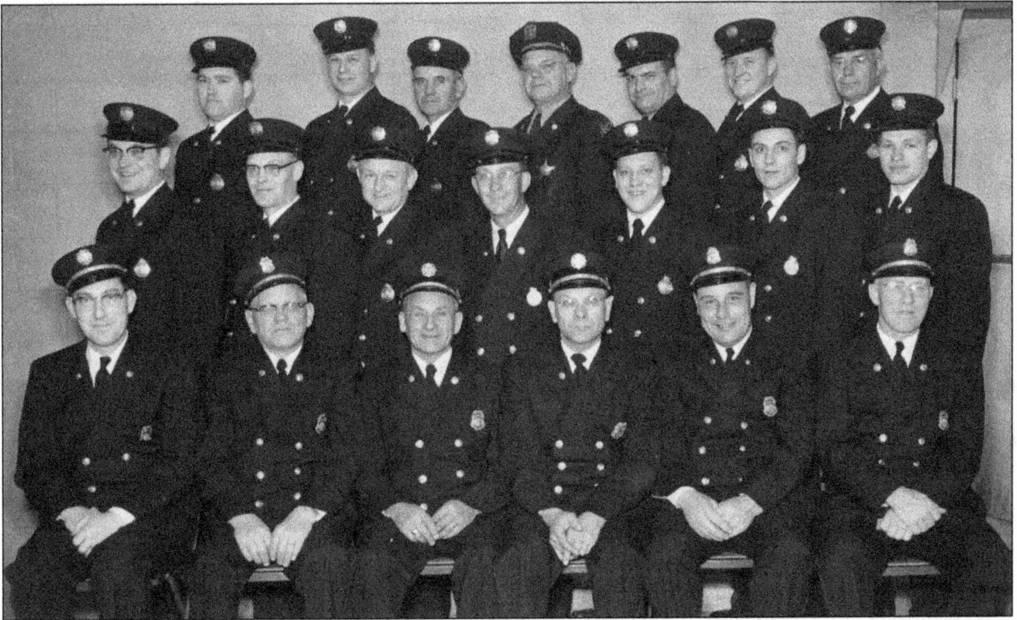

Pictured here in 1954, the Bensenville Fire Department continued to expand to keep up with the demands of a modern suburb. Just six years later, the department would be the first to respond to the scene of a crash of an airplane that had just taken off from O'Hare. Unfortunately, all on board had been killed. The Bensenville Fire Department was cited for its efforts in the face of a dangerous situation by the Illinois House of Representatives.

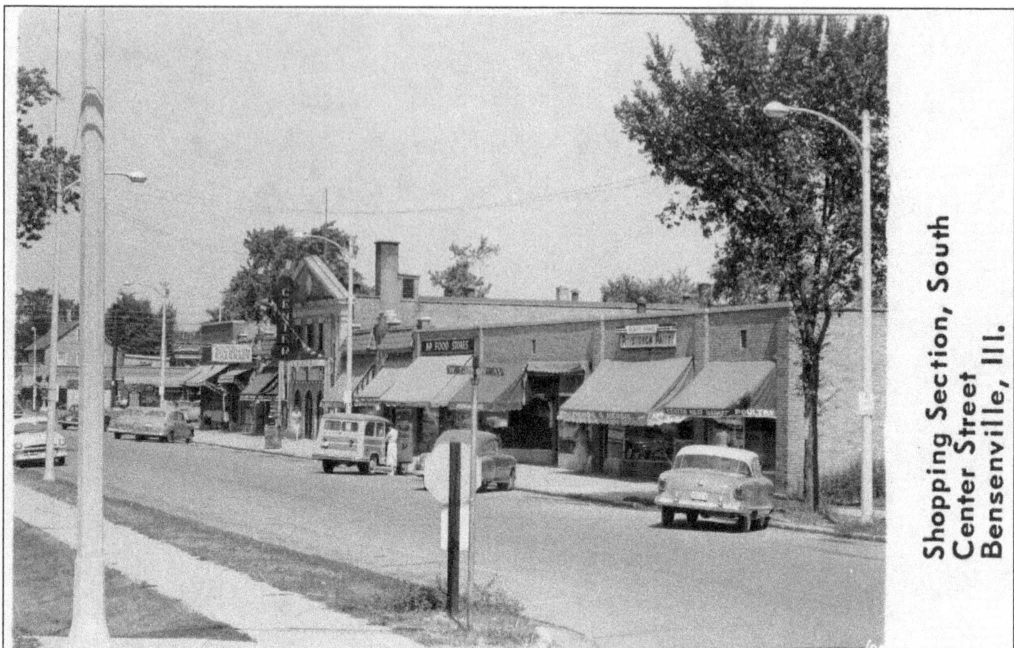

Shown here is downtown Bensenville. The modern suburb was beginning to emerge. The theater, just as popular as before, continued to anchor the businesses on Center Street. There was a chain grocery store, a hardware store, and a pharmacy. The old depot was still there too. It began to serve more commuters than freight.

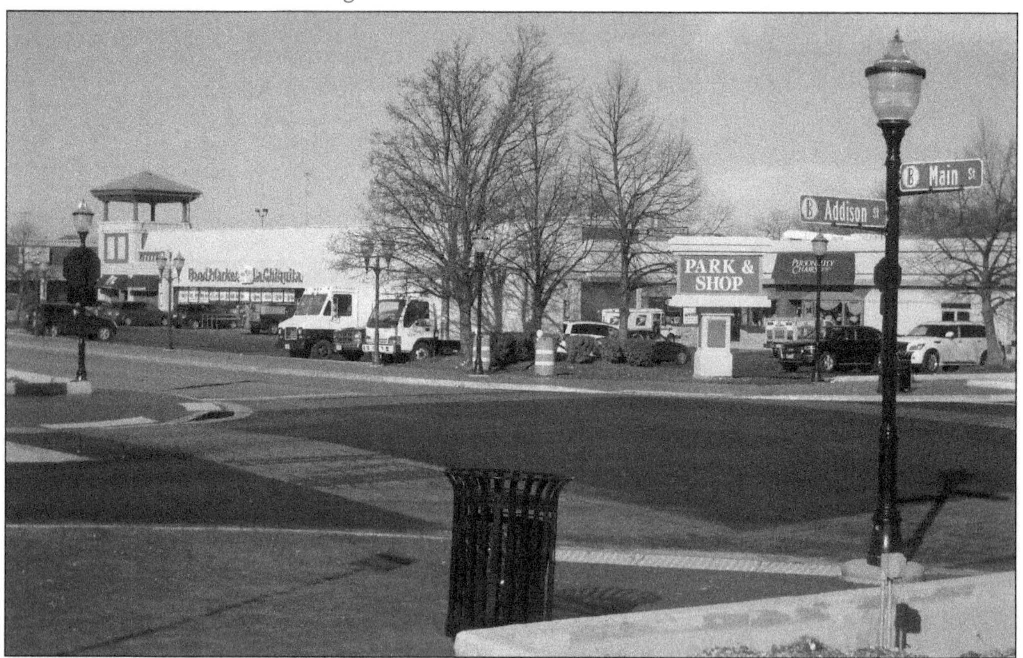

The Franzen Lumber yard had originally occupied this property. That was gone now. A blacktop parking lot filled the space and a line of commercial enterprises lined the parking lot. They were being built in other communities as the impact of the car was being felt on society. Here, it was called the Park & Shop.

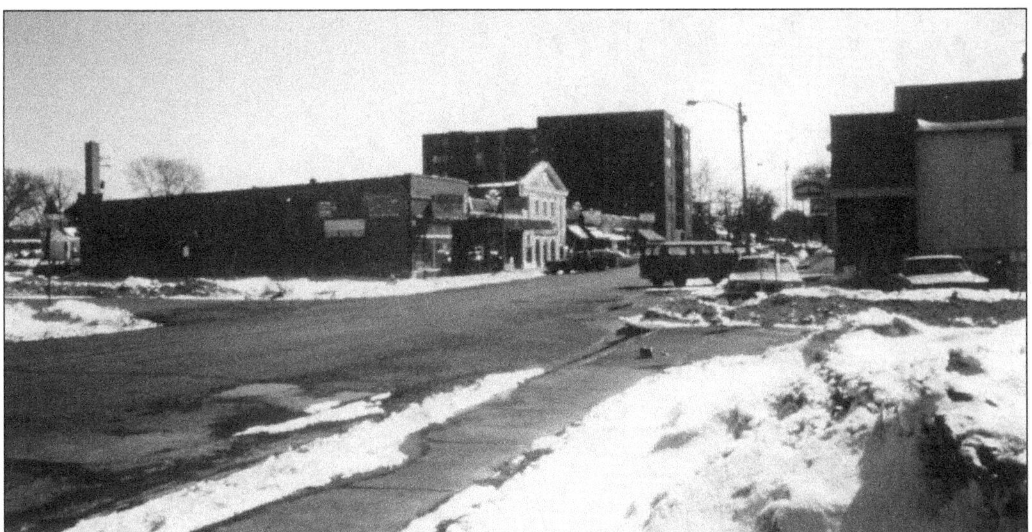

Bensenville had outgrown the old village government by the 1950s. The village purchased eight acres of property on the west side of Church Road between the railroad tracks and Irving Park. Here, a new village hall and public safety building was constructed. The village also adopted a village manager system and began hiring for staff positions to administer the work of the village.

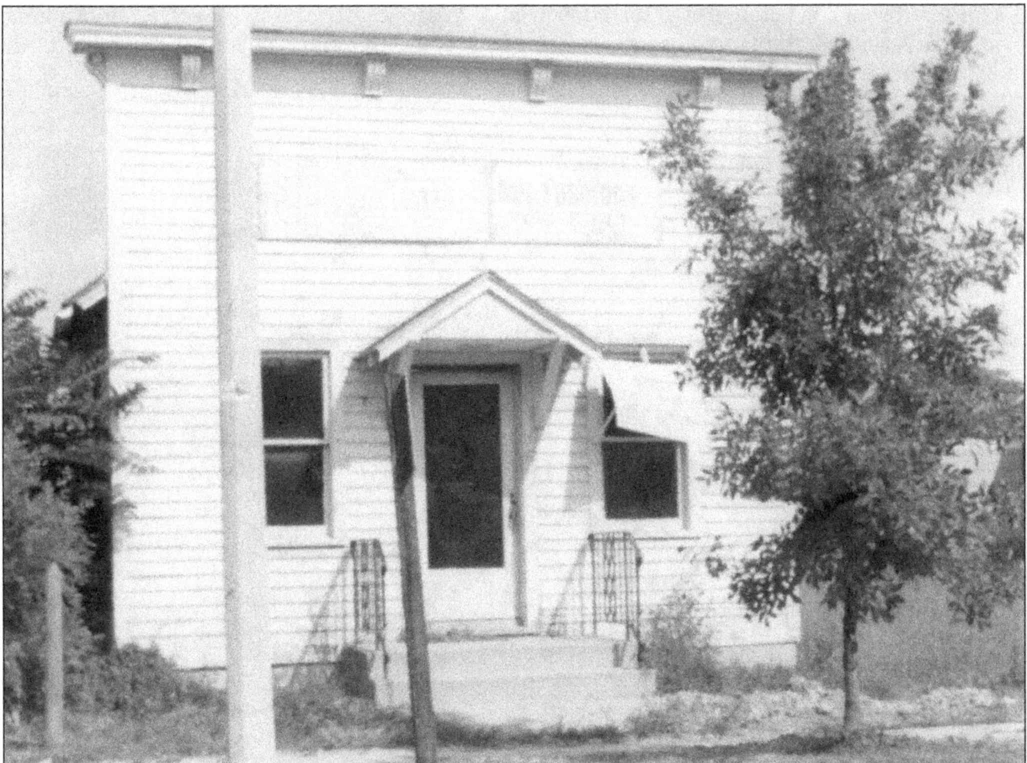

Gustave Gutsche worked as a cobbler in Bensenville. He was also the only lamplighter the village ever had. In 1888, thirty kerosene lamps were placed around the town. Gutsche was hired to light them. Every afternoon, for 22 years, he went around the village with his wagon with kerosene to do the job. In 1910, electricity lit the lamps. Gutsche's house survived until 1975.

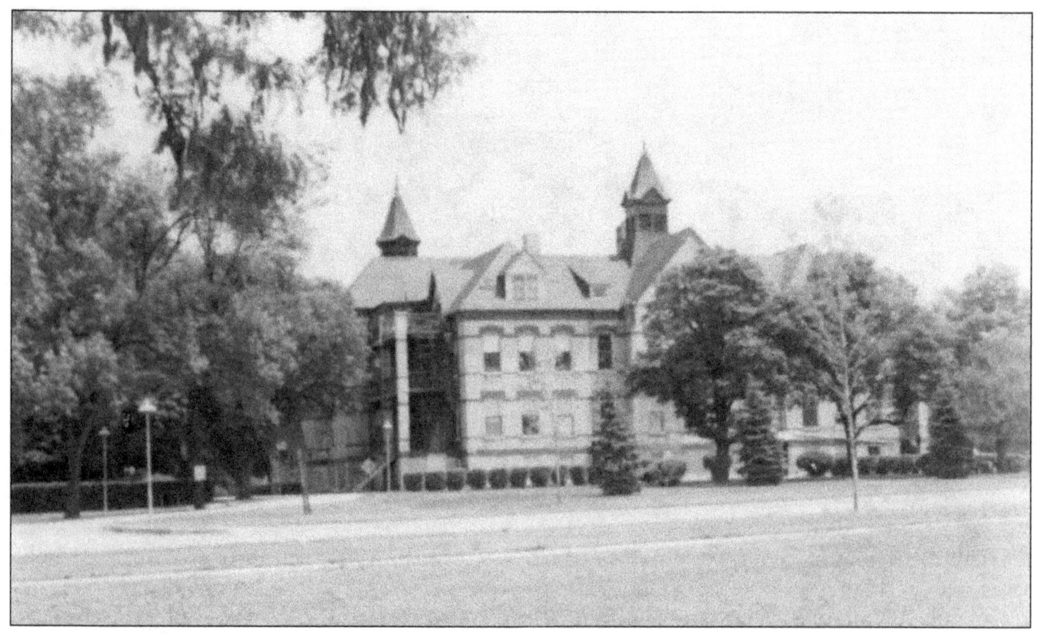

The Bensenville Home Society continued to operate the orphanage until 1978. The building is shown here shortly before it was torn down. In its place stands Castle Towers, a senior living community. Immediately to the south is Bridgeway of Bensenville. This facility houses both independent and assisted senior living.

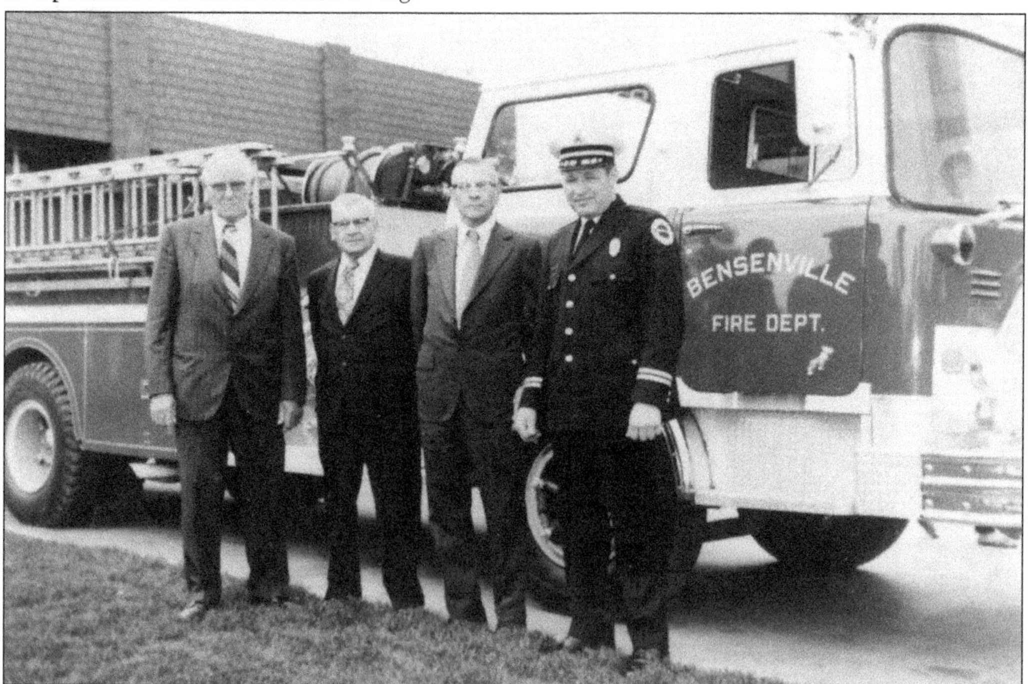

Just as the village government was changed, so was the fire department. In 1949, the rural protection district and the village district were combined. Beginning in 1956, applicants were also put through a formal hiring process and tested. In 1967, George Korthauer Sr. retired as fire chief. He was followed as chief by his brother Armin.

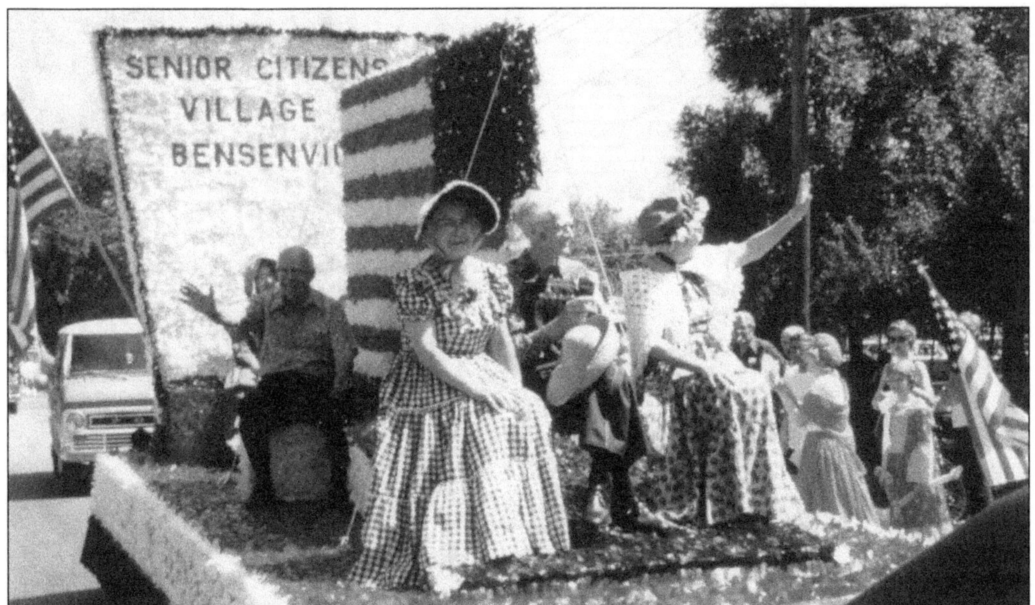

By 1970, the population of Bensenville was nearing 13,000. Horseshoe Bend was no longer used for picnics, but the residents still gathered for celebrations when they could. The Bensenville Park District came into existence in 1960 and took responsibility for the Fourth of July parade and celebration. This image from the 1975 parade shows the senior citizens' float and just a bit of the crowd lining the street.

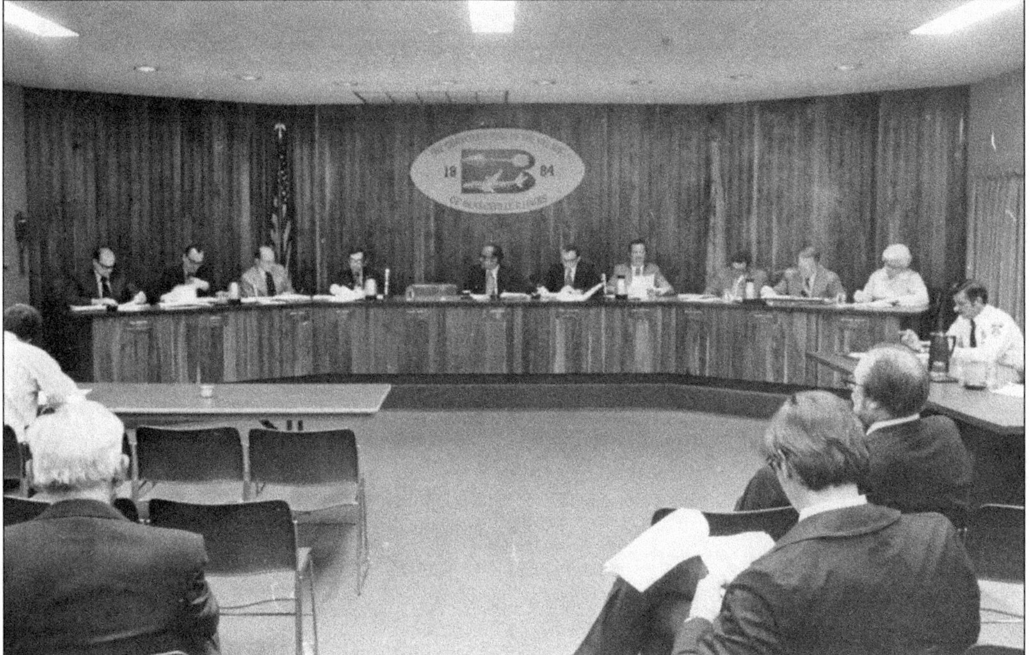

The Village of Bensenville was now operating completely on the village manager structure. More staff was hired to administer the duties of village work. Also, note the presence of the police chief. No longer was there a marshal. Instead, there was a paid police force that was a department of the village. Beginning in 1956, officers were hired under civil service laws.

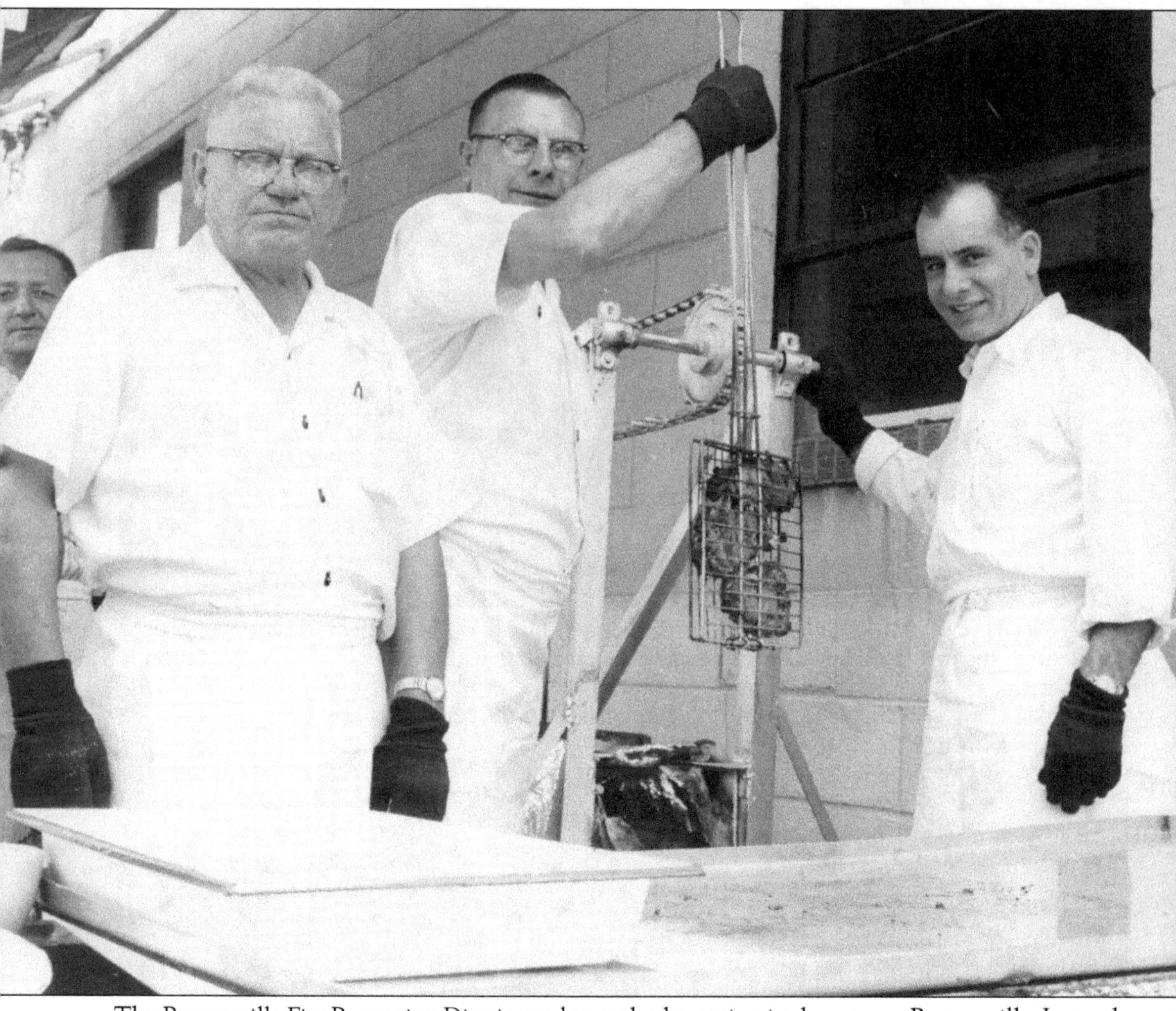

The Bensenville Fire Protection District no longer had a station in downtown Bensenville. Instead, two stations—one to the south at York and Jefferson and one to the north on Foster just east of Route 83—serve the residents of the village of Bensenville and the immediate surrounding unincorporated areas.

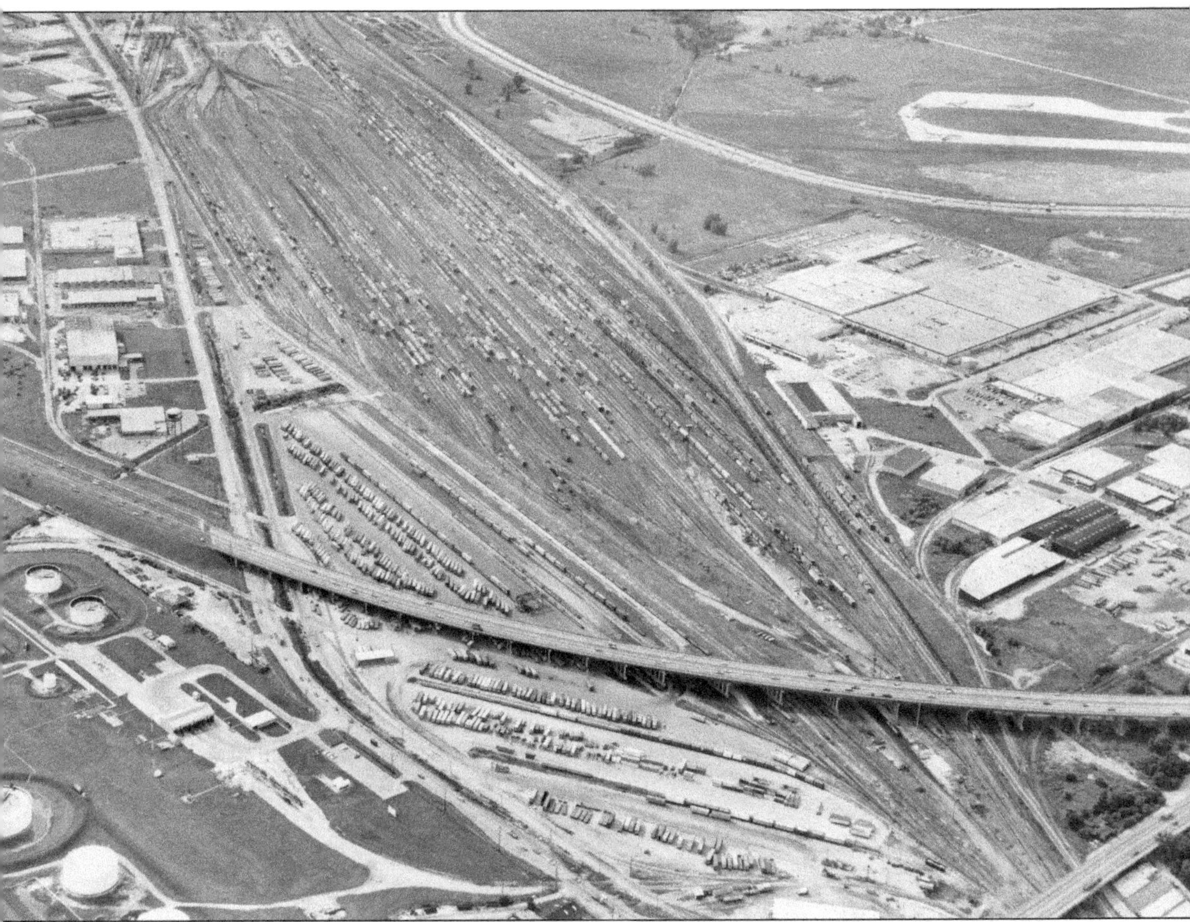

The Bensenville Yard continued to operate and still does today. This image shows the full extent of the yard, reaching from Mannheim Road and the village of Franklin Park at the bottom right-hand corner to the village of Bensenville at the very top of the picture. The Tri-State Tollway, Interstate 294, passes over the top of the trucking facility and the railroad tracks.

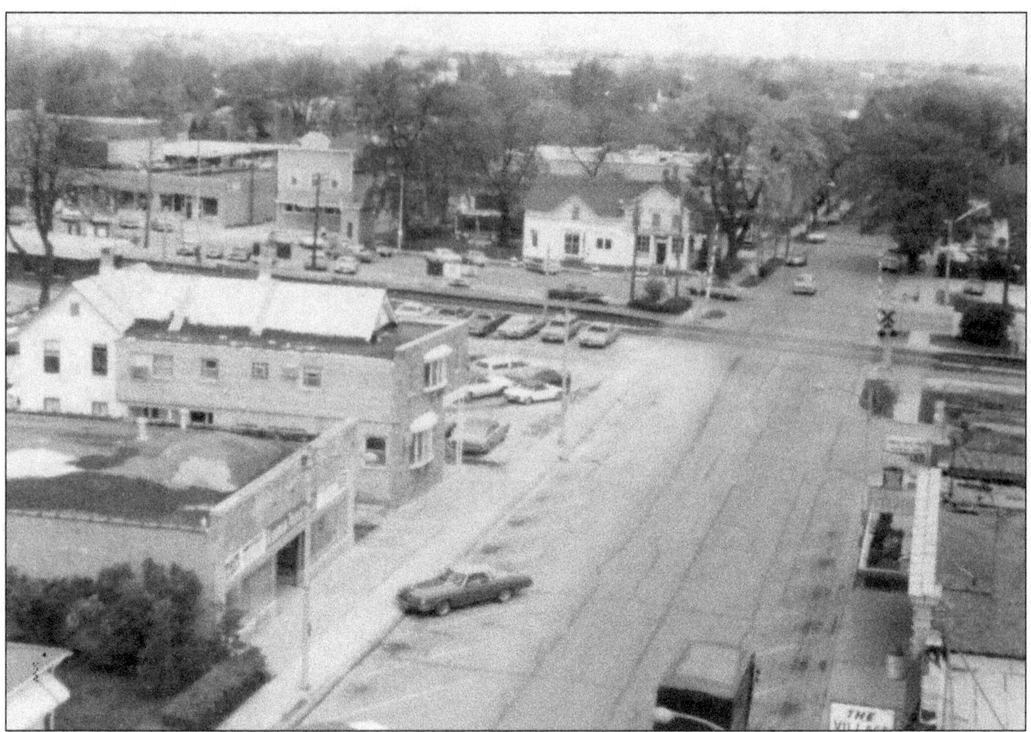

Downtown Bensenville was fully developed, and the buildings now rose several stories. Apartments were built above businesses on Green Street and on the east side of Center and the west side of Addison. There would be more added along the south side of Roosevelt Avenue.

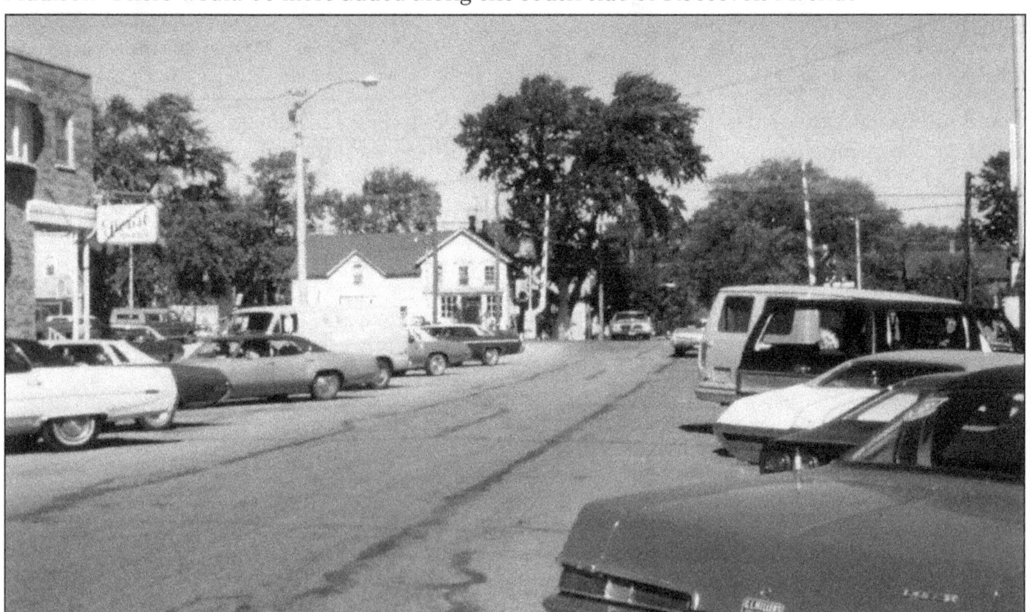

The population of Bensenville continued to grow throughout the 1970s and 1980s and reached over 16,000. The businesses calling the suburb home also continued to increase. Warehouses were built. Industrial equipment manufacturing arrived. Precision metalwork and metal casting was now done here. Rotary die cutting and ultrasonic welding companies are here too.

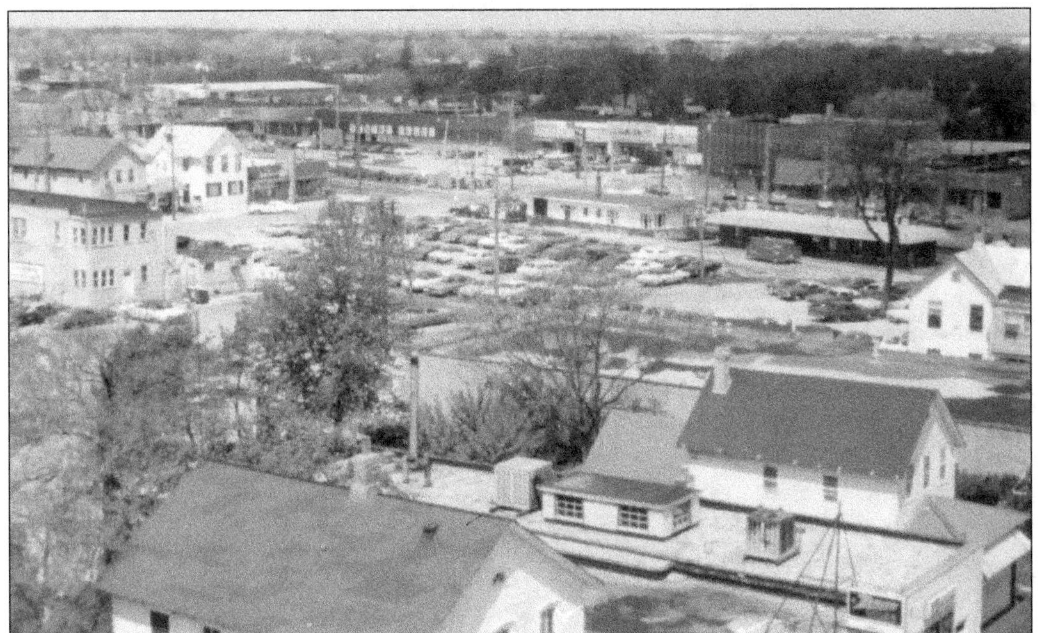

The population had diversified as well. The Latino population had increased dramatically accounting for 48.7 percent of the village, with the majority of these being Mexican. The Asian population accounts for 4 percent, many of whom are Indian. The Polish population in Bensenville has reached 25 percent.

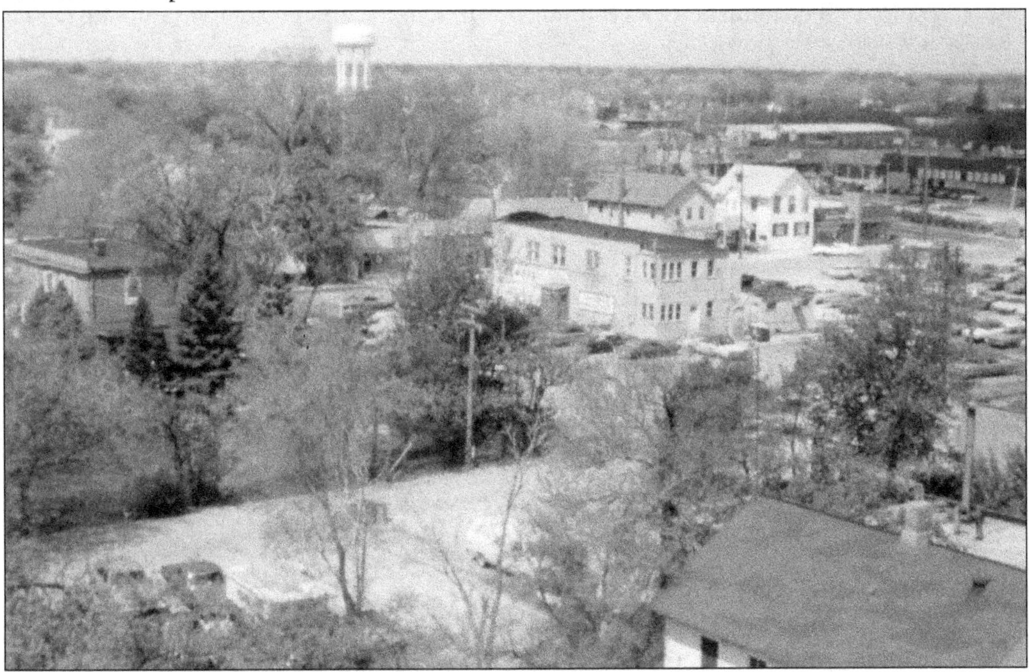

The issue for many in Bensenville and neighboring Wood Dale to the west was the noise from the commercial airplanes. By the 1970s, commercial air traffic was increasing greatly and would only continue to do so throughout the rest of the 20th century. People complained and still do. Fly Quit Committee meets regularly to address this for the residents.

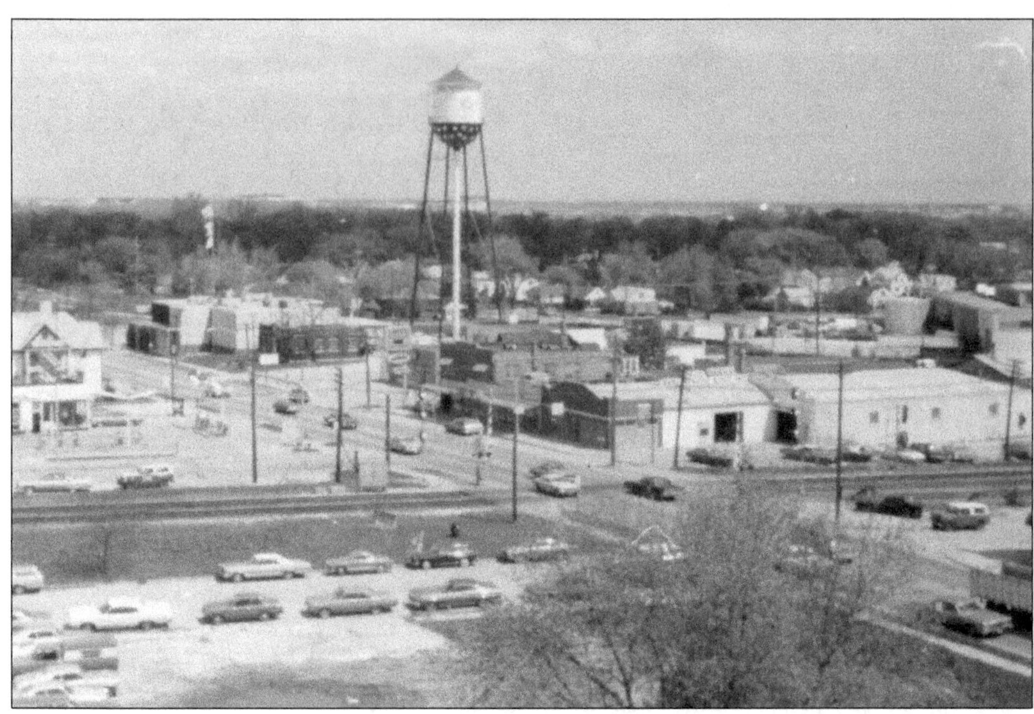

The O'Hare Modernization Program was finally begun in 2010. When it was completed in 2014, three hundred homes were gone and so was a line of businesses that had stood on Irving Park east of York Road. The railroad tracks running north from the west end of the yard were raised. The street was lowered.

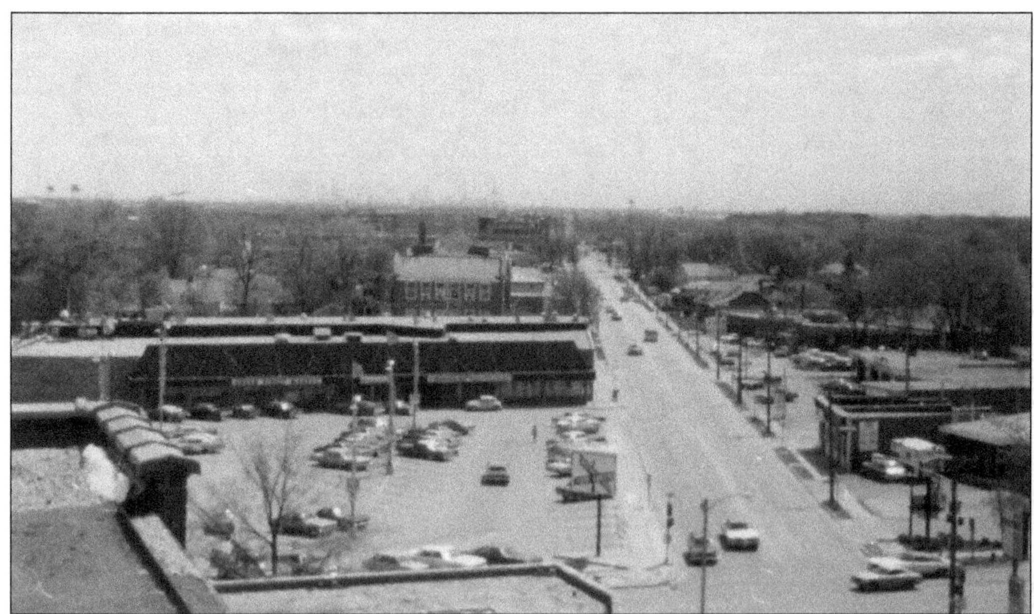

The population of Bensenville has shown some growth since falling to 18,352. Recent US Census Bureau estimates put the population at 18,403. The town center is still full on summer evenings for Music in the Park. Libertyfest at Redmond Park is crowded. Heritage Day at Fischer Farm continues to be enjoyed by hundreds.

Four

The Community Public Library

With Bensenville growing rapidly following World War II, the need for a library was realized. In 1956, a committee was formed and space was set aside at the newly opened Fenton High School. Open only Tuesday and Thursday afternoons and without a real source of financial support, this proved only a temporary solution. A library district was created in 1958 and began renting the farmhouse on the southwest corner of Irving Park and Church Roads from the village.

The election making the district commission official was held in May 1960. The library operated at the farmhouse for four years. With the library board looking for more space, a location at Deer Park and one at Lions Park were selected but voted down. Then the real estate office directly across the street went up for sale and the library found a new home. Two other buildings were erected at this location to expand services, and a community center was opened at Green and Addison Streets to provide a space for the library theater group to perform.

Later, it was decided that more room and a more suitable location were needed. At the west end of Deer Park Forest, as it was called, the new library building opened in November 1978. The hours of operation had expanded as had the staff. Book discussion groups, special guest lecturers, and children's programs were all taking place at the library, but that is not all the library would do.

In 1989, as a home on what had been Horseshoe Bend was being demolished, it was discovered that the living room had actually been a house of its own. The Korthauer family had arrived in 1838 and constructed their log home in 1844. It was subsequently moved and later enclosed inside a larger house. The library board and Bensenville Historical Society, which worked closely, took the lead to save the structure. The building was dismantled, with the logs numbered and transported to property owned by the library, where it was reassembled in 1990. The library staff and volunteers maintain the log house and provide interpretation sharing the history of Bensenville.

The library board also partnered with the local elementary school district and completed a large addition called the Lifelong Learning Center in 1999. In 2016, yet another addition was built: the early childhood learning classroom.

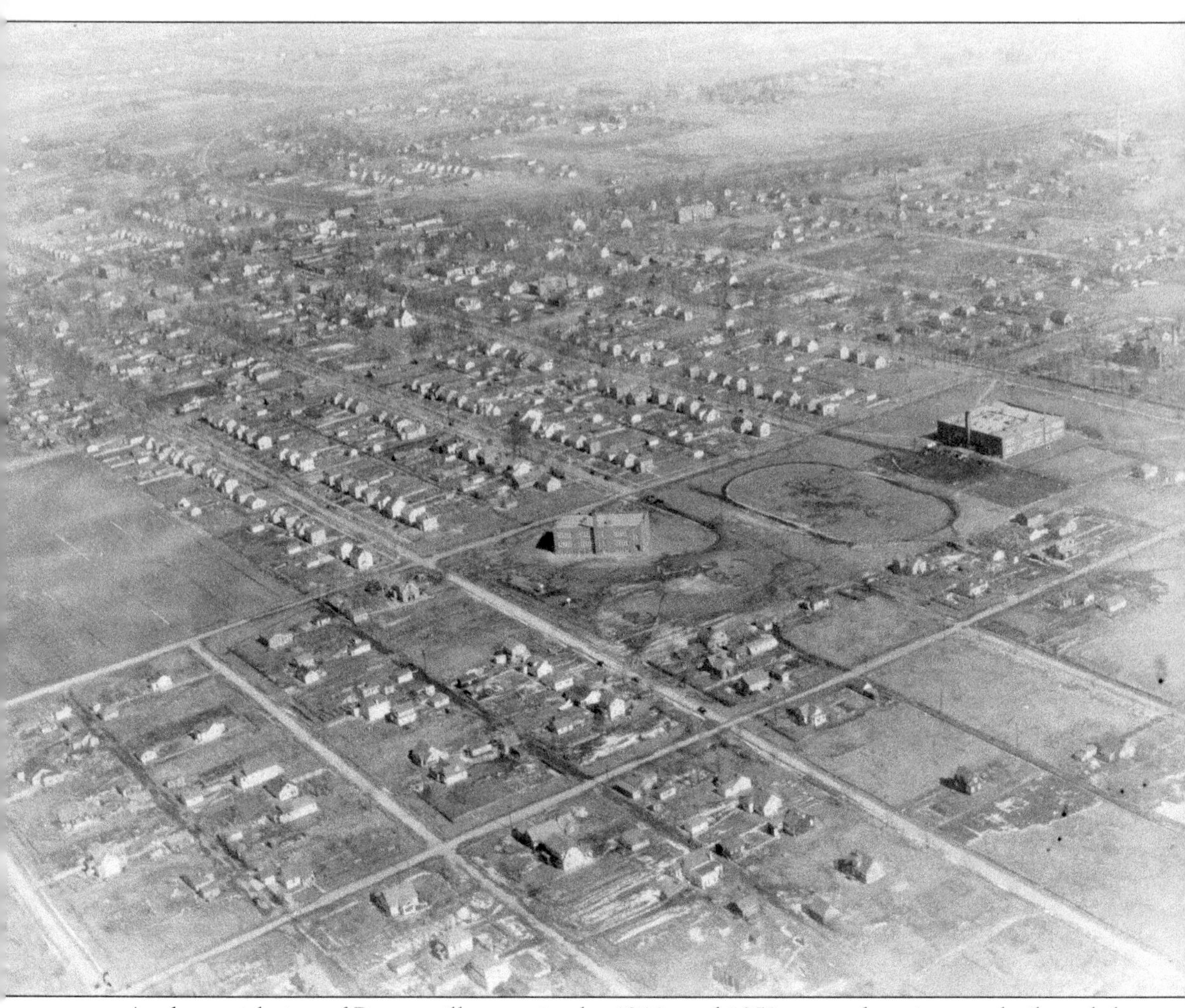

As the population of Bensenville grew in the 1940s and 1950s, more housing was built and the boundaries were moved. The original southern boundary was Mason Street and then Memorial Street. In some places, it eventually reached Grand Avenue. The southern part of the village was almost entirely residential. The exceptions are the block of stores at York Road and Jefferson Street and the shopping plaza at York and Grand.

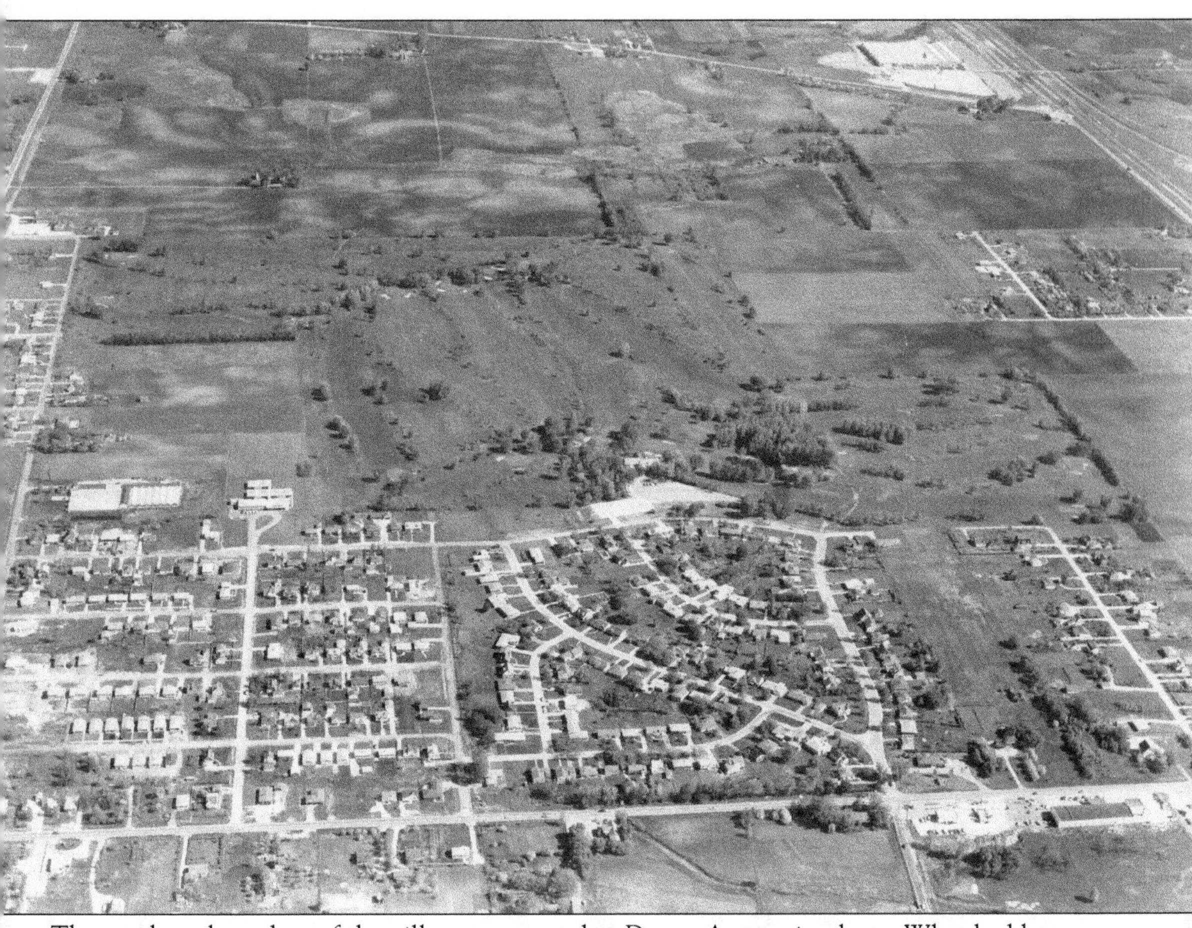

The northern boundary of the village was moved to Devon Avenue in places. What had been the Mohawk Country Club was slated for an industrial park beginning in 1960. Over the next two decades, precision machining, industrial equipment manufacturing, and storage facilities were established in this northern part of the village.

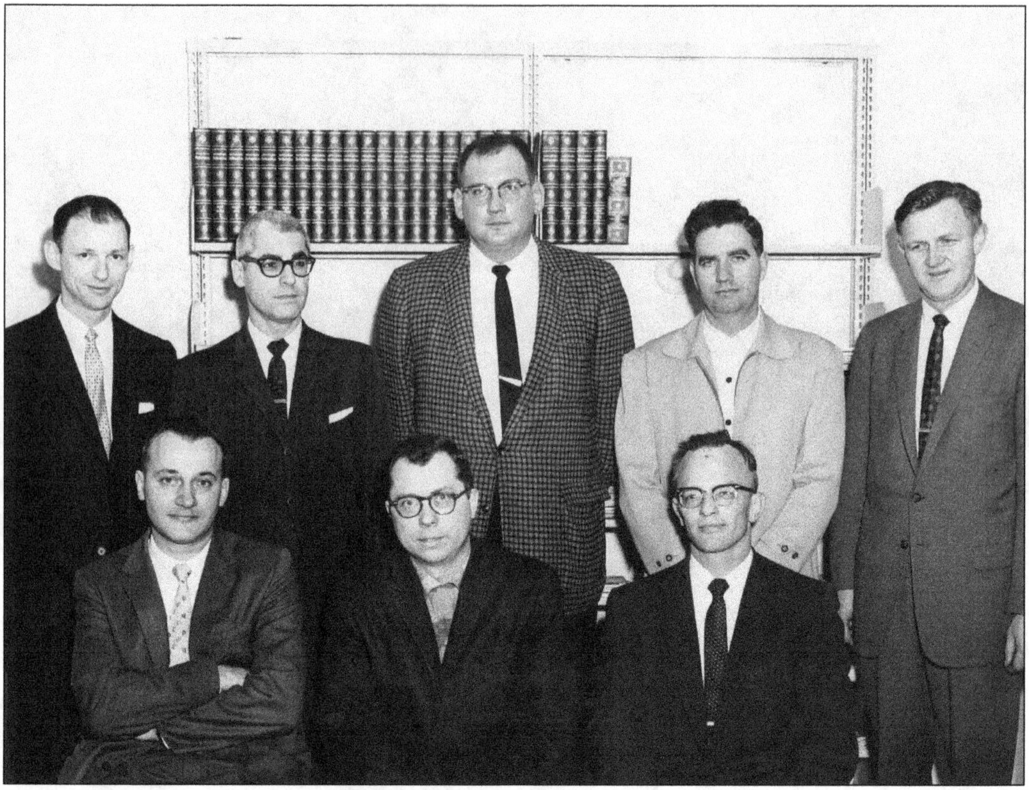

The first library in Bensenville was in the newly constructed Fenton High School. It was open Tuesdays and Thursdays from 6:00 p.m. to 9:00 p.m. This was the result of a committee, seen here, established to organize a public library in March 1956. Initially, the library district corresponded to School District 100 and thus included part of Wood Dale. In 1958, a library board was established and the residents of Wood Dale separated to create their own district.

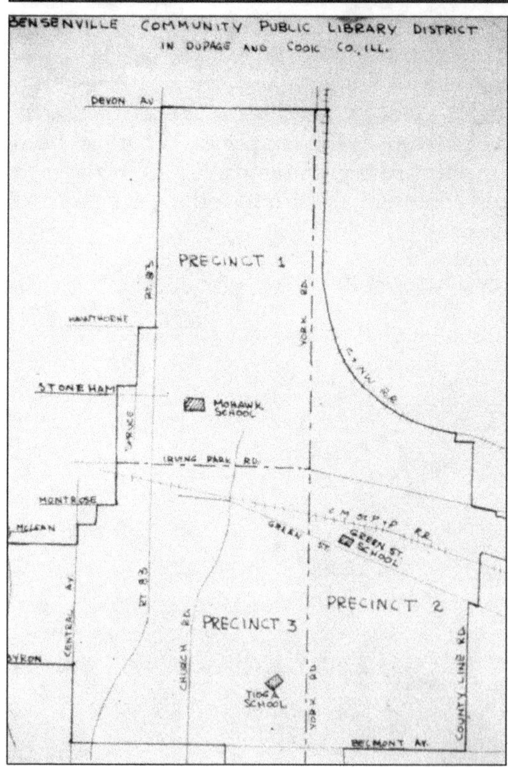

A map of the resulting Bensenville Library District is shown here. The school library needed to utilize the space at Fenton and so there really was not room to operate a public library out of this space. The library board asked the village for any space that might be available.

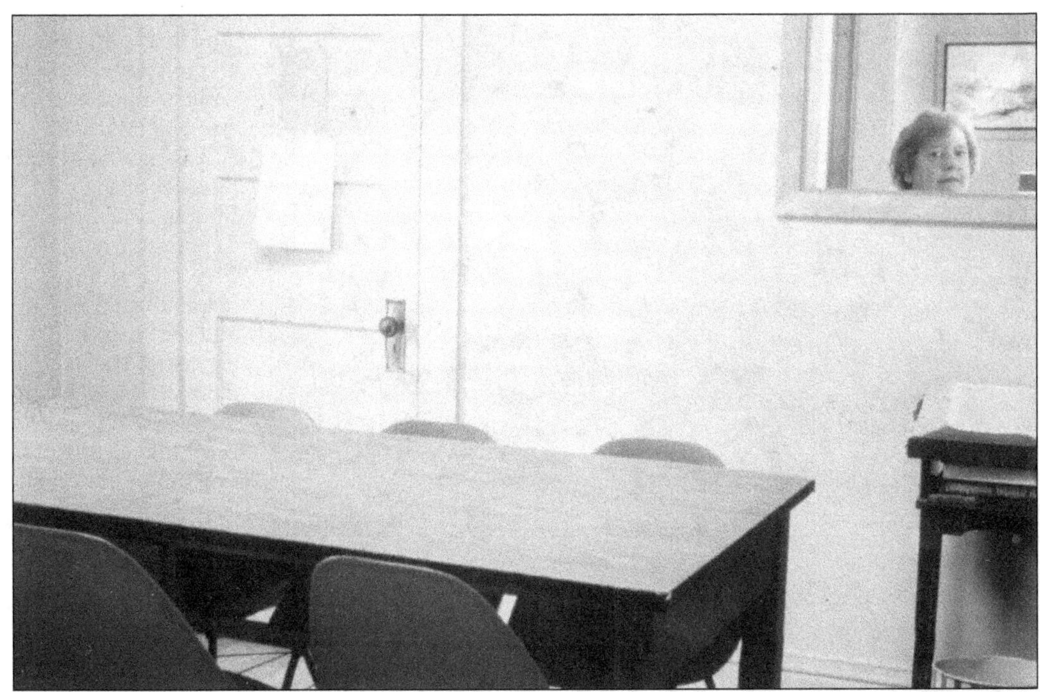

The village told the school library board that there were no plans to use the Kolze farmhouse on the property purchased by the village from that family, as a new police station was being built at the south end of the property. The Kolze house stood at the corner of Church and Irving Park Roads.

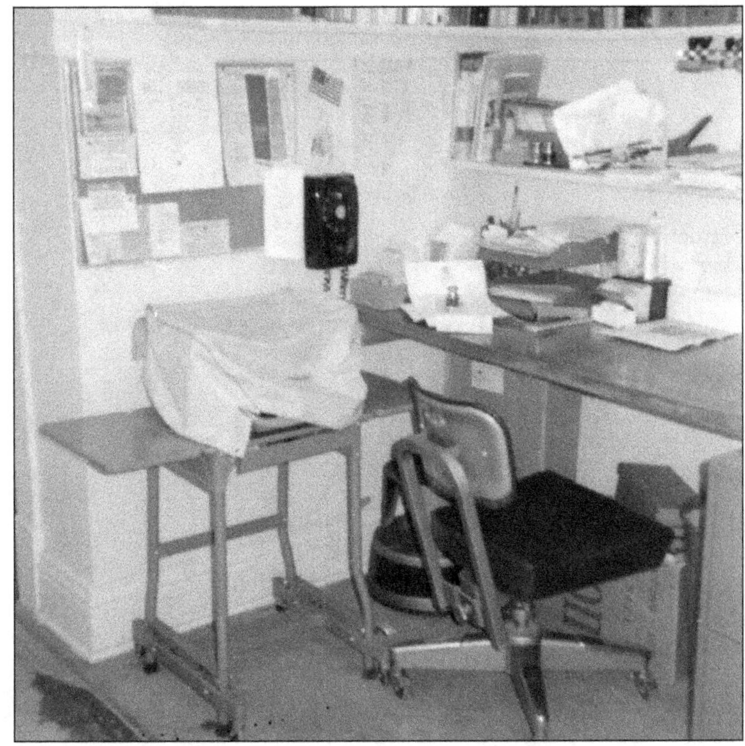

The village reinforced the floors and purchased the office equipment. The library board paid $1 per year to rent the building. After several months of work, including time by members of the Bensenville Jaycees, the library was ready for patrons in January 1960. Here, the former kitchen now served as an office.

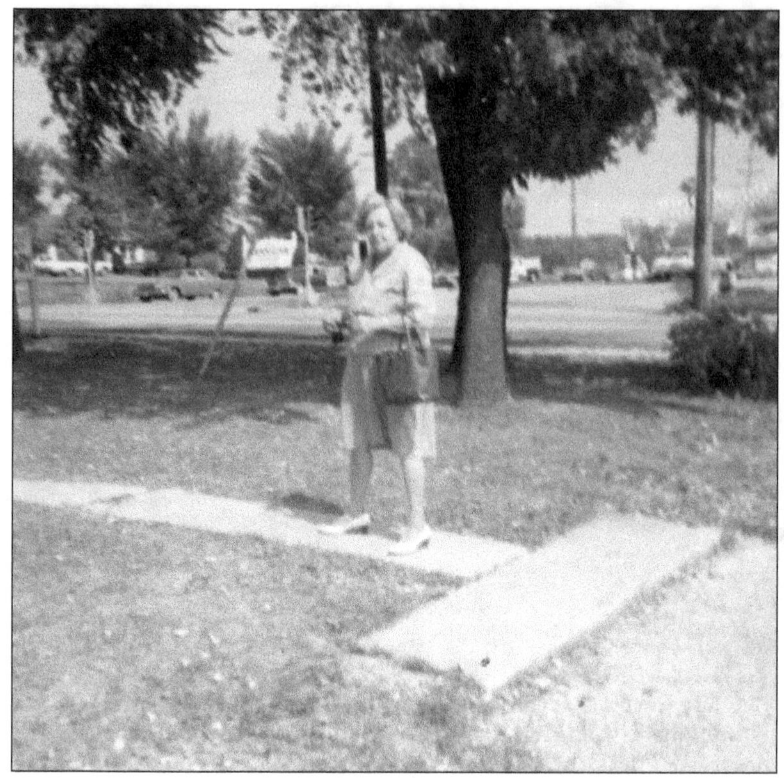

The first year, the commissioners and the library attorney, William A. Redmond—also Speaker of the Illinois House of Representatives—gave their time to help move books and set up and even staff the library. In July 1961, Dorothea Schmidt was hired as full-time librarian. She would continue in this capacity for the next six years.

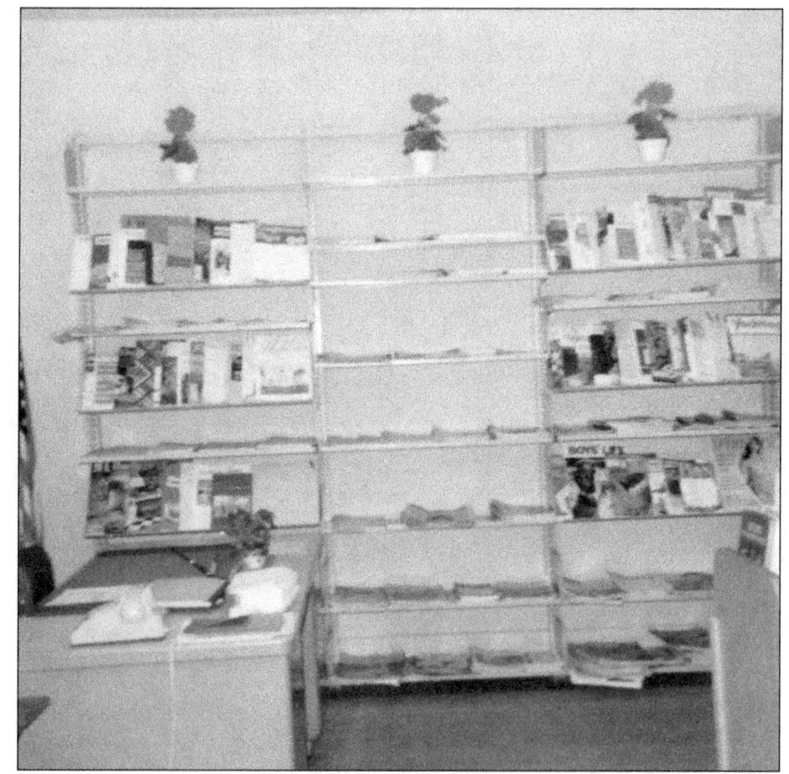

Formerly a branch library manager in Chicago, Schmidt set to work creating some organization. Books were housed on the first floor, down the steps, and in the basement. The kitchen served as the processing area. Patrons would bring their books to the kitchen counter to check them out or to return them. Librarian Schmidt's desk is pictured here.

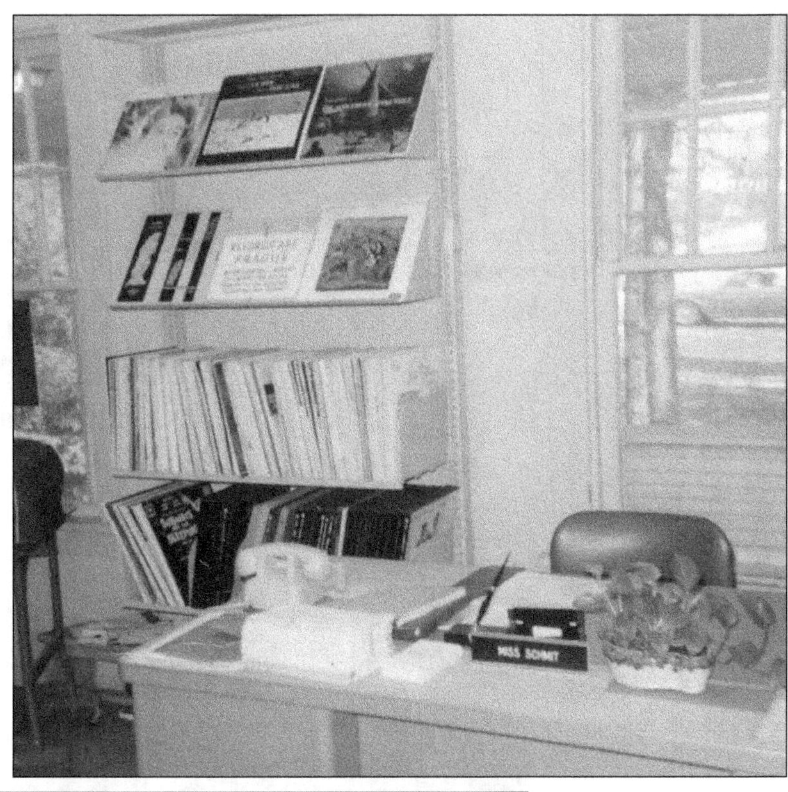

Schmidt established the card catalog at the library. She trained others how to process, sort, and catalog books. She even held the first programs at the library. This image shows her desk from the front.

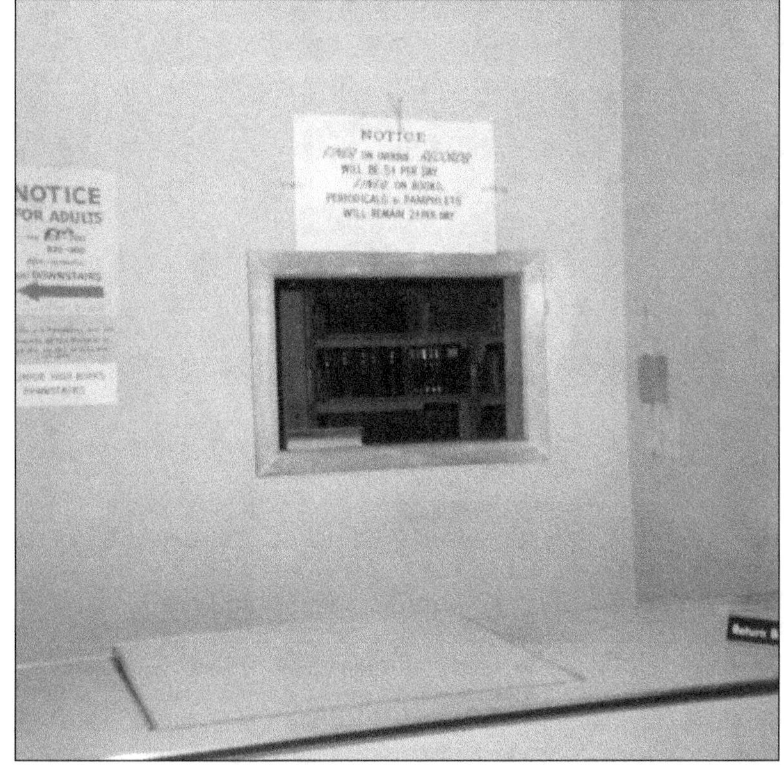

The library board was concerned about support for the future operation of the library. The board placed a referendum on the ballot in May 1960 asking for the creation of a taxing district. This measure passed, allowing the library to tax its residents. Soon, another issue would be faced.

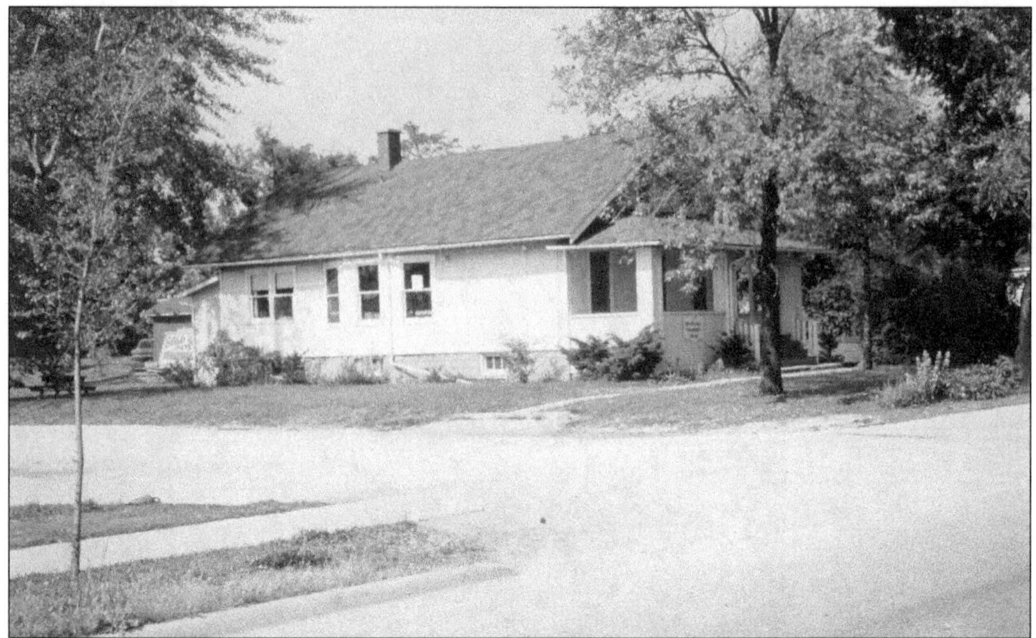

Meanwhile, the village had decided to construct a village hall on the Kolze property. The farmhouse would have to be torn down. The library board now had to search for another location. The board first looked at property on the south side of Wood Avenue in what was called Deer Forest. A referendum to build a new library was placed on the ballot in 1964. This did not pass.

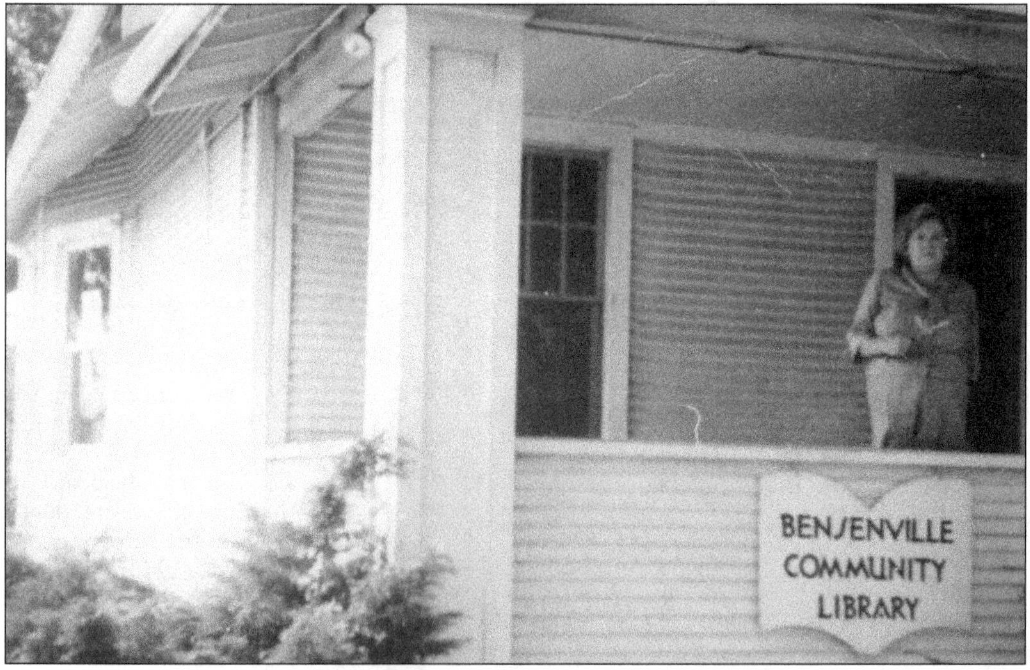

In the general election of 1964, the referendum was again on the ballot. This time, it was to finance the building of a library at Lions Park. The voters responded just as they had earlier in the year. The next year was spent trying to find another location. In 1966, the library board turned its attention to the Branigar Realty Office on the northeast corner of the intersection.

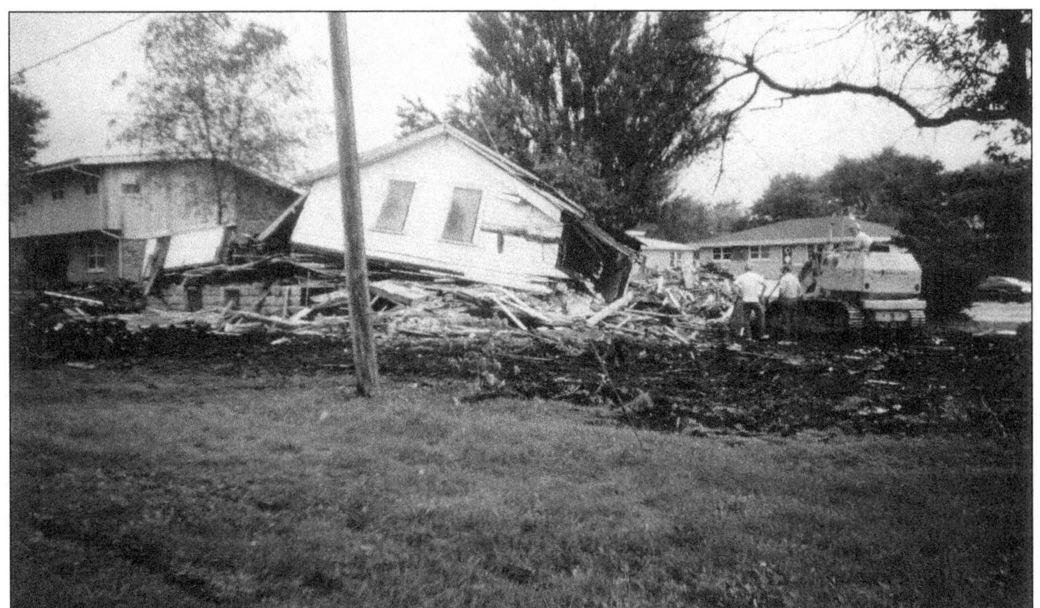

The building was for sale and could be purchased without having to resort to a referendum. The purchase was made and the library had found a new home. In 1967, all the books, office supplies, and furniture were moved across the street. Having overseen the formative years of the library and its move to a new home, Dorothea Schmidt retired from her work. She was succeeded by Dorothea Holland.

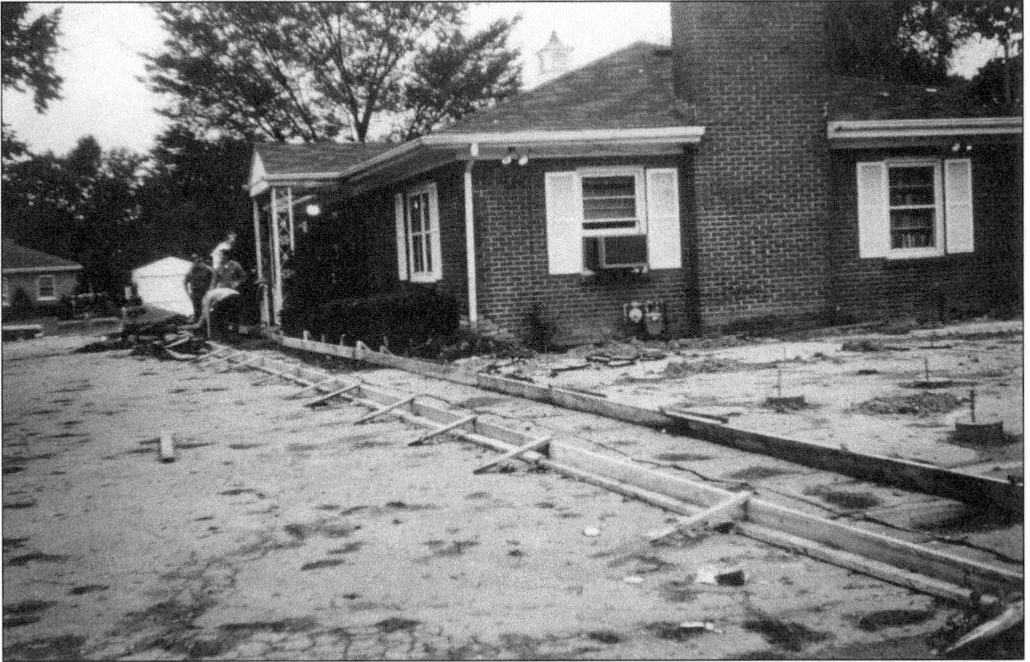

The real estate office was larger than the Kolze farmhouse and initially provided sufficient space. The library, however, continued to grow in collections and in programs offered. More space was needed. An addition was built onto the building. Back across the street, the Kolze farmhouse was torn down, and the village hall was constructed.

OLD BUILDING		NEW BUILDING
	Size	
1,200 sq. ft.		11,500 sq. ft.
	Seating Capacity	
6 Chairs		64 Chairs
	Shelving	
8,500 volumes (.6 vol./cap.)		40,000 volumes (2.5 vol./cap.)
	Service Space	
NO SPACE		Adequate space for reference reading, browsing, children's area, etc.

The library hosted a variety of programs. There were adult book discussion groups and children's story hours. Then it was decided to host art shows at the library as well. The collections continued to grow. Soon, space was an issue again. A second addition was constructed.

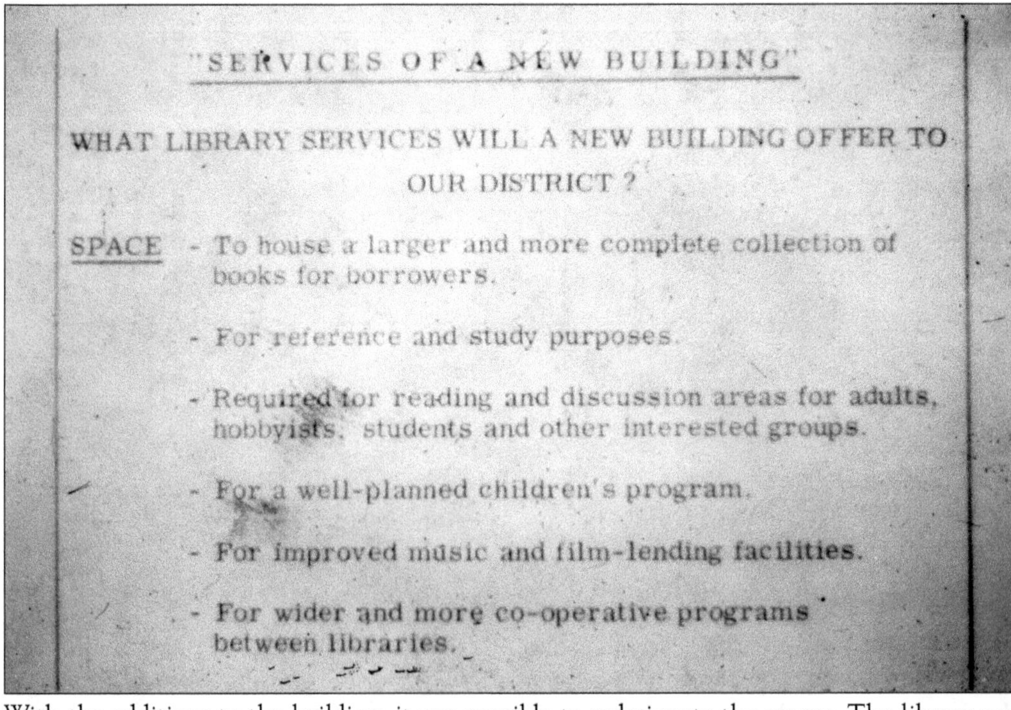

"SERVICES OF A NEW BUILDING"

WHAT LIBRARY SERVICES WILL A NEW BUILDING OFFER TO OUR DISTRICT ?

SPACE - To house a larger and more complete collection of books for borrowers.

- For reference and study purposes.
- Required for reading and discussion areas for adults, hobbyists, students and other interested groups.
- For a well-planned children's program.
- For improved music and film-lending facilities.
- For wider and more co-operative programs between libraries.

With the additions to the building, it was possible to redesignate the spaces. The library now consisted of a formal children's wing, a reference room, and separate office space. The residents of Bensenville continued to embrace the library and all it offered, but space would continue to be an issue.

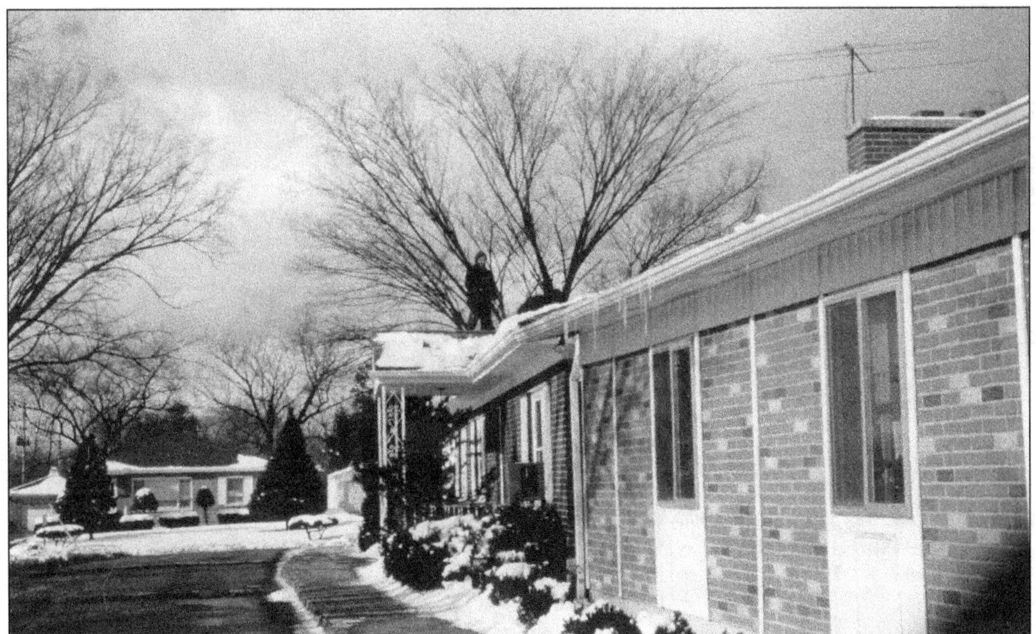

In 1975, the library board opened a separate community center at Green and Addison Streets. A theater group performed there. Concerts were held, and it provided space for children's and senior citizens' activities. For the library, the property adjacent to Plentywood Farm was considered. However, the referendum failed to pass, so the search for a new location continued.

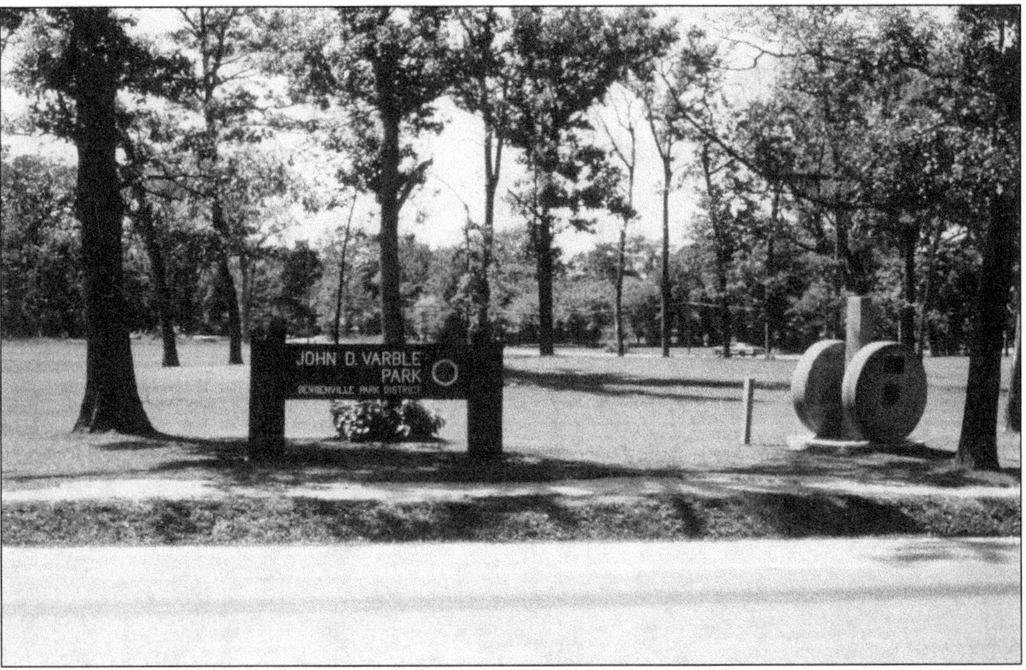

Attention focused on an area that had been considered 12 years earlier. This was the Deer Forest property owned by the park district. The library needed land, and the park district a building. A trade was arranged. The library gave the community center to the park district in return for 6.75 acres of land fronting on Church Road just south of Wood Avenue.

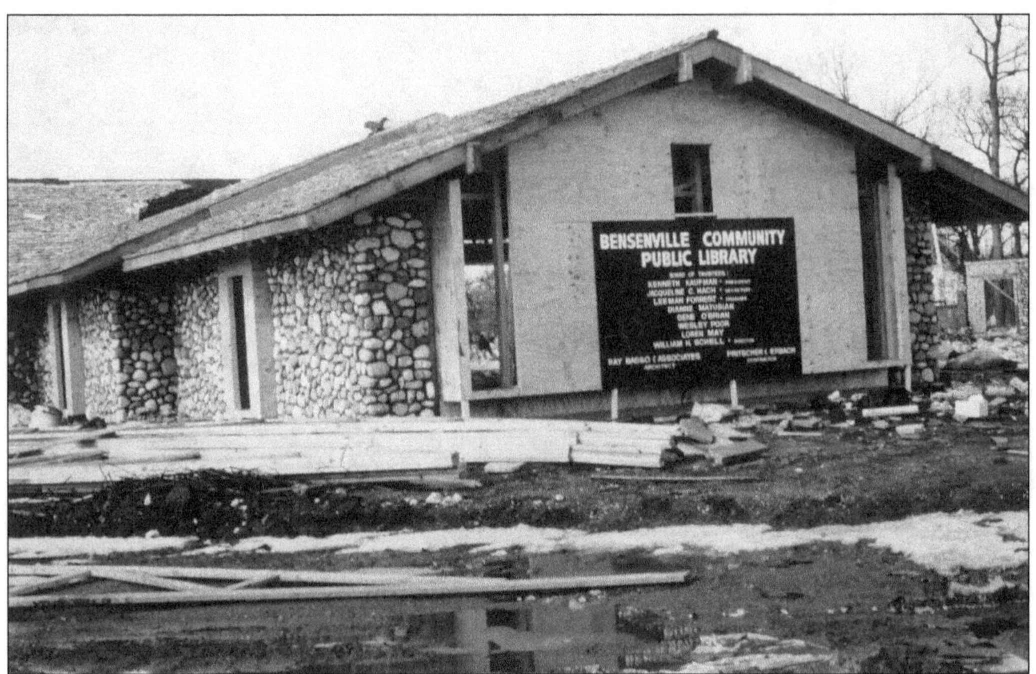

The referendum was rewritten for a lower cost as now the land was already in the possession of the library. It passed and construction began on the 19,000-square-foot building in the spring of 1978. It was to have a rustic look with the use of timbers and stones. The work proceeded quickly, with the building being completed that fall.

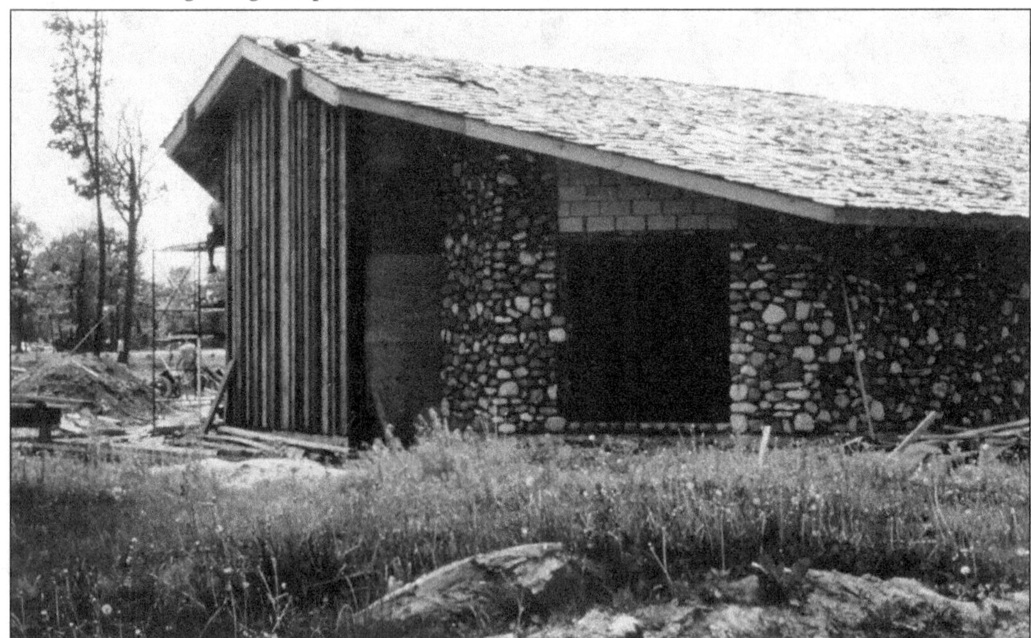

The roof went onto the structure with shakes to complete the rustic appearance of the building. It opened in November 1978. The library was much more modern than either of its predecessors. The expanded collection had now found a home. Historical artifacts had also been collected, and a local history section was taking shape. Soon, there would be a computer lab as well.

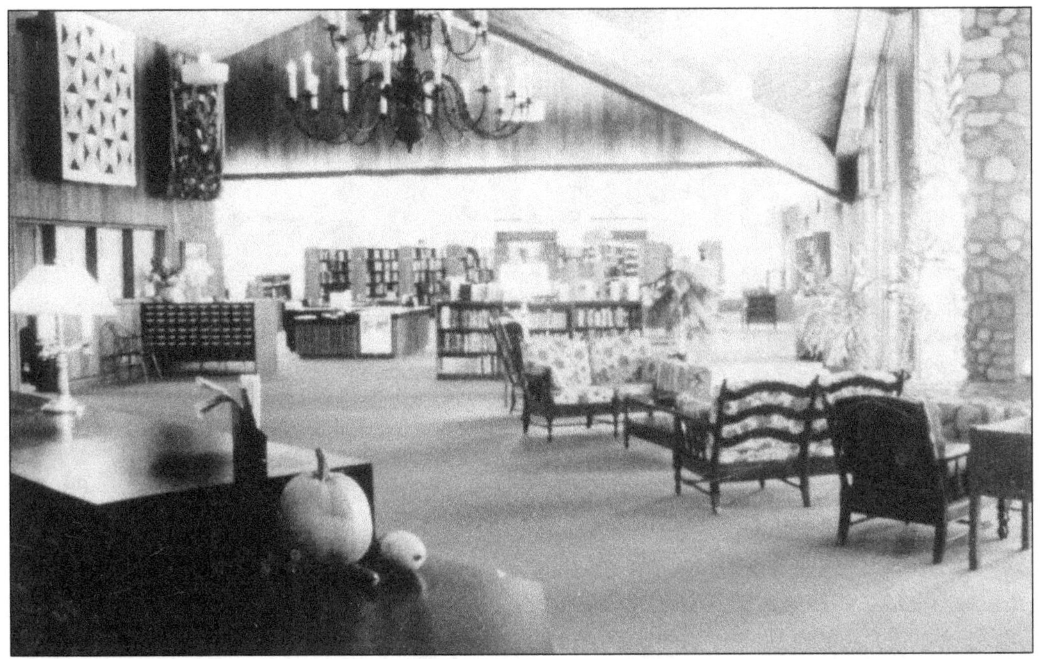

The Bensenville Library has continued to develop. The staff has since grown to 30 full- and part-time employees. In addition to the book discussion clubs, there are computer classes offered. A digital media lab and scanning station are a part of the library, as is the electric charging station in the parking lot.

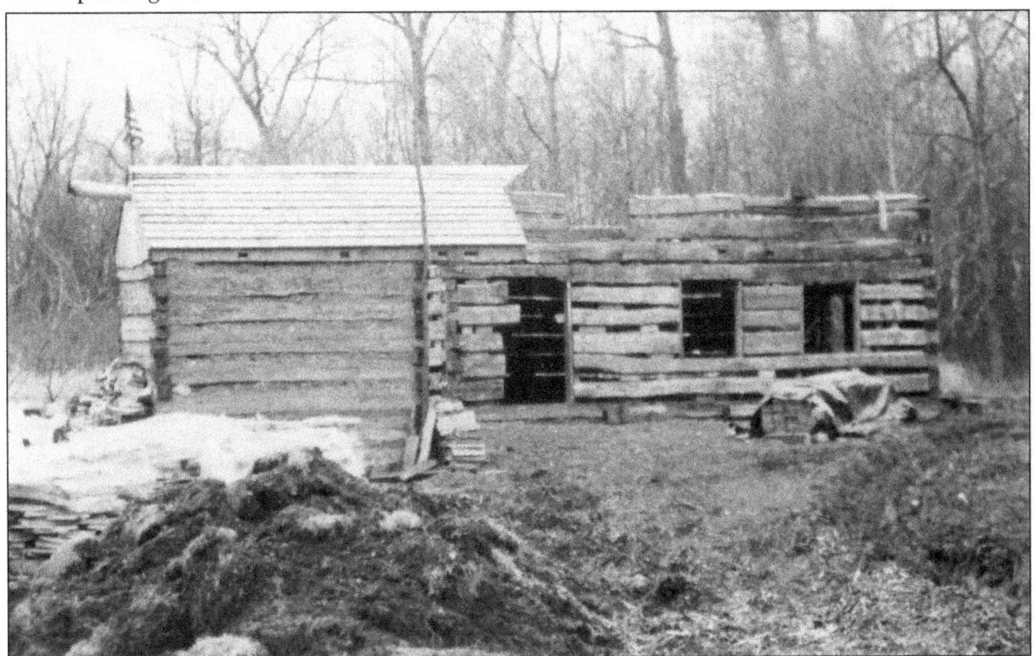

In 1989, the Korthauer family planned to tear down the house on the east side of Evergreen a tenth of a mile south of Green Street. They had said that if the historical society performed the demolition, it could have the old house that had been enclosed and added on to over time. A few timbers were visible in one interior wall.

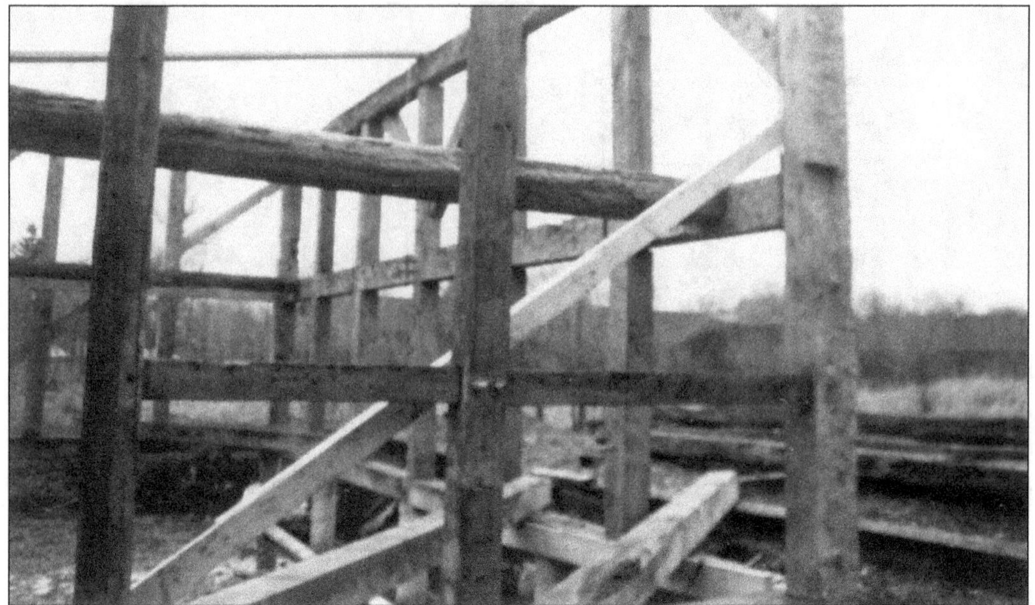

The process was begun in December 1989. It was unusual from the beginning. The process started with the roof, which proved to have six layers of asphalt shingles and a layer of shake under those. At the height of the effort, there were 30 volunteers involved. They got down to the drywall and began to pull it apart.

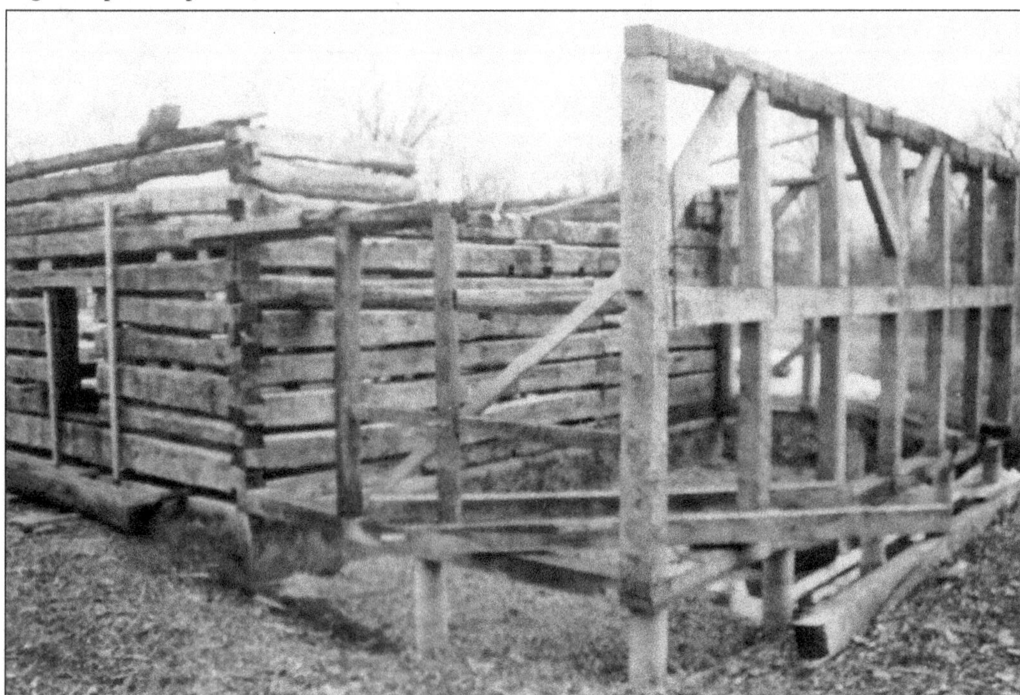

Soon, more timbers were discovered. There was a section of brick wall as well. The staff at the Bensenville Library contacted the Illinois State Historical Society. Ultimately, it was confirmed that this was a very significant structure. With this assessment, it became paramount to the library not only to save it but also to operate it to further interpret the history of the village.

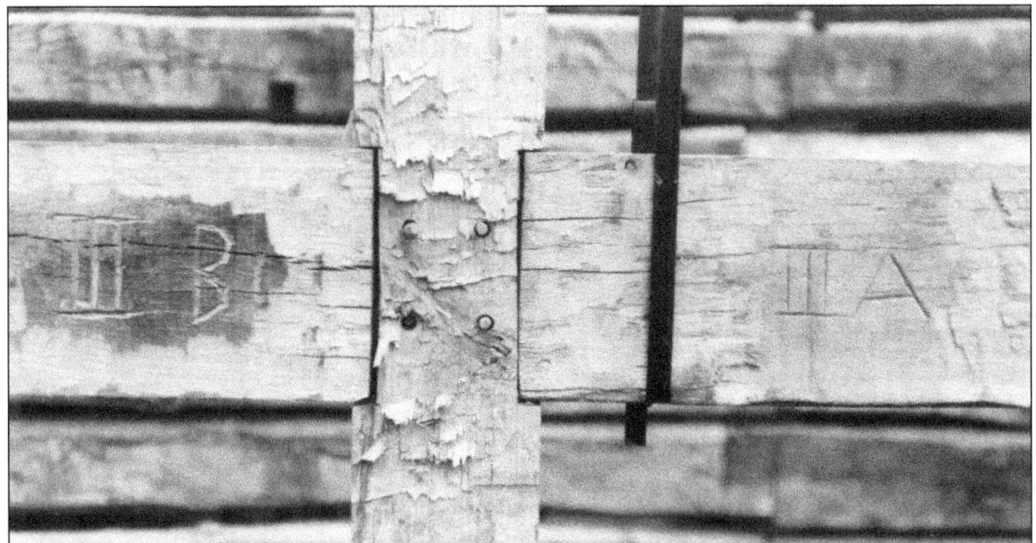

This meant moving it to property owned by the library. This would necessitate disassembly, which would then require knowledge to reassemble it. Every log was numbered with two numbers at each end so it would be known where each log went and which end was to be fitted to which end of the adjoining logs. Additionally, a detailed blueprint of the log house was drawn with all of the logs drawn and numbered on it.

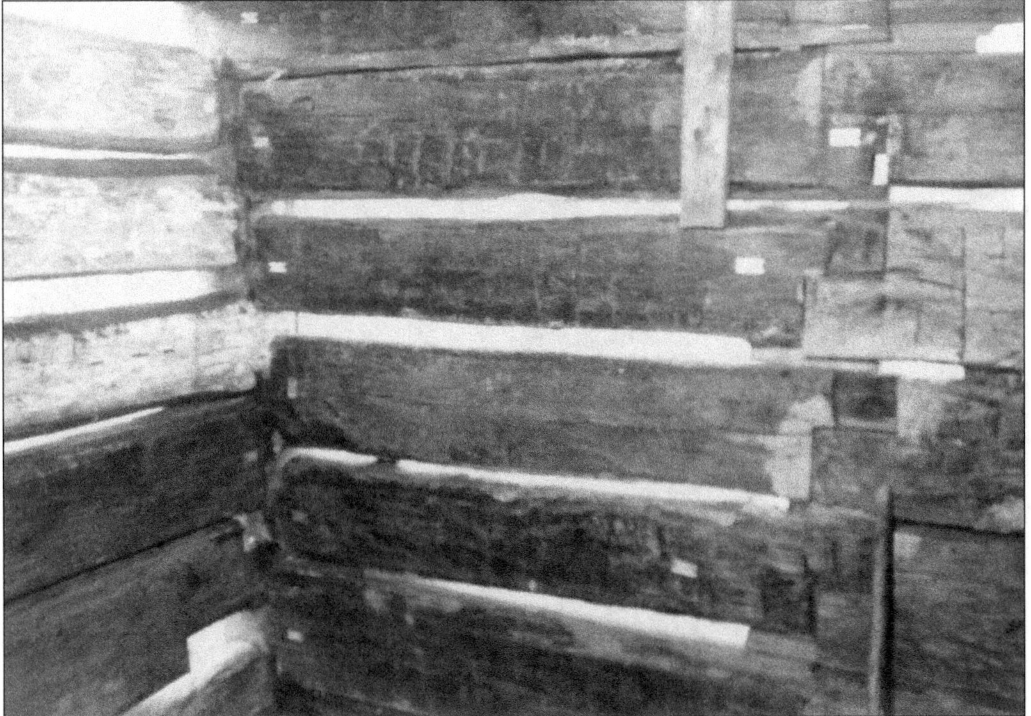

A crane was brought over to lift the logs onto a flatbed truck, which then drove the load to its present location on the south side of Wood Avenue. There, the logs were unloaded and the house was reassembled. The library hosts field trips and offers living history demonstrations. In 1992, Bensenville received the Governor's Hometown Award for these efforts.

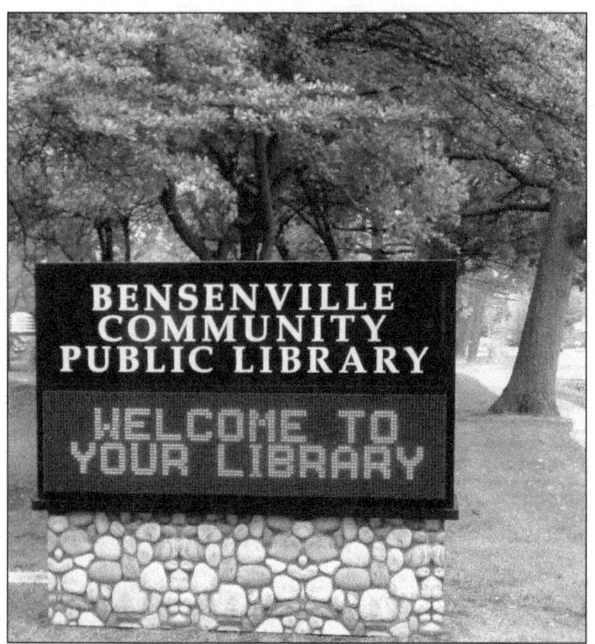

In 1988, the five governing agencies in Bensenville created the Bensenville Intergovernmental Group (BIG) to facilitate better communication and cooperation among the agencies. Using this framework, library director Jill Rodriguez and School District 2 superintendent Cesare Calderelli discussed plans to create a space for the district's administrative offices and also provide space to facilitate learning.

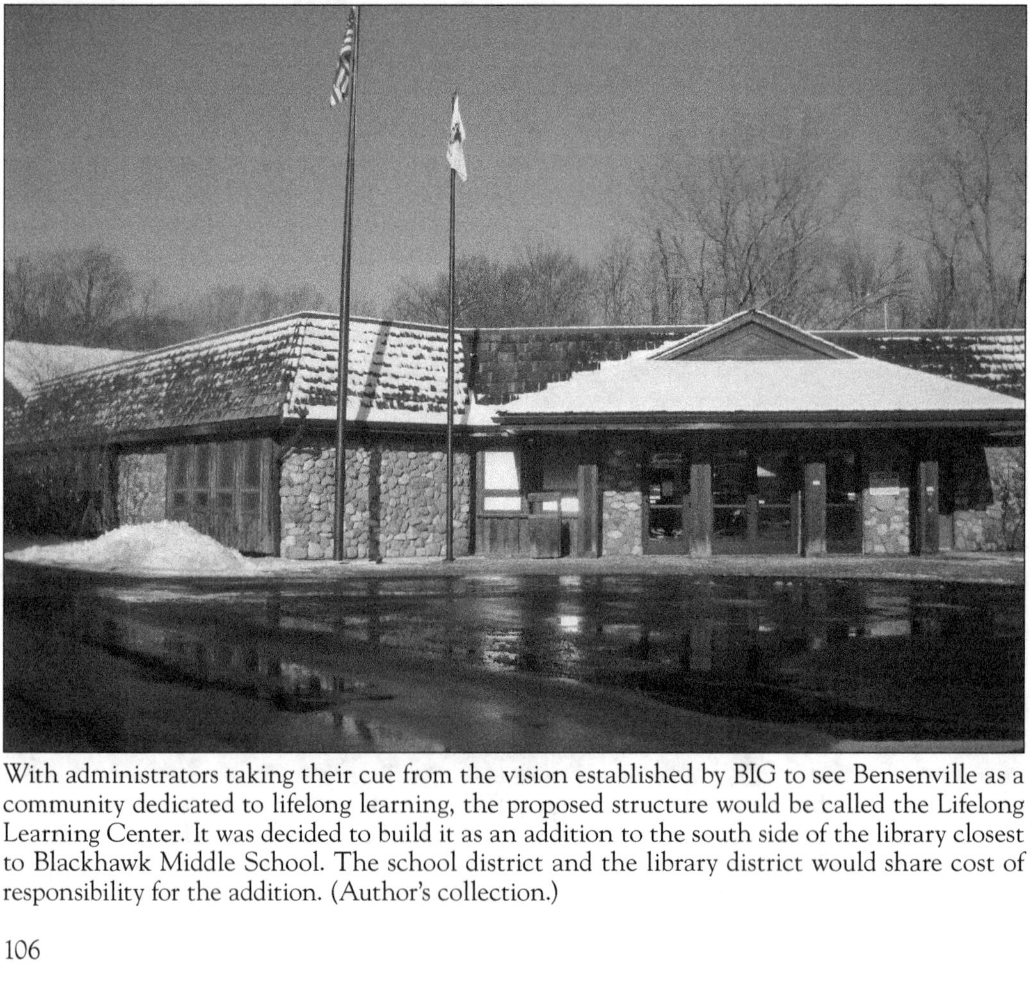

With administrators taking their cue from the vision established by BIG to see Bensenville as a community dedicated to lifelong learning, the proposed structure would be called the Lifelong Learning Center. It was decided to build it as an addition to the south side of the library closest to Blackhawk Middle School. The school district and the library district would share cost of responsibility for the addition. (Author's collection.)

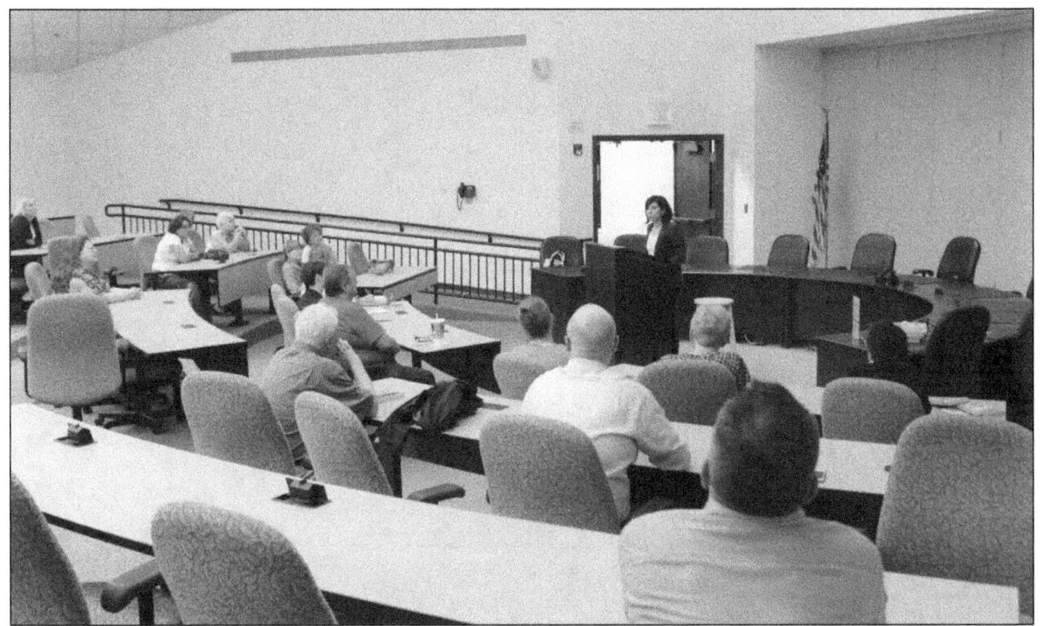

A Secretary of State Live and Learn Construction Grant was applied for and received. The Lifelong Learning Center became a reality in 1999. This has facilitated much greater communication between teachers and staff of School District 2 and the staff of the library. Classes and meetings are regularly held here.

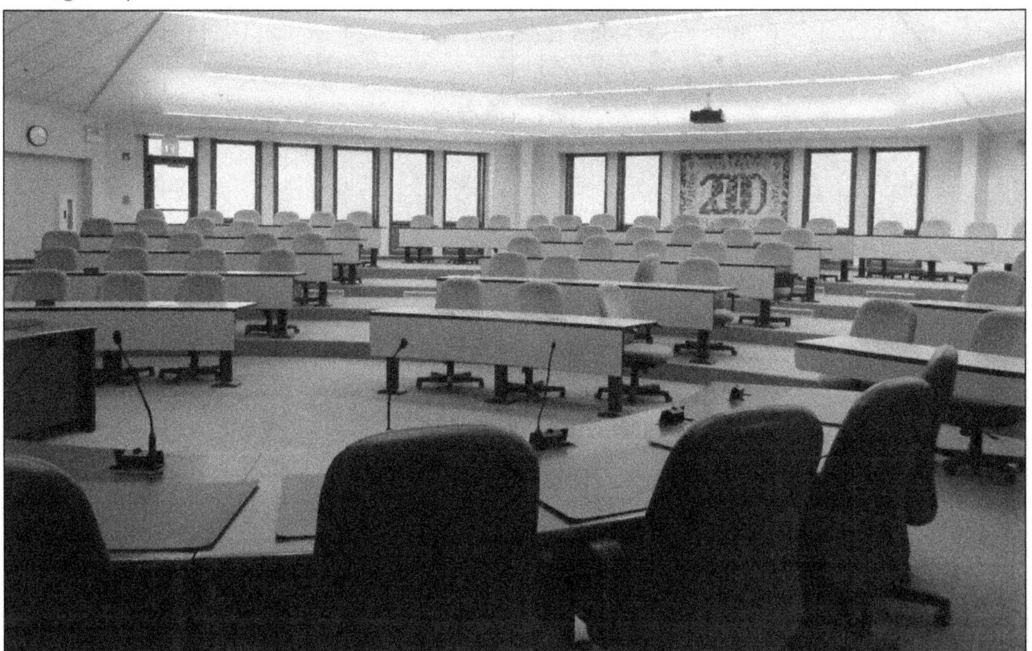

Additionally, the library is able to use the space for special events and programs. Guest speakers to art programs to movies for children all make use of this room. John Borowski, documentarian known for his film on H.H. Holmes; Leslie Goddard, known for first-person presentations; as well as scholars from the Oriental Institute at the University of Chicago have all spoken here. (Author's collection.)

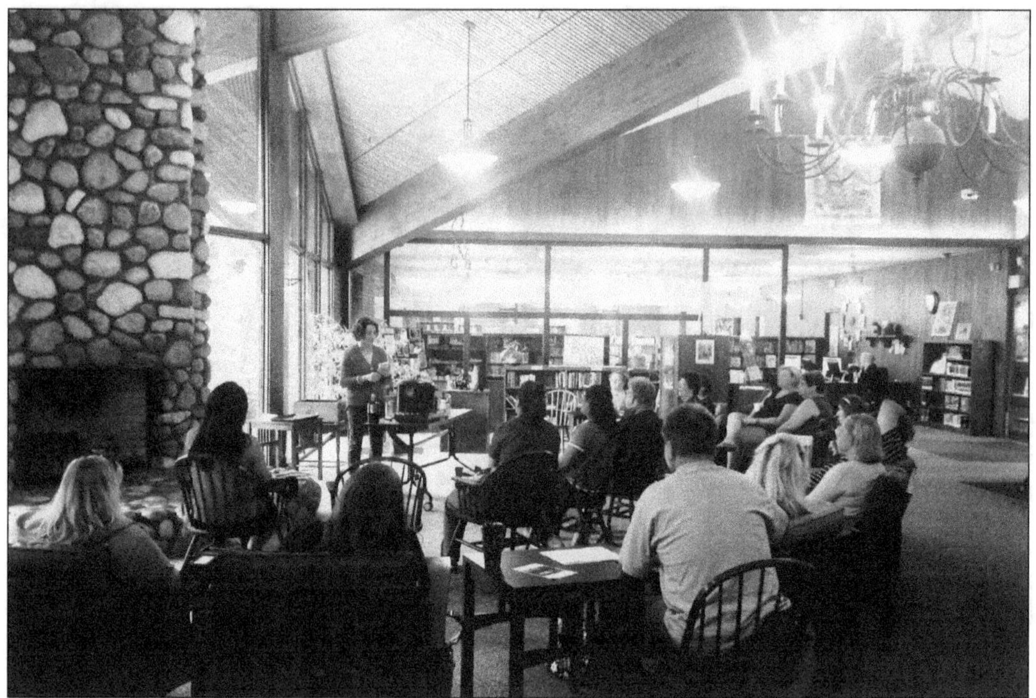

The garden series programs are also popular. Here, a do-it-yourself program introduces participants to techniques and benefits of home canning. Sometimes, the programs are held inside, but often they are held in the Garden of Knowledge, the area immediately west of the library building.

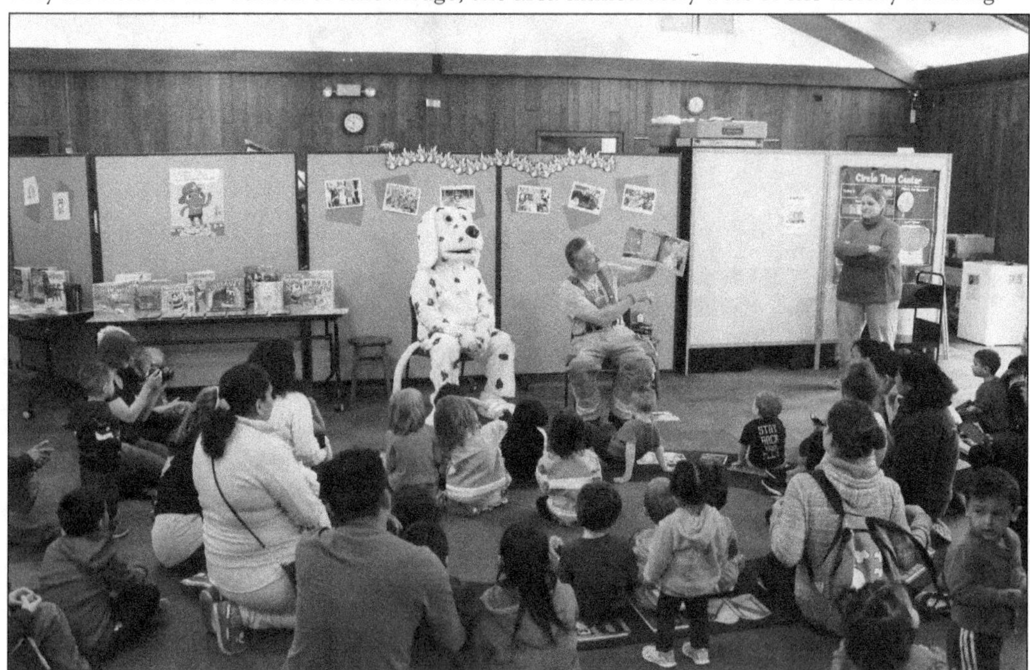

The library brings in several community members to present. On International Firefighters Day, a local Bensenville firefighter, Hank Mandizara, read aloud to children assembled and also spoke about fire safety. Visitors were also able to inspect a fire truck that was brought for the program.

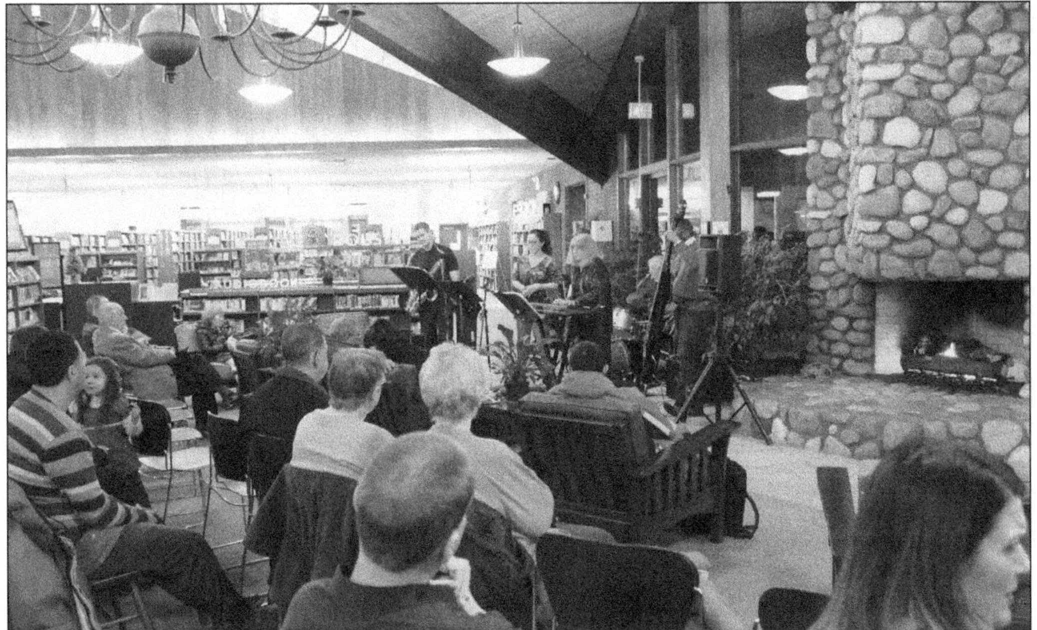

The children's programs offered at the Bensenville Library have only continued to expand. This includes art classes and reading clubs for all age groups from prekindergarten through middle school. There is Little Builders as well as Toddler Tales. In the evening, there are opportunities to try out musical instruments and various media of art.

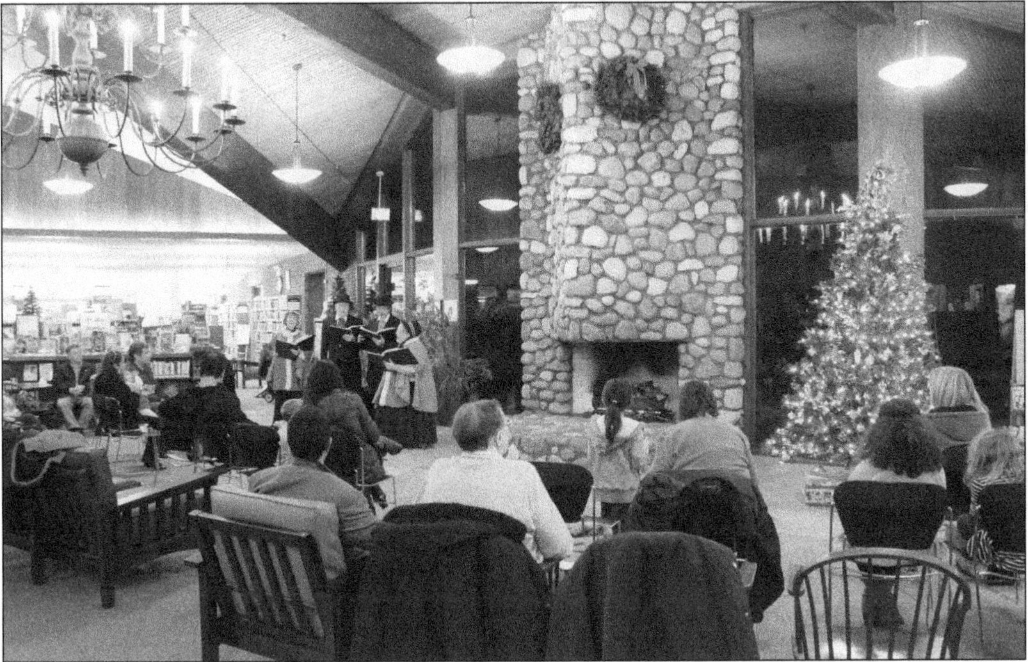

The library also offers special programs for all seasons of the year. Halloween-Boo-Tacular invites families to wear their costumes to participate in the activities planned. There is a Valentine's card–making party in February. In December, there is a holiday card–making party, a visit from Santa, and (pictured here) a Holiday Open House.

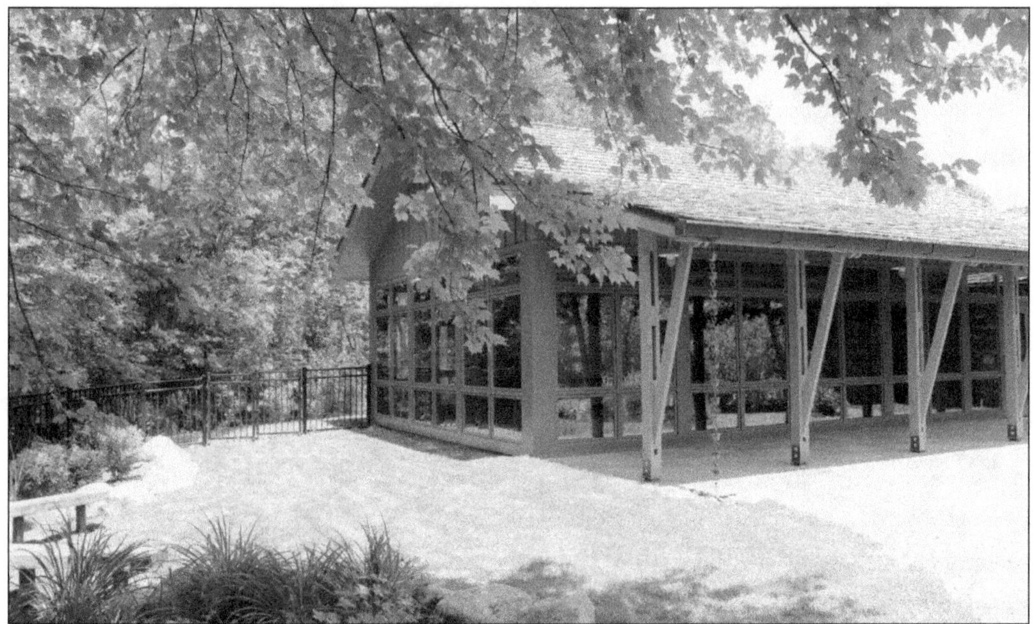

Feeling the need to add more early childhood programs, the library board applied for an Illinois State Library Live and Learn Construction Grant. This was received in 2015. Bensenville Library was one of only two in the state to receive the full amount. Construction was undertaken that same year. This addition extends off of the children's wing of the library.

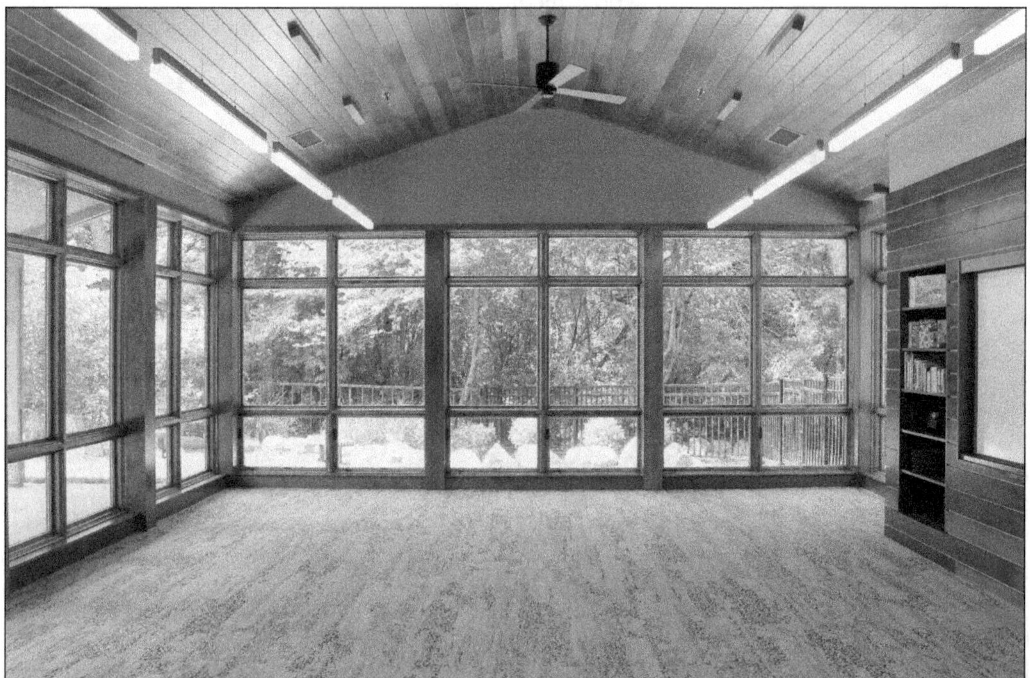

The wing also has access to the Garden of Knowledge, the space immediately outside of the library on the west side of the building. It was specifically designed with this in mind to foster connection to the natural environment and facilitate indoor/outdoor programs for preschool-aged children in the summer.

Five

The Park District

During the 1950s, the population of Bensenville reached 9,141. Houses had gone up on open lots throughout the village. Seeking to provide services to the residents, the Greater Bensenville Recreation Association was created in 1956, and a swimming pool was constructed. Just three years later, funds were running out. From the fall of 1959 through the spring of 1960, a series of public meetings were held to discuss the creation of a separate taxing district that would be responsible for maintaining parkland and providing recreation opportunities for the residents of Bensenville. The Illinois Association of Park Districts was also consulted concerning the creation of a park district. A study committee recommended in favor of pursuing such plans. On August 17, 1960, an election was held and the referendum to create a park district passed with 444 votes in favor and 232 against. Commissioners were also voted for at this time in the event that the referendum would pass. Ten candidates ran for five seats. Just 10 days later, the commissioners met for the first time and the Bensenville Park District had officially come into existence.

The Village of Bensenville deeded the five existing parks to the newly created park district. Then, in light of the impact of the railroad on Bensenville, many residents thought it should have a permanent monument. This became a reality in October 1961 when the money had been raised to transport locomotive No. 18 to Bensenville and to build a set of tracks on which it would sit. The village in turn donated the locomotive to the park district, which had set aside a part of Veterans Park on which to house and maintain it. This was followed by the acquisition of White Pines Golf Club in 1967. Then more parks were created. The Bensenville Water Park was built in 1985, and the Deer Grove Leisure Center opened four years later. This facility covers 50,000 square feet and houses a park district–run preschool, before- and after-school care during the academic year, summer day camps, fitness classes, and athletic leagues.

The park district also took the initiative to save and preserve Fischer Farm, one of the oldest homesteads in the county.

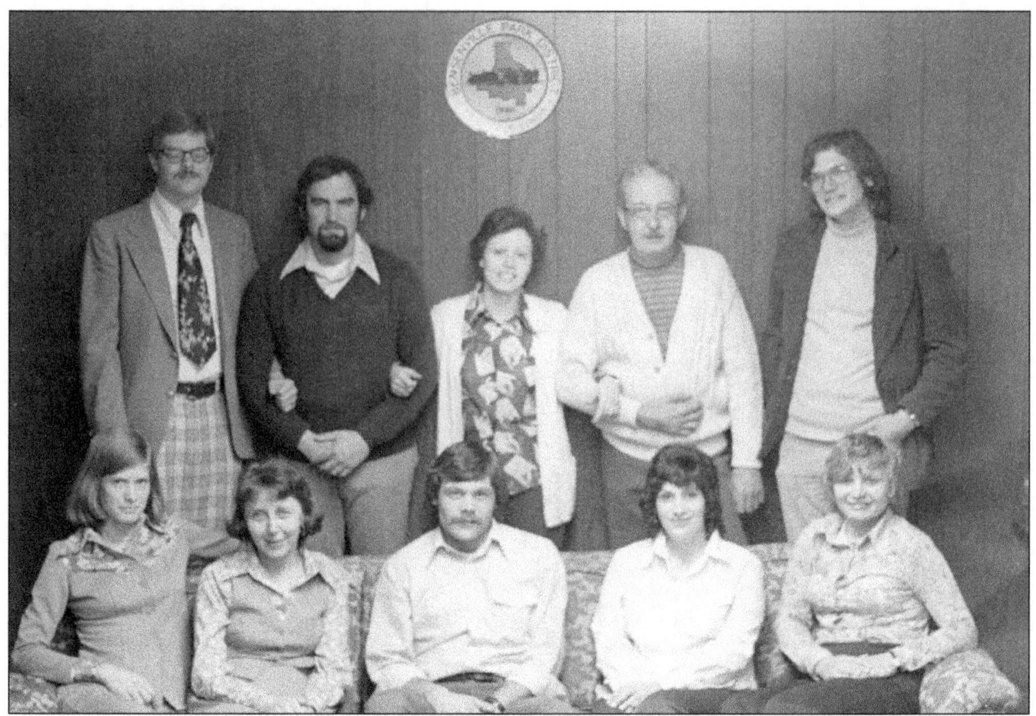

The recreation association, created in early 1956, was already facing a serious shortage of funds by the beginning of 1959. It maintained five parks—Kremples, Rose, Seekarr, Sunset, and Veterans—and operated the Richard D. Thomas Pool at Veterans Park. The issue was brought to the residents, resulting in the discussion of the creation of a park district.

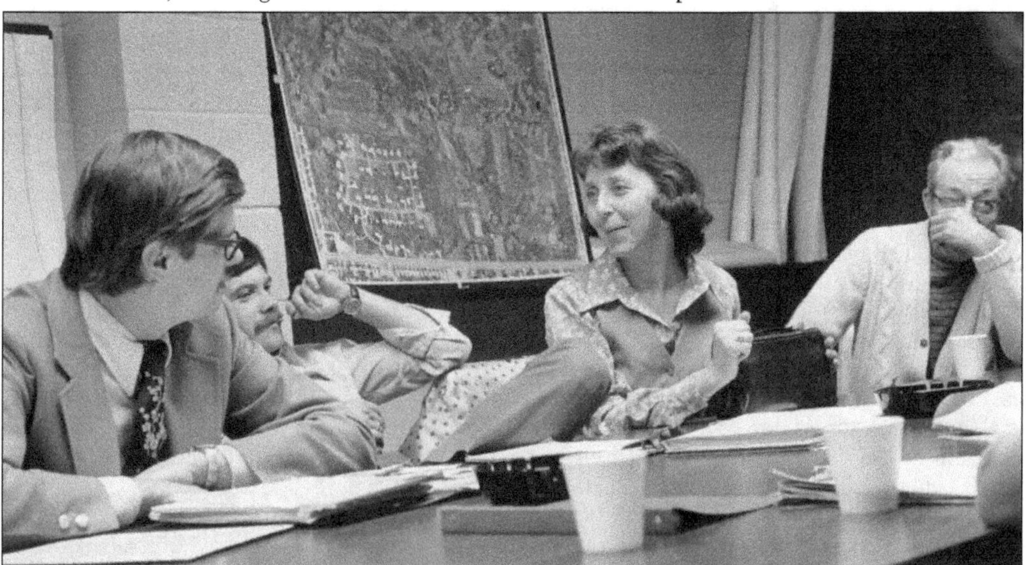

On August 27, 1960, the commissioners met for the first time and drew the boundaries. The board consisted of Rudolph Kremples, Wayne Schepple, Robert Nichols, John Varble, and Maxine Geils. The borders reached from Devon Avenue on the north to Grand Avenue on the south and from the Chicago & North Western Railroad tracks on the east and into Wood Dale on the west using the boundary of School District 2.

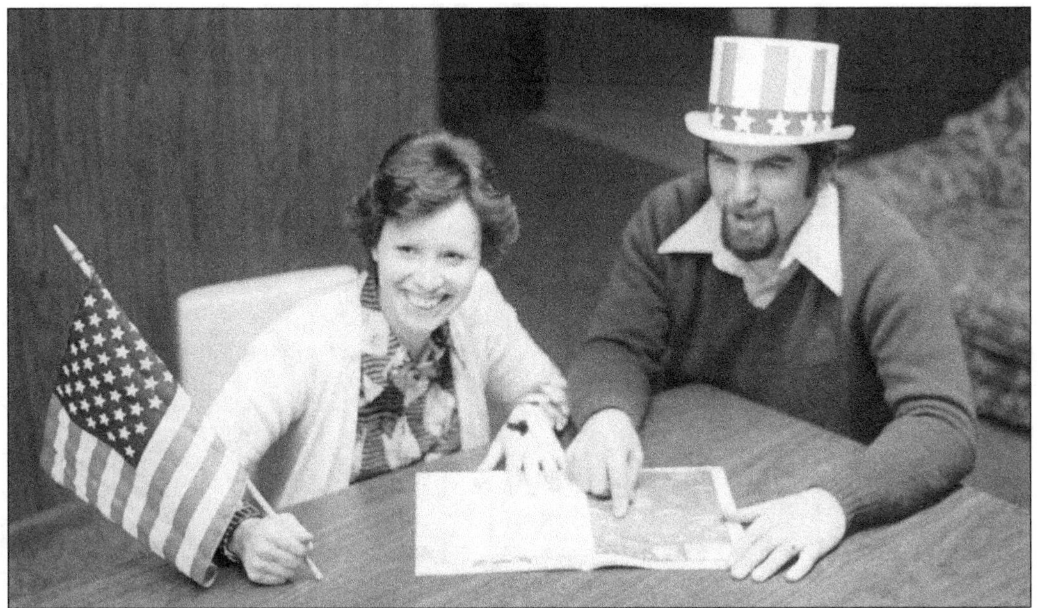

The village deeded the five existing parks to the park district. The revenue from the first taxes collected was used immediately for park maintenance and improvements. The next year, the park district purchased the property on the southeast corner of Route 83 and Wood Avenue. In 1965, the remainder of the Deer Forest property along Wood Avenue was purchased.

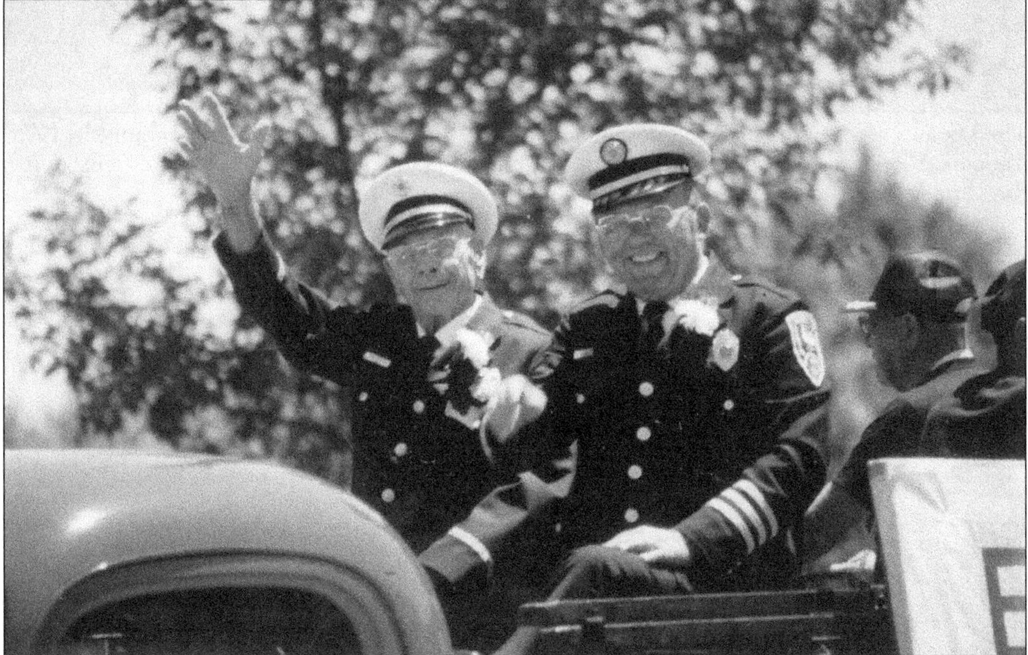

The park district also took over the operation of the Fourth of July festivities. Bensenville residents had a tradition of holding big celebrations, from the picnics and concerts at Horseshoe Bend to Gold Rush Days to the firemen's picnics. The Fourth of July began with a parade down Church Road from Irving Park to the White Pines Golf Course. There, activities were held with a firework display at night.

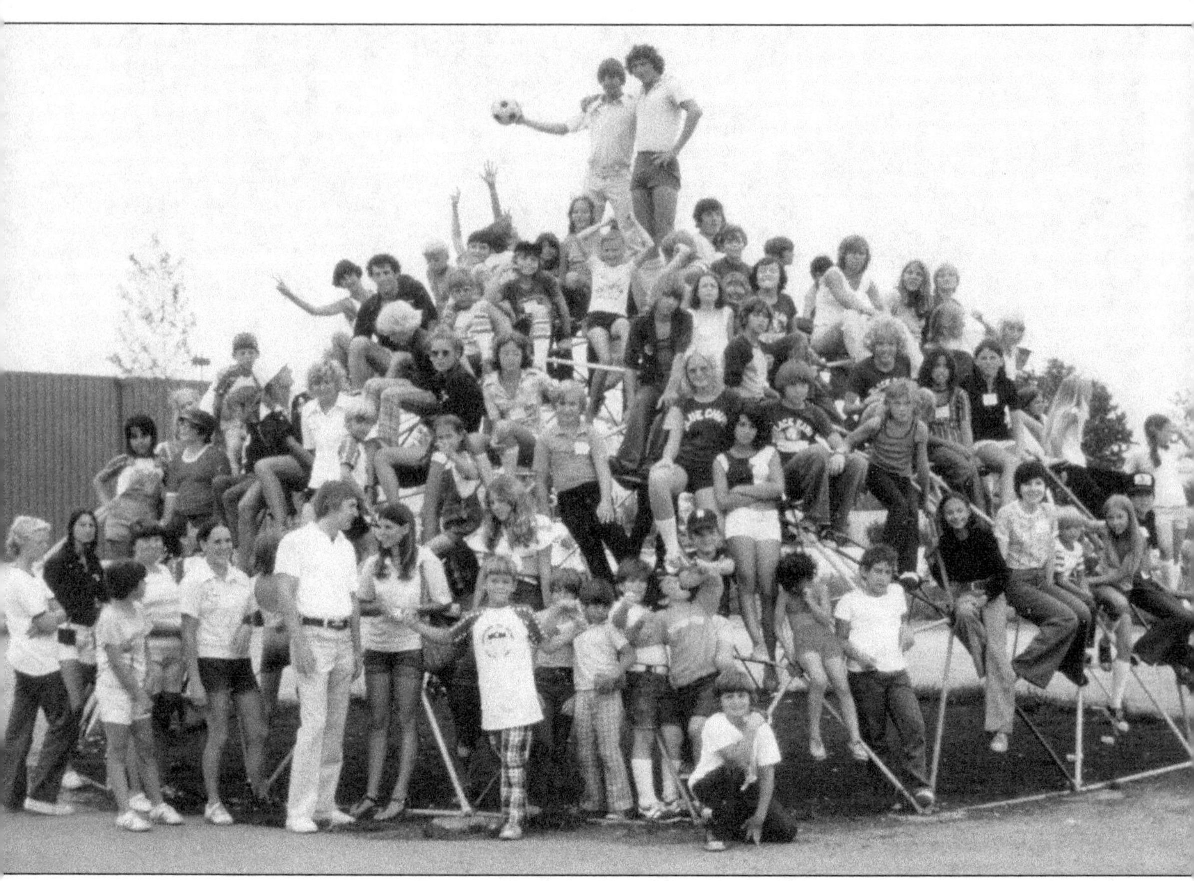

The tax levy received in 1970 was designated, for the first time, to recreation programs. In 1975, the park district also bought DiOrio Park, which it had been maintaining for the Bensenville Boys and Girls Athletic Association since 1962.

The Richard D. Thomas Pool that had been constructed by the Greater Bensenville Recreation Association in 1956 remained under the ownership of the village after the recreation association ceased to exist at the end of 1959, and the park district was created the following year. This was to honor the original agreement between the village and the recreation association. Now, however, the park district was maintaining and operating the pool.

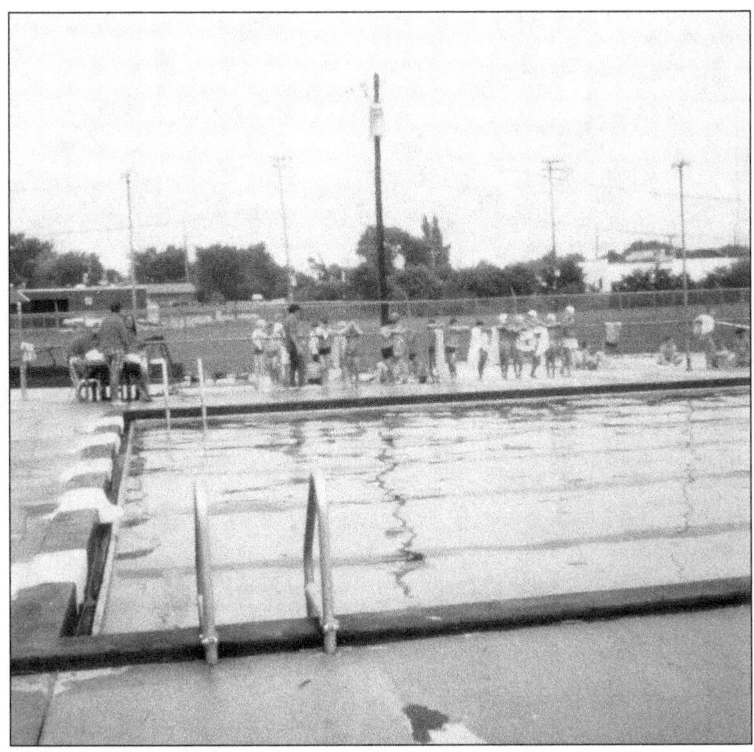

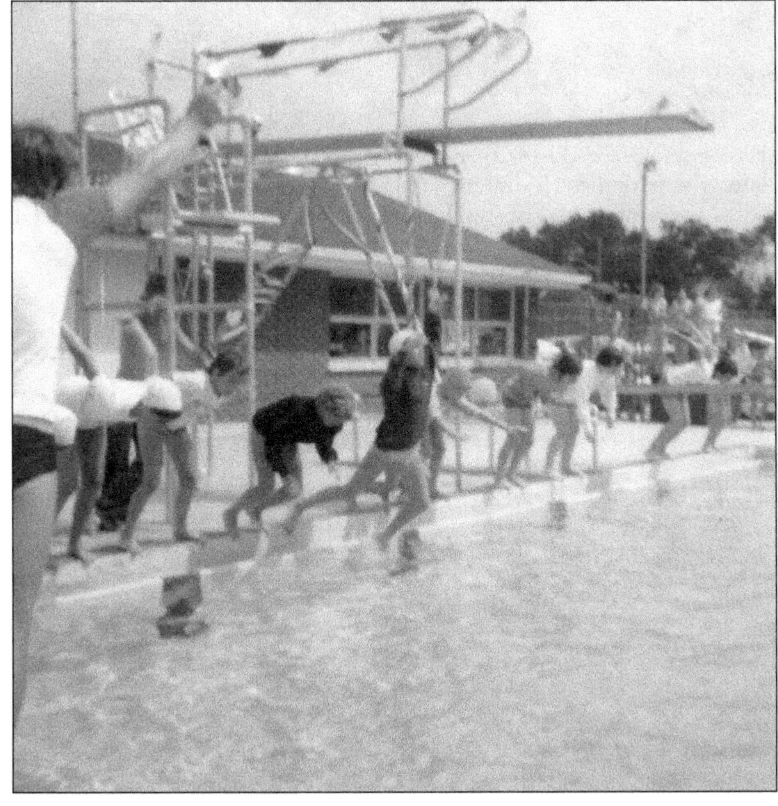

This situation would exist for five years. The village then sold the pool to the park district in 1966. It would continue to operate the pool at this location until 1977. The pool was located on the west side of the building at Veterans Park.

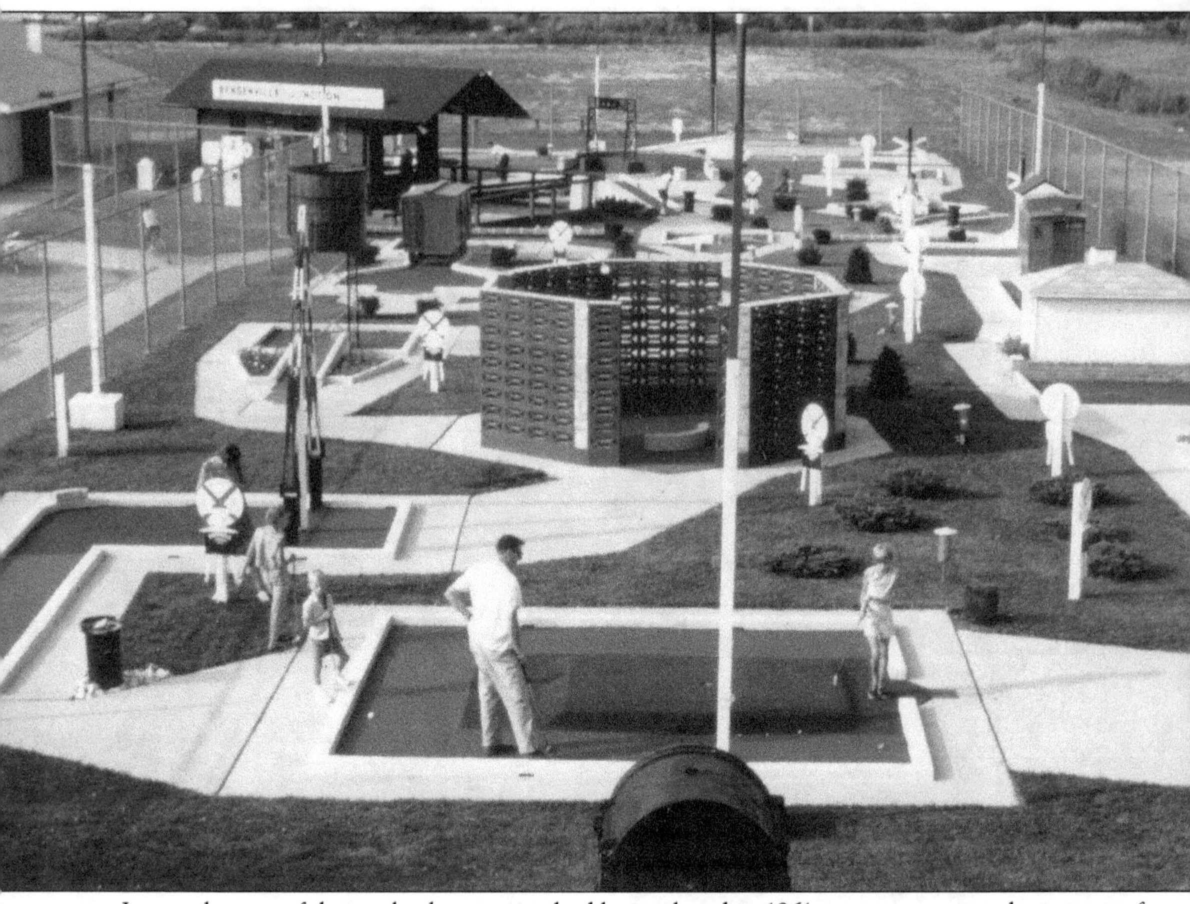

Just to the east of the pool, a locomotive had been placed in 1961 as monument to the impact of the railroad. Three years later, the park district designed a miniature golf course with a railroad theme immediately north of the locomotive. This operated for almost 20 years. It was replaced in 1985 with a course adjacent to the new water park. This course remained until 2012 when it was replaced by the splash pad.

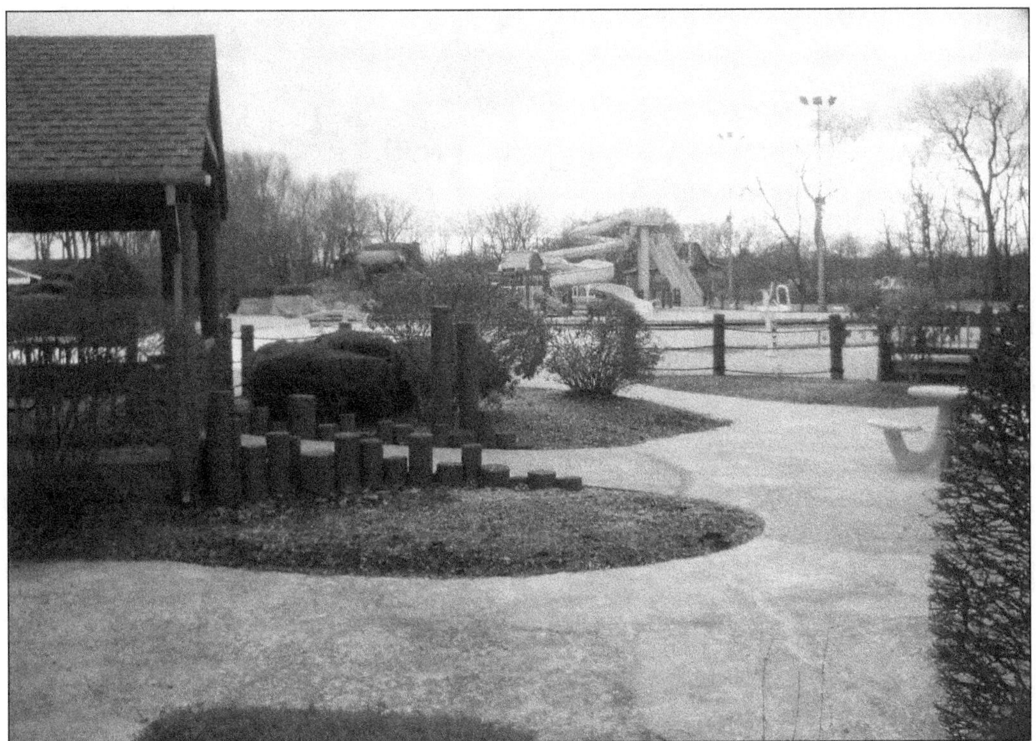

By the early 1980s, the park district was looking to replace the pool and began raising money for this purpose. In 1984, a water park was constructed on the southeast corner of Route 83 and Wood Avenue. The Bensenville Park District Water Park opened to the public in June 1985. (Author's collection.)

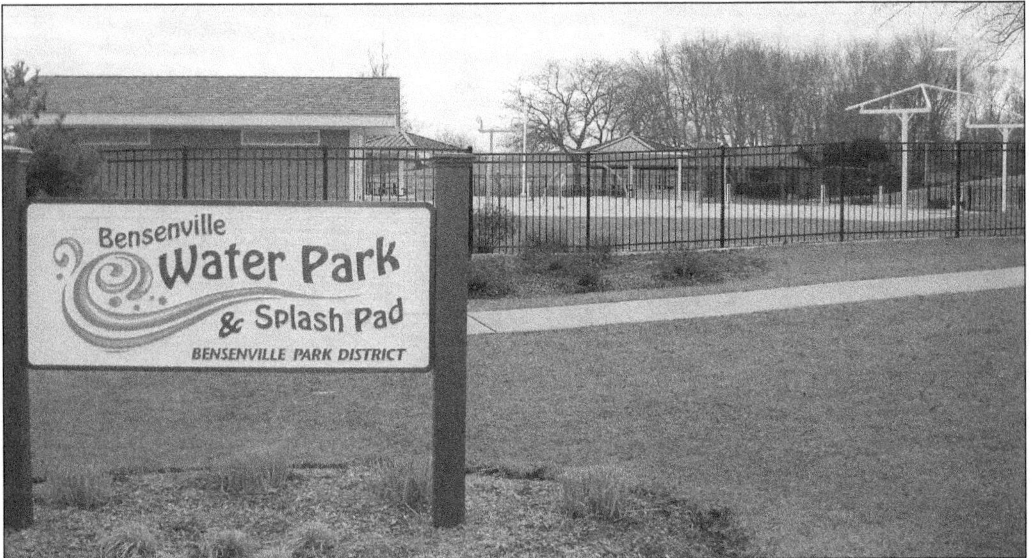

The water park still serves the community today. Home to three slides, a sand volleyball area, concessions shop, and locker rooms, it is enjoyed by many. In 2012, the decision was made to remove what had come to be called Golf Waters mini golf and replace it with a splash pad addition to the water park. This was completed in 2013. (Author's collection.)

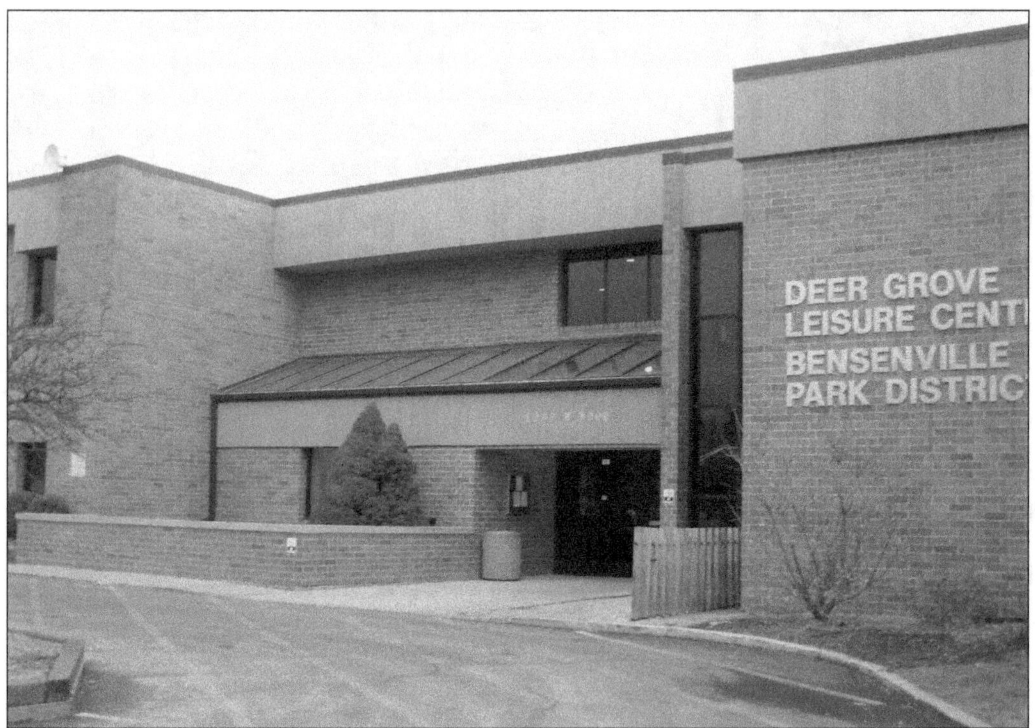

The park district also needed space. The primary location was the building at Veterans Park. Athletic programs were run out of the school gyms. This limited greatly what the park district could offer. Then, in 1978, the park district traded property to the library in return for the community center at Green and Addison Streets. This allowed for the introduction of a preschool in addition to the dance classes. (Author's collection.)

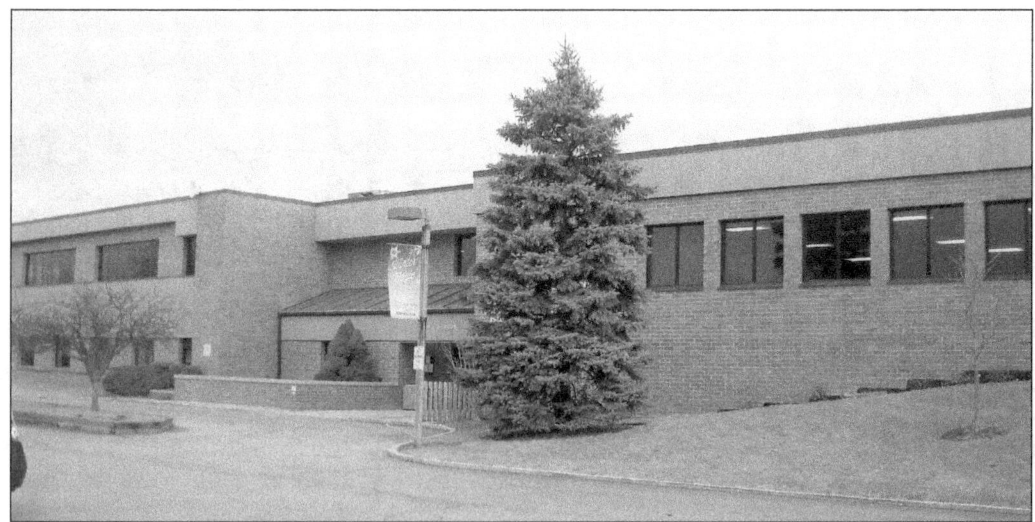

Program development here resulted in a full-fledged recreation department for the park district. A new building was needed. Designs were submitted and employees of other park districts that had built recreation centers were asked to review the plans and offer suggestions. The community center went through other owners. Currently at that location is the Green Street Grille, which opened in April 2017. (Author's collection.)

Ground was broken in 1988 just east of the water park. Named after the property, the Deer Grove Leisure Center houses not only the administrative offices, but also a gymnasium, weight room, racquetball courts, an indoor walking and running track, and classrooms. The Tiny Tot Preschool, as it is known, has been loved by more than one generation in Bensenville now. (Author's collection.)

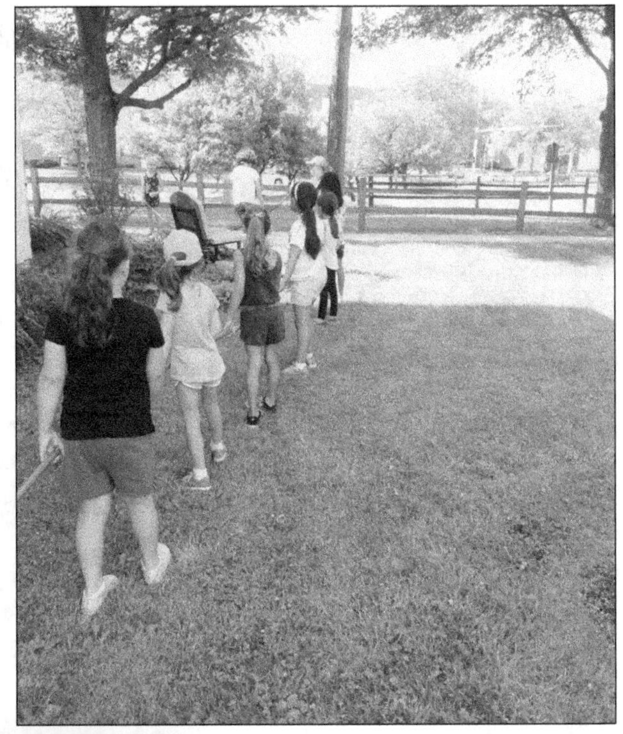

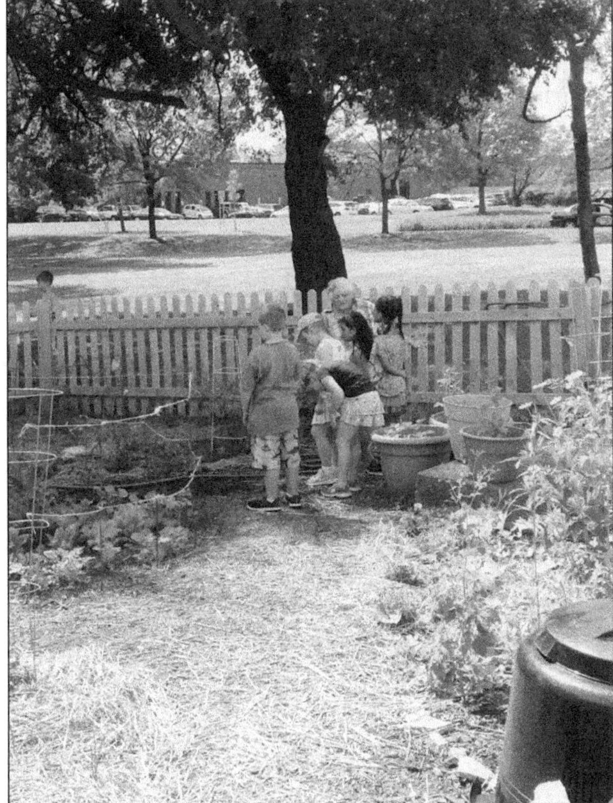

The tot program was largely redesigned beginning in 2015. Now, additional classes are offered for two-to-three-year-old children as well. There are evening classes too and a peewee gym time. The Tiny Tot Preschool holds an annual Christmas program in December and then a graduation in May. It also a tradition to purchase eggs that are placed in an incubator and allowed to hatch. (Author's collection.)

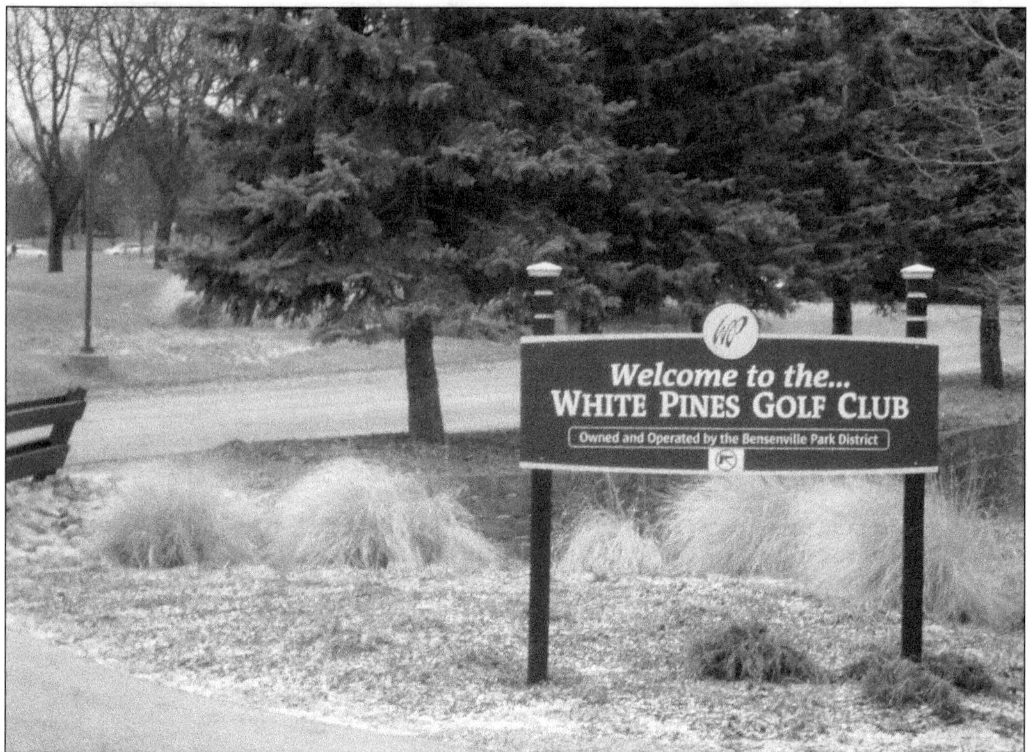

The park district had desired to purchase the White Pines Golf Course and secured an option for this in the spring of 1966. Federal matching funds for the outright purchase of the golf course were also sought, but these could not be secured. The decision was made to find an alternate source of funds through revenue bonds.

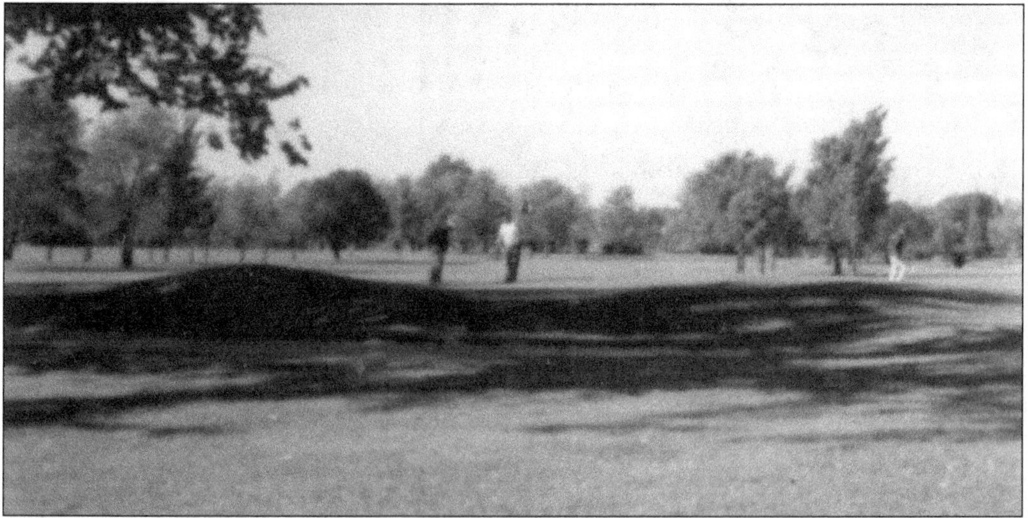

In 1967, the park district raised $1.68 million in bonds allowing for the purchase of the golf course that fall. It contracted with the Branigar Organization to operate the course, which it did for the next four years. In January 1972, the park district took over operation of the course. A new clubhouse and banquet facility was constructed in 1979. The j123
37 Bar and Grill was renovated and reopened in April 2014.

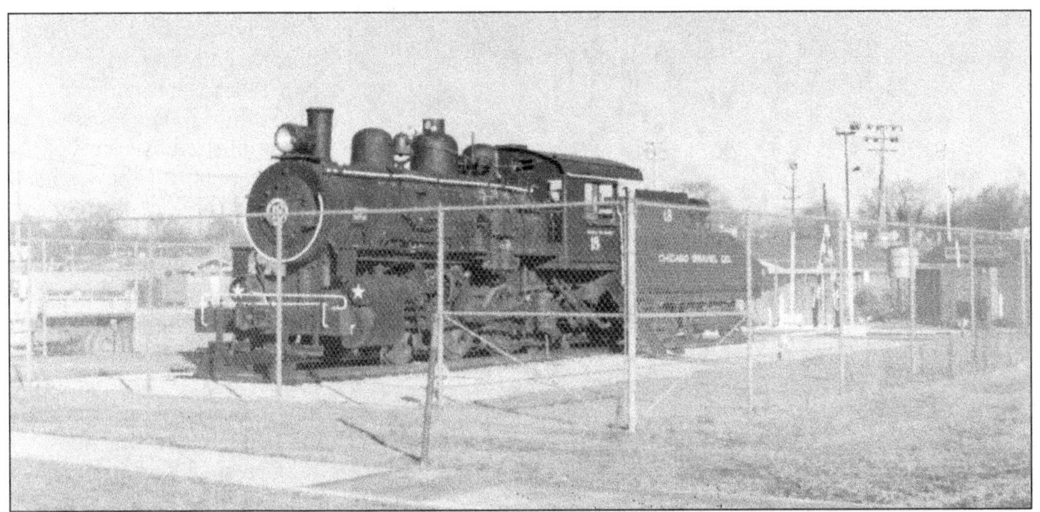

The Fourth of July celebration in Bensenville in 1960 was just as big as any other. In fact, the Chicago Gravel Company had driven a locomotive and tender to the village as a part of the festivities. Several residents, knowing the importance of the railroad to Bensenville, thought it desirable to have a permanent monument commemorating this.

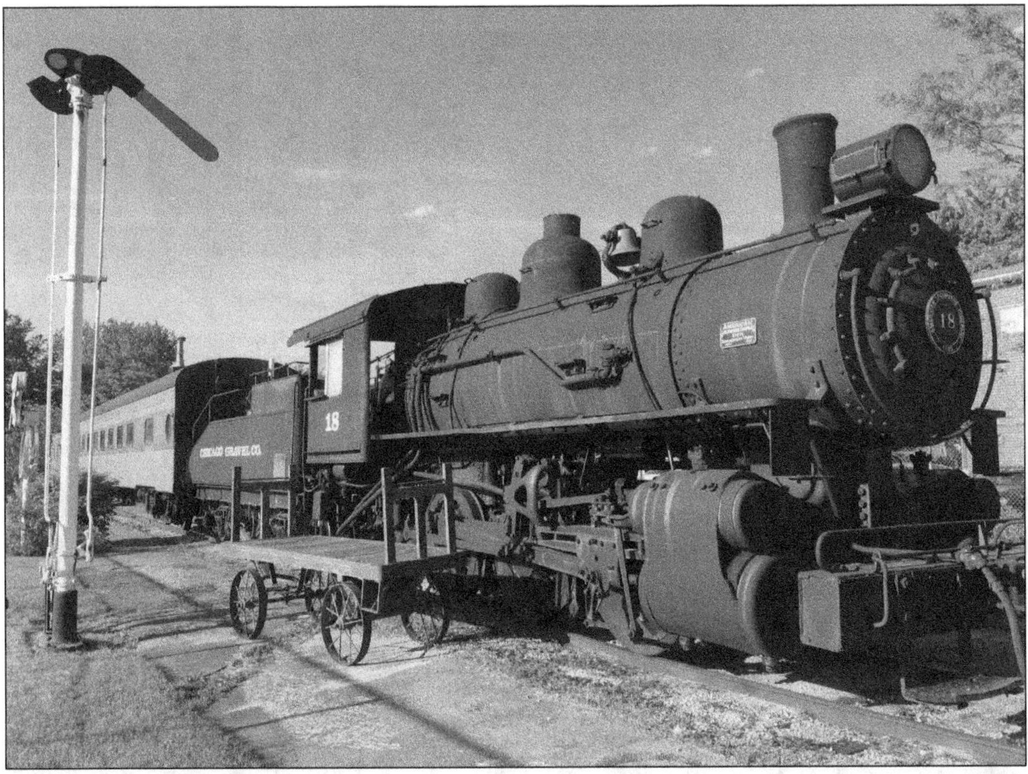

It was learned that the Chicago Gravel Company would be scrapping engine No. 18, which had been brought to the Fourth of July celebration because of the shift to diesel. Here seemed an opportunity to create the desired monument and save the engine from its fate. Fundraising efforts began immediately to have a section of track constructed in order to locate the engine and tender. (Courtesy of Karl Joost.)

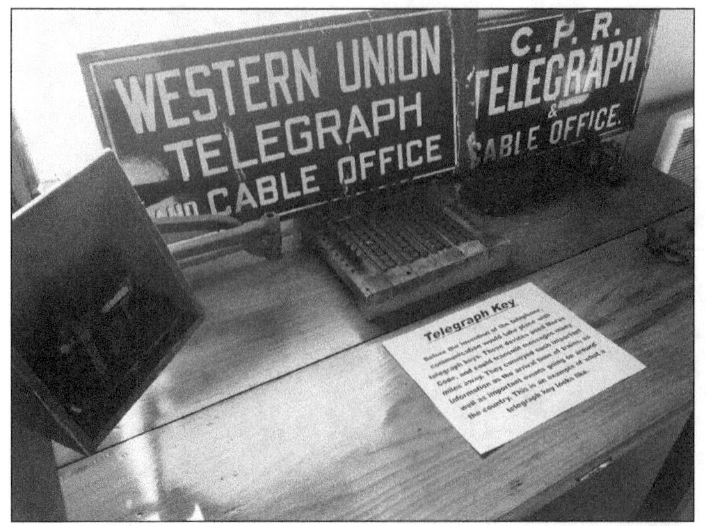

On June 1, 1961, the village purchased locomotive No. 18 and the tender for $1. Fundraising was accomplished by October of that year and the village donated the locomotive and tender to the park district, which placed the cars at Veterans Park. In April 1990, the park district purchased a Milwaukee Road caboose manufactured at the Bensenville Yard and created a display inside. (Courtesy of Karl Joost.)

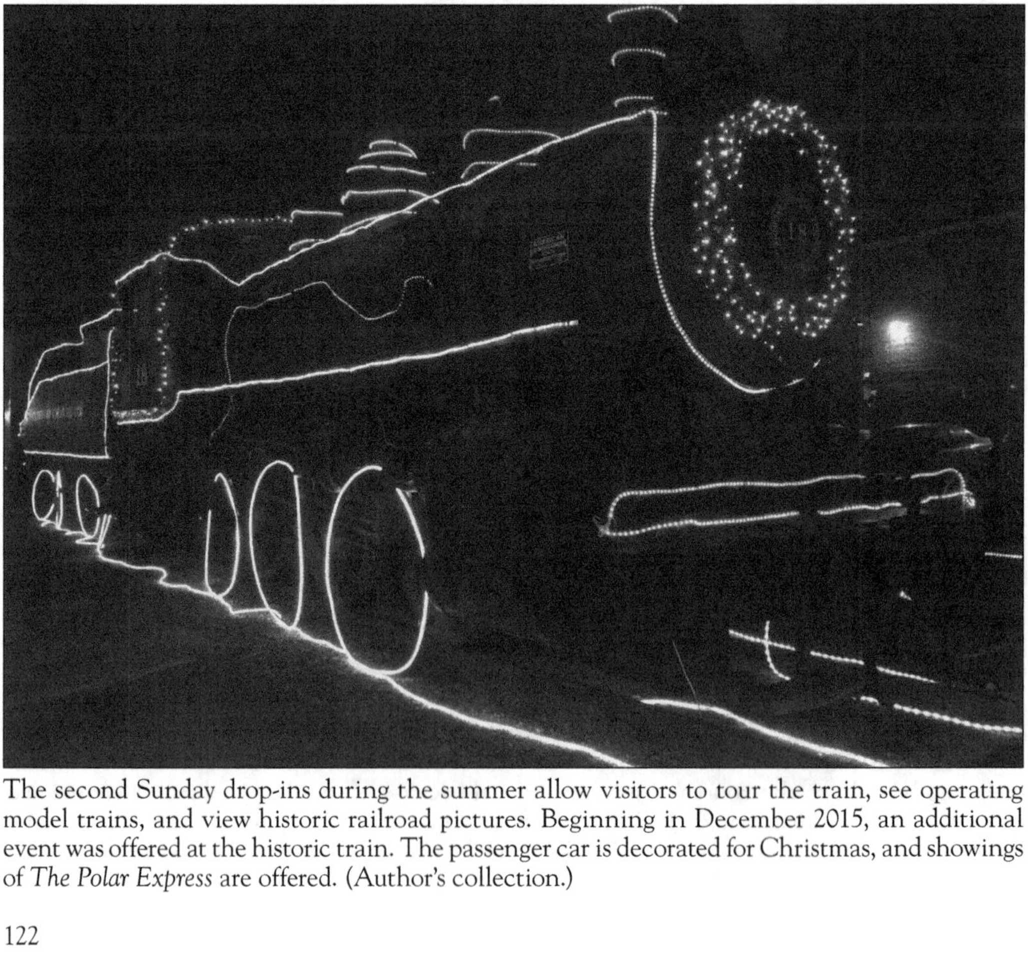

The second Sunday drop-ins during the summer allow visitors to tour the train, see operating model trains, and view historic railroad pictures. Beginning in December 2015, an additional event was offered at the historic train. The passenger car is decorated for Christmas, and showings of *The Polar Express* are offered. (Author's collection.)

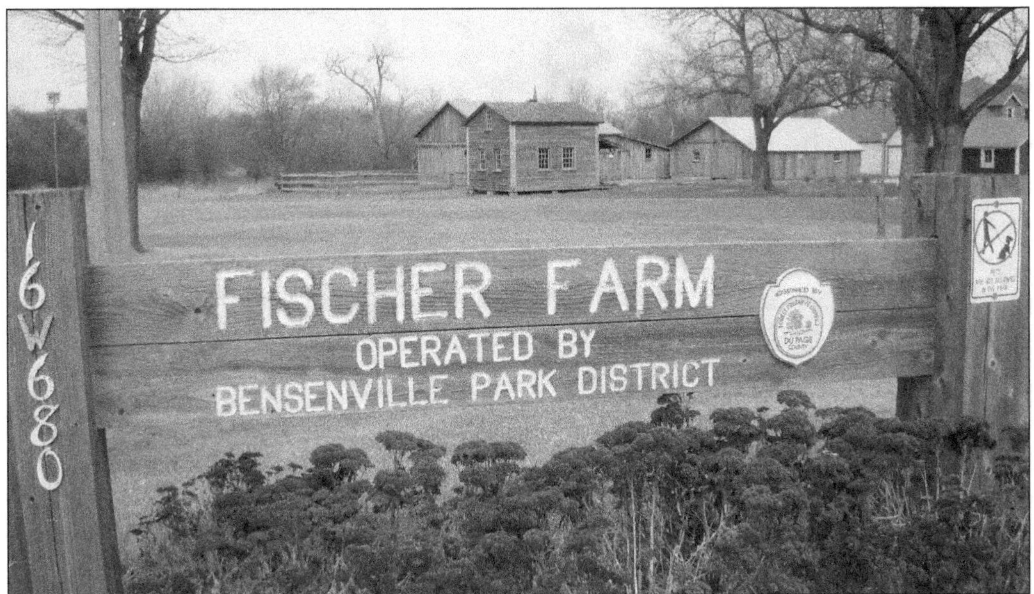

The Bensenville Park District became involved with another historic property in 2000. The remaining undeveloped parcel of the Fischer Farm still owned by the family had been purchased by the Forest Preserve District of DuPage County through eminent domain. With the district already operating a living history farm and having purchased the property for its ecological value, demolition of the structures was intended. (Author's collection.)

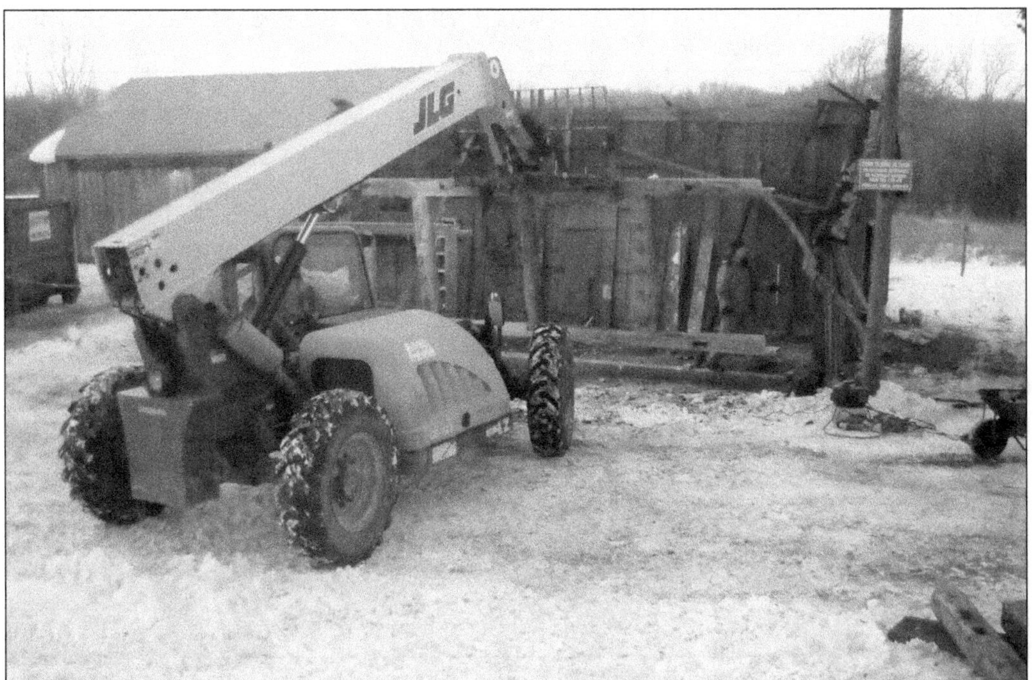

The park district placed the saving of Fischer Farm on the ballot in March 2000, where it failed to carry. The same result was obtained in November. Not wanting to lose this landmark, the park district offered to enter a lease agreement with the Forest Preserve District in order to operate the property. (Author's collection.)

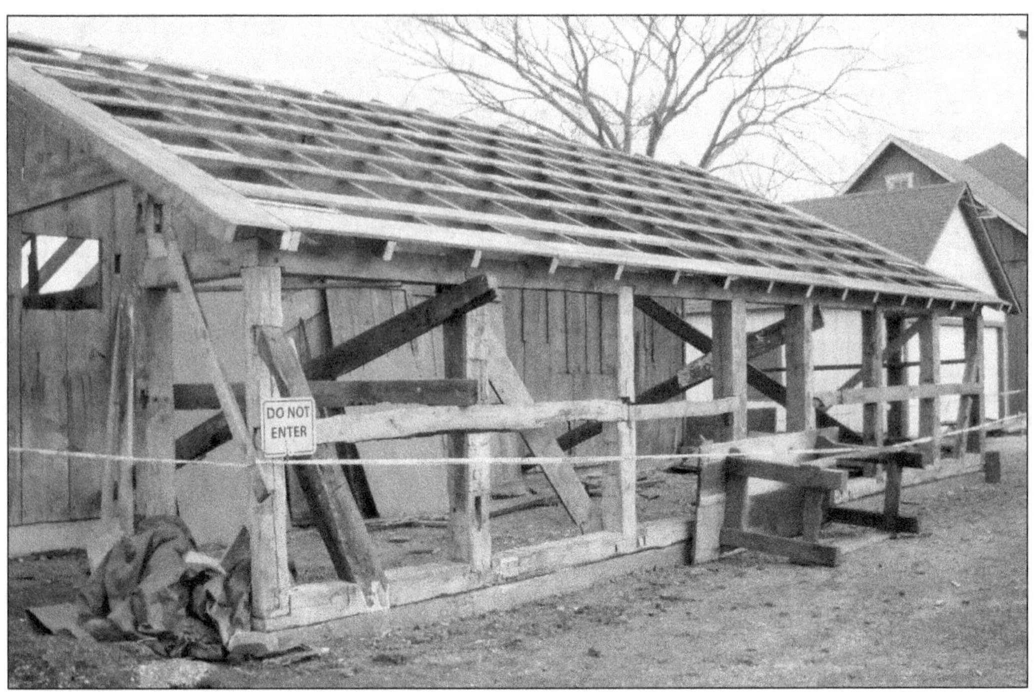

The Forest Preserve District did not agree to this unless the park district could show cash on hand. The board of commissioners made the decision to do this and cancelled the Fourth of July celebration. In December 2000, the lease was signed. The village has since offered Fourth of July celebrations. (Author's collection.)

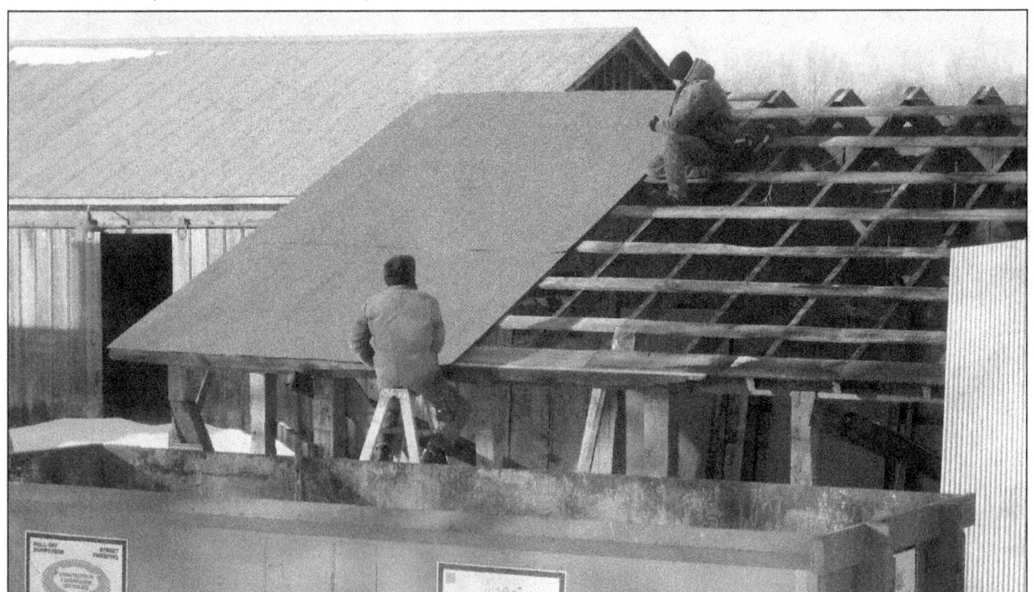

After the park district interviewed representatives from three restoration firms, Preservation Trades, Inc. was hired in 2002. This firm ultimately conducted the restoration of seven of the structures and the reconstruction of an eighth over the course of the next 13 years as the park district was able to secure funds. A community garden program was offered from 2004 through 2007. (Author's collection.)

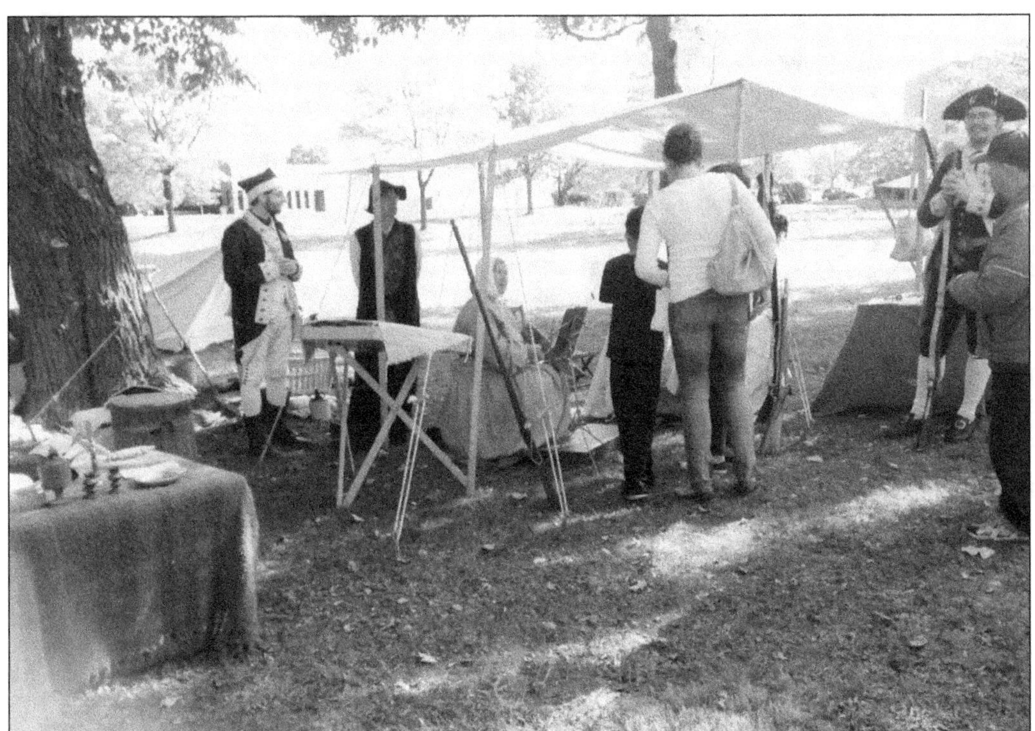

The largest and longest-standing event at Fischer Farm is Heritage Day. In fact, the first iteration of this event was held in September 2000 in order to demonstrate the park district's commitment to the site. This event includes historical reenactors and living history displays, pumpkin patch, pony rides, petting farm, and much more. Eighteen years later, the event continues to a be increasingly popular. (Author's collection.)

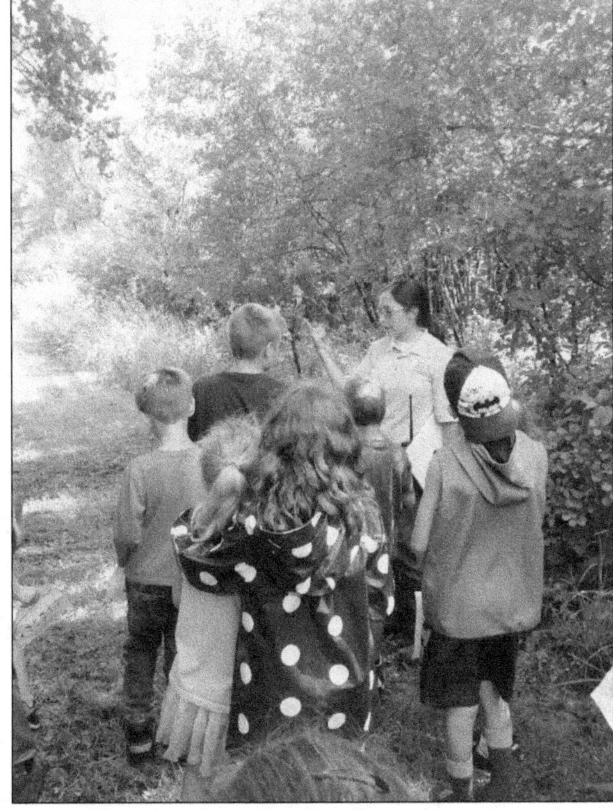

Beginning in late 2005, the nature and heritage education supervisor had responsibility for the farm. A single session of summer day camp was offered along with a handful of standalone programs. Heritage Day continued and was joined in 2007 by a second large-scale event, the All Around the House Quilt Show. (Author's collection.)

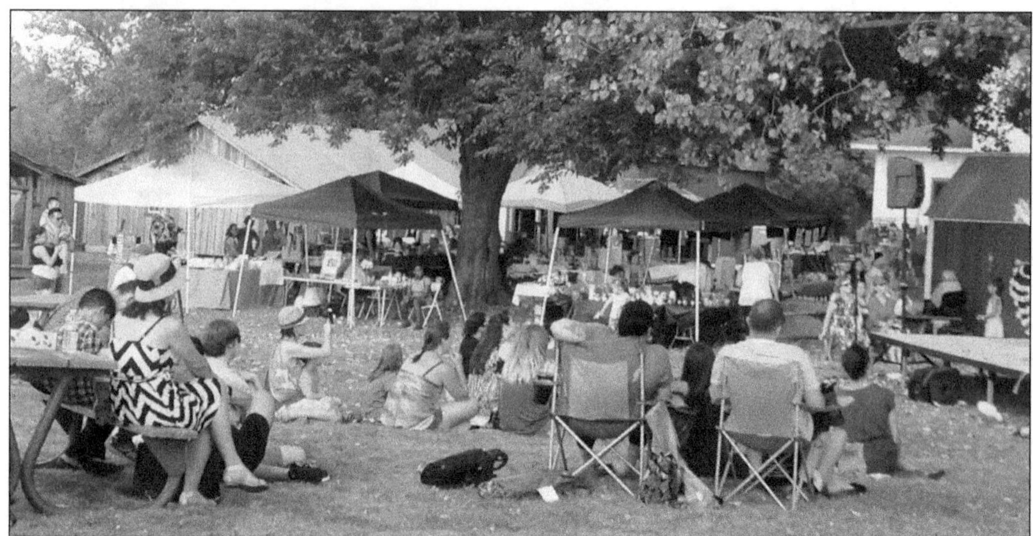

When the employee occupying this position left to take another job, a new position was created. This was the Fischer Farm curator. On June 1, 2011, Jonathan Sebastian was hired for this position. He added four additional events. Now, 10 events are offered, and the summer camp continues. Sebastian also undertook the establishment of a museum. (Author's collection.)

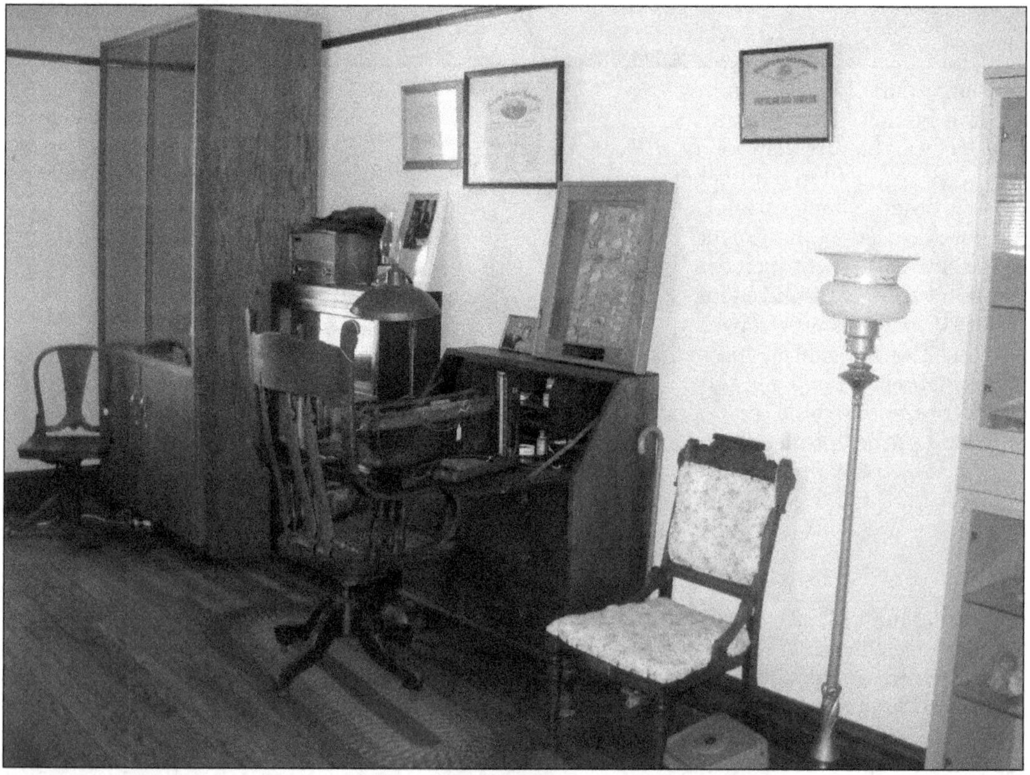

This work has included research, accessioning of artifacts, and the writing of core documents. The collection of oral histories and an archival collection are also maintained. A kitchen garden has been added along with other cultivation. An ecological restoration program is under way. Chickens, bees, and for a few months at a time, sheep, all call the farm home. (Author's collection.)

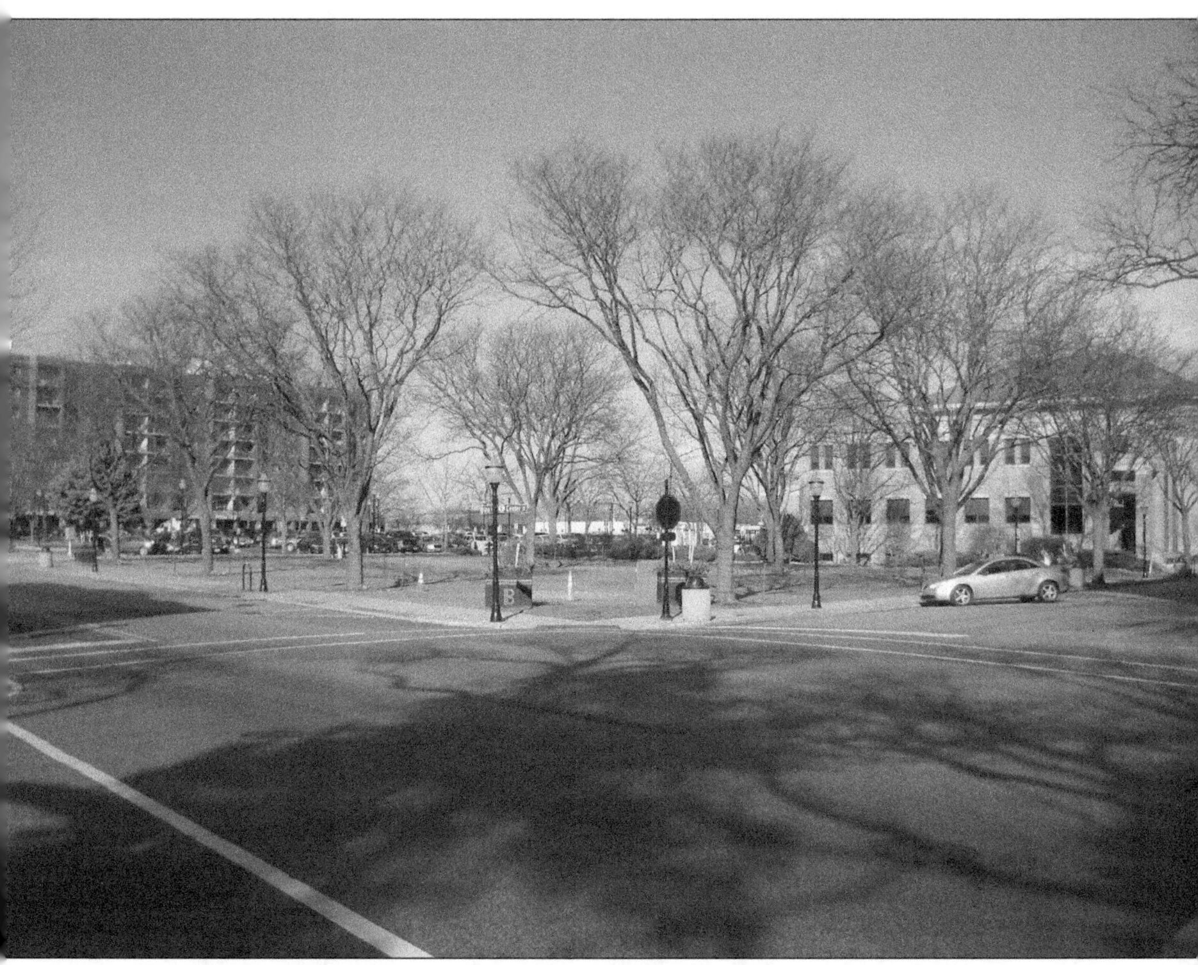

The opportunity for education at the newly built and always adapting schools, both public and private, and the opportunity for work can be found here. It is the neighbor to O'Hare Airport and the city of Chicago, with truly global connections. Here is the opportunity to engage with the community. Libertyfest and Music in the Park are ever popular events offered by the Village of Bensenville. The library offers programs for all ages. The park district runs leagues, teams, camps, and various classes for all those 2 and up. The history here has not been lost. Instead, it has been built upon as a solid foundation. Through the preservation and operation of the Korthauer Log House and the historic locomotive the history of the village becomes apparent. The Fischer Farm, and in cooperation with the Elmhurst History Museum, the Churchville Schoolhouse, and the larger property on which both sit allow for a remarkable opportunity in both ecological and historical interpretation. Bensenville is not the fastest-dying town in America. It is not dying at all—it is just starting to thrive. (Author's collection.)

www.ingramcontent.com/pod-product-compliance
Lightning Source LLC
LaVergne TN
LVHW081530100826
845153LV00004B/247

* 9 7 8 1 5 4 0 2 3 5 5 1 0 *